D0567446

BLOOD IN THE SNOW, BLOOD ON THE GRASS

BLOOD IN THE SNOW,
BLOOD ON THE GRASS

TREACHERY, TORTURE, MURDER AND MASSACRE – FRANCE 1944

DOUGLAS BOYD

First published 2012
by Spellmount, an imprint of The History Press
The Mill, Brimscombe Port
Stroud, Gloucestershire, GL5 2QG
www.thehistorypress.co.uk

© Douglas Boyd, 2012

The right of Douglas Boyd to be identified as the Author
of this work has been asserted in accordance with the
Copyrights, Designs and Patents Act 1988.

All rights reserved. No part of this book may be reprinted
or reproduced or utilised in any form or by any electronic,
mechanical or other means, now known or hereafter invented,
including photocopying and recording, or in any information
storage or retrieval system, without the permission in writing
from the Publishers.

British Library Cataloguing in Publication Data.
A catalogue record for this book is available from the British Library.

ISBN 978 0 7524 7026 9

Typesetting and origination by The History Press
Printed in Great Britain

CONTENTS

ACKNOWLEDGEMENTS

It is not surprising that few people in France wished to remember, let alone talk or write about, their experiences during the awful years of the German occupation of their country. I have to thank historian Robert O. Paxton, sometime professor of Columbia University, for breaking down 'the wall of silence' in 1973 and forcing into the light of day many events that have since been investigated in greater depth.

On a personal level, my thanks are due to Max Lagarrigue, indefatigable editor of *Arkheia* magazine, for repeated access to information on the war years in south-west France; to Marie-Françoise Roth and her husband at Le Noirlac Hotel in St Amand-Montron for background on what did happen in 'the town where nothing ever happened'; to Palu Fourcassié for an account of his time in Le Service de Surveillance des Voies; to Dédée Fourcassié for persuading 'Marie-Rose Dupont' to trust a historian she had never met before and talk about the terrible price she paid for the affair with her Austrian SS lover Willi, of which she had previously never spoken to anyone; to Joseph la Picirella for keeping alive the history of the Vercors betrayal – a story that no one in France or the Allied countries wanted to be known; to Fabrice Vergili for sharing his research on the shame within the shame of the occupation – the many thousands of French women who bore babies by German fathers and were publicly humiliated for this.

Many others who survived these years contributed – but with the plea that their names not be revealed. Some asked this from guilt at what circumstances forced them to do and some from shame at what happened to them. Among the museums that contributed significantly are: le Musée de la Résistance at Clermont-Ferrand; le Musée de la Poche at Royan; le Musée de la Résistance du Vercors; le Centre Jean Moulin at Bordeaux; le Musée de la Résistance at Limoges; le Musée de la Résistance at Cahors. On a professional level, at The History Press, I have to thank Jay Slater for commissioning the book and editor Chrissy McMorris for pulling everything together and making a book out of a pile of paper. My personal thanks go to Jennifer Weller for help with maps and otherwise and, as always, to my partner Atarah Ben-Tovim who suffers with good humour the loneliness of living with a historian who is forever somewhere and sometime else.

Douglas Boyd
Summer 2012

LIST OF ACRONYMS
AND ABBREVIATIONS

Abwehr: German military intelligence and counter-espionage organisation

Allgemeine-SS: the organisation headed by Himmler that ran the concentration and death camps

BCRA (Bureau Central de Renseignements et d'Action): the Free French intelligence organisation

CDL (Comité Départemental de la Libération): committee in each *département* coordinating Resistance actions before and during the liberation

CNR (Conseil National de le Résistance)

COMAC (Comité d'Action Militaire): action committee of MUR (see below)

COSSAC: Chief of Staff to the Supreme Allied Commander

deuxième bureau: French military intelligence

FAFL (Forces Aériennes Françaises Libres): Free French air force

FFI (Forces Françaises de l'Intérieur): blanket term covering all Resistance and Maquis groups in build-up to, and during, the liberation

FTP (Francs-tireurs et Partisans): a communist Resistance movement

Kriegsmarine: German navy

malgré nous: term for Alsatians and Lorrainers compulsorily enlisted in German armed forces, meaning literally 'we had no choice'

MAAF: Mediterranean Allied Air Forces

MAT (Manufacture d'Armes de Tulle): arms factory in Tulle

Milice: paramilitary Vichy police force

MLN (Movement de Libération Nationale): successor to MUR

MUR (Movements Unis de le Résistance): the first nationwide coordinating body of the Resistance

OAS (Organisation Armée Secrète): a Resistance movement headed by ex-army officers

OKW (Oberkommando der Wehrmacht): German High Command

PCF (Parti Communiste Français): French Communist Party

ORA (Organisation Résistance Armée): Resistance movement headed by ex-army officers

OSS: United States Office of Strategic Services

PH: Purple Heart

SAARF: Special Allied Airborne Reconnaissance Force

SAS: British Special Air Service

Section F: department of SOE dealing with France

Section RF: department of SOE liaising with BCRA

SHAEF: Supreme Headquarters, Allied Expeditionary Force

SIS: Secret Intelligence Service, also known as MI6

Sipo-SD (Sicherheitspolizei/Sicherheitsdienst): German 'ultra' anti-partisan troops

SOE: Special Operations Executive

SPOC: Special Projects Operations Centre

STO (Service du Travail Obligatoire): compulsory conscription for labour service in Germany

USMC: United States Marine Corps

Waffen-SS: the elite parallel German army controlled by Himmler, which carried out atrocities

PART 1

THE BUILD-UP
TO BLOODSHED

1

RAISING THE RESISTANCE – TRACTS AND TERRORISM

Tourists visiting France are often surprised by the number of Second World War memorials in towns and villages and beside country roads, dedicated to men shot by the German forces occupying the country in 1940–45 or deported in atrocious conditions to concentration and death camps in the Reich, from which the few who did return came back broken in health and spirit. Although many who suffered and died under the occupation have no memorial, the tourist wandering down a side street of a peaceful town, perhaps looking for a shady bar on a hot afternoon, is confronted far too often by a little shrine bearing the inscription *Ici est tombé un maquisard*, followed by a date in summer 1944.

Each of these shrines marks the spot where a young civilian – usually male but sometimes a woman – was gunned down by battle-hardened soldiers in German uniform, to die in a pool of blood with a parachuted pistol or Sten gun in hand. Even that word 'die' is often a euphemism for a savage beating that ended with his or her body twisting on a rope hanging from a nearby tree or street lamp.

But who exactly were the *maquisards* and why were so many of them killed? And what exactly was the Resistance? Two clear generations after the tragedies to which the memorials bear witness, many French people ask themselves these questions, confused about the difference between the Resistance and the Maquis.

In the summer of 1940, after Hitler and his generals had taken just six weeks to conquer the country with the biggest standing army in Europe, the new government of Marshal Philippe Pétain signed an armistice agreement on 22 June. It was a humiliating defeat, after which a few patriots immediately sought to assuage the shame that their military and political leaders had been found so sadly wanting. In full knowledge that the penalty for being caught was death, they decided to work against the occupation in defiance of the armistice agreement signed by their legal government. A clause in the armistice agreement was quite explicit:

> The French government will forbid French citizens to fight against Germany in the service of states with which the German Reich is still at war. French citizens who violate this provision are to be treated by German troops as insurgents.

Should they be caught, as many were, their own government would do nothing to help them. On the contrary, the Gestapo and German Security Police were aided and abetted by Vichy's Police Nationale, Gendarmerie Nationale, the Milice and the Groupes Mobiles, including their Reserve, which was the ancestor of today's Compagnie Républicaine de Securité riot police.

In the First World War, which ended just over two decades before the defeat of 1940, France and the British Empire each mobilised between 8 million and 9 million men, but total French casualties were twice as high as those for the whole Empire. From a population of 40 million, France lost 1,357,800 men killed, with 4,266,000 wounded and another 537,000 taken prisoner or missing in action. At the other end of the scale, the decisive but late entry of the USA into that war cost only a total of 116,516 Americans killed and 206,502 other casualties.[1]

After the 1940 armistice the vast majority of French people were simply relieved that the fighting was over with no more bloodshed and no more loved ones' lives to be pointlessly lost by France's inadequate generals and wavering politicians. Numbed by the speed at which their nation had been defeated and its British allies driven out of the Continent, people spent hours every day in the long queues outside the few bakeries and food stores still open. The problem was not so much shortage of food as disruption to food production and distribution caused by 8 million refugees being far from home, butchers, bakers and other shopkeepers among them.

Once the fighting stopped, most French people were surprised at the good behaviour of the German soldiers. Taking refuge with friends in the Loire valley after fleeing the capital, Simone de Beauvoir wrote of their arrival there:

> To our general surprise, there was no violence. They paid for their drinks and the eggs they bought at farms. They spoke politely. All the shopkeepers smiled at them.

Further north in Cherbourg, General Erwin Rommel wrote home to his wife:

> The war is turning into a peaceful occupation of the whole of France. The population is calm and in some places even friendly.

Likewise, they were in the British Channel Islands, where the Wehrmacht landed on 30 June without opposition, the islands having been judged impossible to defend and demilitarised a week earlier.

Even Hitler's ambassador in Paris, Otto Abetz, commented upon the apparent apathy of the general population. Like all German officials and civilians in France, Abetz was well fed – as were some privileged or dishonest French people, but the majority of the population was preoccupied with getting the next meal, or extra clothing coupons, or 'grey' market food at the weekends. The diary of a Parisian housewife for October 1942, when commerce was far more stable than just after the defeat and prices were controlled by the government, goes some way to explaining this:

7.30   At the baker's. Got bread. Rusks maybe available later.
9.00   Butcher says will only have meat on Saturday.

9.30   Cheese shop. Says he will have some cheese at 5 p.m.
10.00   Tripe shop. My ticket No. 32 will come up at 4 p.m.
10.30   Grocer's. Vegetables maybe, but only at 5 p.m.
11.00   Return to baker. Rusks, but no bread this time.[2]

At 4 p.m. she had to be back at the tripe shop. At 5 p.m. came the dilemma: a small portion of cheese or a handful of vegetables? And so it went on, day after day. In addition, there were effectively three price levels for food and most other things: the official price decreed by Pétain's government in Vichy, which only applied to purchasers who possessed the right number of coupons; the 'grey' market where peasants could be persuaded to sell a few eggs or some meat; and the black market, where everything could be obtained – at a price. If the housewife keeping the diary was rich enough, she had the following choices:

	Legal price	Grey Market	Black Market
1kg butter	42F	69F	107F
12 eggs	20F	35F	53F
1kg chicken meat	24F	38F	48F

On some items the mark-up was grotesque: farmers sold potatoes for cash at 3F per kg; in Paris they cost five times as much. With average wages frozen at 1,500F per month for men and 1,300F for women, shopping around was time-consuming and exhausting.[3]

The chaos immediately after the defeat was unbelievable. In many areas under no military threat from the German advance, the population had been ordered by local authorities, the police or Gendarmerie officers to leave their homes, taking only three days' provisions with them. In many of the half-empty villages and towns German soldiers set up for the hungry stay-at-homes and returnees a soup kitchen and distributed bread to them. German railwaymen were driving the few trains that enabled the first refugees to return home. On the bandstands in public parks and in front of town halls, Wehrmacht musicians played afternoon concerts, whose programmes included a token French composition like an extract from Bizet's *Carmen* to calm the population and show them what German *Kultur* was all about.

Compounding the confusion, France was now divided in two. Hitler did not wish to occupy the whole of France, because this would have required keeping hundreds of thousands of men there on garrison duty, men he needed for his planned invasion of the USSR. Under the June 1940 armistice, he therefore annexed the industrial northeast *départements* rich in mineral deposits and heavy industry and declared the border provinces of Alsace and Lorraine, also known by their historic German names of Elsass und Lotharingen, to be part of the Reich. For strategic reasons, the coastline from the Belgian border to the Pyrenees was occupied, and this Occupied Zone stretched so far inland in the north as to absorb more than half of France. The remaining two-fifths of the country, governed from Vichy, was known euphemistically as the Free Zone, with the exception of some pockets in the south-east that were occupied by Italian forces as a result of Mussolini's 'stab in the back' incursions after *Il Duce* had waited to make sure that the main French armies had been beaten by the Wehrmacht.

Zone attached to German military government of Belgium

Cherbourg

Forbidden zone

Paris

Zone annexed into the Reich

Brest   OCCUPIED
          ZONE   Orleans

Reserved zone

Tours   Bourges

Demarcation Line

                        Lyon
            Vichy

            FREE   Grenoble
Bordeaux   ZONE

Italian-occupied pockets

Bayonne

          Toulouse
                    Marseilles

France divided by the armistice agreement.

On the hoardings all over the Occupied Zone, the tattered general mobilisation notices from the previous September had been covered by more recent posters boasting, 'We shall win because we are the stronger'. These, in turn, were now covered up by thousands of German posters showing a valiant Wehrmacht soldier holding a grateful small child in his arms above the message, 'Abandoned by your leaders, put your trust in the German soldier'. For many French civilians, there was no one else they could trust, with their civil servants, police and even the local firemen far away and uncertain when they could return.

An acting brigadier named Charles de Gaulle, who had briefly served as Minister of Defence in Paul Reynaud's government that handed power to Marshal Pétain on 16 June, disagreed. On 18 June he issued over the BBC French Service from London a call to arms that was heard by very few French listeners, but swiftly reproduced clandestinely in print all over France. It read:

To the people of France

France has lost a battle, but France has not lost the war!

Unworthy leaders have capitulated through panic and delivered the country into servitude. However, nothing is lost! Nothing is lost because this war is a world war. The immense forces of the free world have not yet come into play. One day, they will crush the enemy.

On that day, France must share in the victory to recover her liberty and her prestige.

That is my sole aim, and the reason why I invite all Frenchmen, wherever they may be, to join me in action, in sacrifice and hope.

Our fatherland is in danger of dying. Let us all fight to save it.

Vive la France!

The writer François Mauriac, later a strong supporter of de Gaulle, remarked at the time: 'Purely symbolic, his obstinacy. Very fine, but ineffectual.'[4] The reaction of most of his audience to the radioed call to arms, or its clandestinely printed copies, was bafflement. They reasoned that France's two most famous soldiers President Philippe Pétain and Chief of Staff General Maurice Weygand must have considered all the possibilities and have a better grasp of the situation than this unknown renegade in London. There was also the worrying thought that, should de Gaulle lose his solitary gamble – which seemed only too likely at the time – his supporters could legally be condemned to death for high treason by the French government, as was de Gaulle himself shortly afterward.

It was one thing for a career soldier like him, safely across the Channel in London, to call upon his countrymen to resist the German invader, but what could ordinary people at the mercy of Hitler's victorious war machine do about it? The first individual acts were limited to disobedience of German proclamations, which invited reprisals to serve as lessons to the general population, and a scattering of acts of unthinking desperation. In Rouen, Epinal and Royenne lone protesters cut German telephone lines and were executed by firing squad. In Bordeaux a distraught Polish refugee shook his fist at a military band, for which he too was shot on 27 August.

At the time, most French people were saying that the British Expeditionary Force had 'fought to the last drop of French blood' before running away in the Dunkirk evacuation, although a few resolute souls in the north-eastern *départements*, who recalled the Tommies fighting alongside their fathers in the previous war, did shelter and help British servicemen on the run out of humanitarian instinct. They took this risk in defiance of ubiquitous German posters warning that the penalty for doing so was death.

A few patriots and political activists opposed to fascism braved the dangers of duplicating and distributing anti-German tracts bearing news from abroad, especially the BBC French Service, but most people considered this sort of activity to be *un refus absurde* – a ridiculous refusal to face the facts. In the larger towns of the Free Zone exiled Alsatians and Lorrainers who could not return home and intellectuals from the north whose political reputations made it inadvisable to return to the Occupied Zone – as well as Jews and others with good reason to fear German racial policy – all formed their own groups where resistance was talked about, but little of their hopeless frustration was translated into action in the early months of the occupation.

One of the very few people to respond immediately to de Gaulle's call by thinking in terms of espionage that could be used against the Germans was Catholic farmer Louis de la Bardonnie, who lived in an elegant château above the sleepy Dordogne village of Le Breuilh. A pre-war member of the far-right Action Française party, whose members supported the collaborationist government in Vichy headed by Marshal Philippe Pétain, Bardonnie's personal sense of honour obliged him to resign from Action Française after the defeat, stating in writing that he withdrew his support from Pétain, whom he regarded as a traitor for capitulating to Hitler. There was little else that Pétain could have done, except leave France and continue the war from French North Africa, as a minority of officers and politicians – the latter mainly Jewish – urged him to do.

With the aim of collecting intelligence that could be used against the forces occupying his country and transmitting it somehow to de Gaulle's intelligence service in London, then known as *le deuxième bureau*, Bardonnie contacted a small group of trusted friends who shared his patriotic feelings. De Gaulle's *deuxième bureau* was commanded by André Dewavrin, who took the *nom de guerre* of 'Colonel Passy'. One of his first recruits inside occupied France was Gilbert Renault, a thickset, balding, dynamic 35-year-old film producer with a prodigious memory, whose alias was 'Colonel Rémy'. He regularly crossed the Demarcation Line from the Occupied Zone carrying military intelligence collected by a network of informers in Brittany and along the Atlantic coast. Once in the Free Zone, Rémy gave this to Bardonnie, who passed it to the guard of a train leaving Pau for Canfranc in Spain. From there, a French customs official took it to Jacques Pigeonneau, the Vichy consul general in Madrid, who forwarded the vital envelope to London.

While Rémy risked only his own life, Bardonnie and his friends of both sexes had families to worry about. By keeping in his house a transmitter furnished by Rémy, plus weapons and 10 million francs in secret funds at times, and by allowing his home to be used as a safe house by two other Gaullist agents, Bardonnie was placing at risk his wife Denyse and their nine children. Among his group was Paul Armbruster, a refugee from Alsace who had lived through the German occupation of the province in 1914–18, later studying in Germany and working there for French Intelligence undercover as a journalist. He persuaded Bardonnie to go underground using false identities after initiating proceedings for divorce with the aim of protecting Denyse and their children from guilt by association – as would have been the case because the Nazi code of *Sippenhaft* made all members of a suspect's family equally guilty. Armbruster also assured Louis and Denyse that their children would be left alone by the Germans because of their blue eyes and blonde hair. On several nail-bitingly terrifying occasions, his advice was proved right.

Two other members of Bardonnie's tight-knit *réseau* were Freemasons working as pilots for the port of Bordeaux, who conned the U-boats up the treacherous Gironde estuary into port at the end of each foray and guided them out to sea again. To begin with, the information of this traffic which they sent to London was considered 'too good to be true' and not acted upon. Their greatest frustration was that the immense U-boat pens being built by the Organisation Todt in Bordeaux were never bombed during construction because, once completed in autumn 1942, they were bombproof

– and still stand today, indestructible. Grand Admiral Doenitz considered the British failure to destroy the pens along the Atlantic coast while they were still vulnerable one of the greatest mistakes of the RAF bombing campaign in the entire war.[5]

However, Bardonnie's pilots were eventually able to claim the credit for eleven U-boats destroyed by Allied aircraft after leaving the Gironde estuary, having diverted suspicion from themselves by the daring expedient of repeatedly telling their German employers that the losses must be due to a spy inside their own port administration!

Like the Bardonnie-Rémy operation, all Resistance networks were organised groups of men and women who shared a particular political or religious orientation but, for security reasons, had little or no contact with other groups or individuals likely to take unwarranted risks. At the time of the blitzkrieg invasion in June 1940, Hitler had dismissed his generals' fears of organised resistance to the occupation of France by telling them that the French nation was so irrevocably divided by class, politics and religion as to be unable to create a unified resistance to anything. How close he was to being right is borne out by the many occasions on which different Resistance networks worked against each other to the advantage of their common enemy.

Eventually the most tightly, indeed punitively, disciplined Resistance networks were the various communist factions. Because of its very efficient propaganda machine, Le Parti Communiste Français (PCF) was later believed by many to have been an important force in the Resistance from the first day of the occupation. In fact, far from opposing the arrival of German troops on occupation duties, it obeyed the spirit of the German-Soviet Non-Aggression Pact signed in August 1939 and supported Hitler for the first twenty months of the Second World War. The PCF's daily *L'Humanité* had been banned for its anti-war stance during the phoney war of September 1939 to June 1940 – as had the British Communist Party's organ *The Daily Worker* in Britain. When the German occupation authorities re-authorised publication of *L'Humanité*, editorials followed instructions from Moscow by dubbing the recent conflict 'an imperialist war', for which the capitalists of Britain and France were mostly to blame. De Gaulle was labelled a lackey of the international banking interests in the City of London and readers were urged to regard German soldiers in France as fellow workers far from home, for whom works committees should organise picnics, to make them feel welcome.

On 22 June 1941, Hitler showed what he thought of the paper on which the pact was written by launching Operation Barbarossa, his invasion of the USSR. The Comintern in Moscow immediately ordered the PCF to go underground – its secretary general Maurice Thorez was safely installed in Moscow, working with the Comintern – and execute a 180-degree turn vis-à-vis the occupation forces. Going underground was not too difficult for many members because, when the party was banned during the phoney war, its elected *députés* who were not immediately arrested went underground, as did many less well-known activists. There was thus already a cell structure in which no one member could betray more than a few colleagues.

Reversing the previous love affair with the occupation troops was a more bloody business: orders came swiftly from Moscow to launch a campaign of terrorism, assassinating German military personnel and civilians. This had nothing to do with the French war effort, but was intended to oblige the German forces in France to take reprisals by shooting hostages and thus drive a wedge between themselves and the previously passive population. This in turn would force Hitler to keep in France on garrison duties whole divisions which could otherwise have been transferred to the Eastern Front. Their presence there could have proved critical during the German advance on Moscow when the Soviet armies, badly trained, poorly equipped and purged of most of their commanders from colonels upwards, were collapsing like a house of cards.

Initially, PCF activists worked under a number of banners, but the party's perpetual paranoia regarding individual initiative forced a unification at the beginning of 1942 under the apparently patriotic name Francs-Tireurs et Partisans (FTP), a title borrowed from the patriotic militias that had fought against the German invaders during the Franco-Prussian war of 1870. Although the PCF propaganda machine portrayed its killers as heroic patriots fighting the German enemy, few people outside the party thought the assassinations heroic or even of any value. For example, after a Wehrmacht captain was shot dead on the Boulevard de Strasbourg in Paris on 16 September 1941, journalists of all shades except the communists reflected the mood of the population and publicly deplored the assassination. Author Pierre Audiat summed up their views to this and previous assassinations:

> It is by no means clear how the elimination of a German soldier who is only here in obedience to military discipline might influence the outcome of the war. Had some truly heroic gesture been at stake, the murderer should have fulfilled his patriotism by staying right out in the open, to pay the price.[6]

From London, de Gaulle condemned the assassination campaign as militarily useless.[7] Most other factions in the Resistance regretted the PCF assassination campaign because it achieved nothing for France and simply made life more difficult for everyone. So, the largest single element of the Resistance was frequently at odds with the others from June 1941 onwards.

De Gaulle therefore used a number of politically astute figures in efforts to unite the various groups in the Resistance under his overall control. Socialist politicians Pierre Brossolette and Christian Pineau played their parts but most credit is usually given to a brilliant administrator named Jean Moulin. Parachuted into France in January 1942, this former prefect of Chartres had by the end of the year drawn the three main Resistance networks of the Free Zone – COMBAT, LIBERATION-SUD and the communist FTP – into a loose federation titled 'Les Mouvements Unis de la Résistance' (MUR). As the plurality of the title indicates, command was divided. Charles Frenay, the hard-line escaped POW ex-officer who had founded COMBAT with a core of other military men, refused to collaborate with FTP, with whose pro-Moscow politics he strongly disagreed, while both FTP and LIBERATION-SUD claimed that Frenay was a militaristic dictator. The differences between the various leaders were deliberately played up by the infiltration into the other networks of undercover communists nicknamed 'submarines'.

Frenay, as befitted his military background, sought approval from his superiors – in this case, General de Gaulle. In September 1942 he had travelled to London and met de Gaulle, who gave him a solemn assurance that organised groups in France who wanted to fight the Germans would be supplied from London with arms and other provisions. Although this was in accord with Churchill's desire to 'set Europe ablaze', the Allied military commanders mistrusted the idea of arming civilians in an occupied country where the weapons might fall into German hands and one day be used against Allied soldiers. They also mistrusted the political motivation of many Resistance networks, particularly the communist-dominated ones. Implementation of de Gaulle's undertaking was thus inadequate, irregular and subject to assessment of the recipients by London's Special Operations Executive (SOE).

Since none of the various movements' leaders agreed to work with the others, Moulin harnessed them loosely to his troika by astute manipulation and by doling out subsidies from funds parachuted to him with arms drops – and then withdrawing financial support when someone became too difficult. In the first five months of 1943 his subsidies totalled 71 million francs.[8] As to what was done with this money, researchers run into blank walls, since it was simply written off back at base, with no records kept of the disbursements, and most Resistance operations at this point cost no more than a few bullets or some plastic explosive.

Although Moulin's brief from London ran only in the Free Zone initially, he also made contacts with the PCF hard core in Paris, working directly for Moscow. Shortly thereafter, 'Col Passy', whose intelligence operation was now called Le Bureau Central de Renseignements et d'Action (BCRA), defied all the canons of intelligence work by parachuting into France at the end of February 1943. Moulin chose the moment to return to London and did not return to France until 21 March.

There was considerable friction between BCRA officers and those of Major Maurice Buckmaster's Section F of SOE, on whom BCRA depended for clandestine pick-ups in France and the return of agents to the field, for arms and other supply drops and for finance and communications links. BCRA was, however, kept at arm's length by SOE's creation of Section RF (standing for République Française) whose main function was to separate the two organisations, allegedly because BCRA was riddled with double agents reporting to Vichy. Seemingly justifying SOE's caution, on 9 June 1943 in Paris the Gestapo arrested Moulin's military counterpart General Charles Delestraint, code name 'Vidal'. He was a man so unsuited for the clandestine life that he was caught after signing his true name in a hotel register. Once arrested, there could be no question of denying his mission or using an alibi because he was carrying identity papers in his own name. Detained with him was one René Hardy, who was liberated a few days later with no marks of ill treatment, but did not tell his Resistance comrades that he had been arrested.

The major breakthrough in unifying the many Resistance movements came on 27 May 1943, when the first meeting was held, in Paris, of the Conseil National de la Résistance (CNR). Three of the movements were those of the Free Zone, co-existing uneasily thanks to Jean Moulin; the other five were from the Occupied Zone, brought together by fellow Gaullist Pierre Brossolette, and represented six political parties and two national trade unions.

On 21 June 1943 Moulin committed a fatal error. Although well aware that he was being hunted all over France by the Gestapo and its French collaborators, he called a meeting in Caluire, a suburb of Lyon, of the heads of the eight Resistance networks in the CNR. Any one of the attendees was likely to be under surveillance and thus unwittingly to lead his shadowers to the meeting. It is hard to find a sane reason for such a major error, which may have been due to a disarming sense of triumph at getting this group of powerful men to set aside their internecine conflicts in a common cause.

The venue for the meeting in the afternoon of 21 June was in the house of dental surgeon Dr Dugoujon, chosen because Moulin thought they could enter and leave unnoticed among the coming and going of Dugoujon's patients. Frenay, in London for a briefing, was represented by his deputy Henri Aubry, who brought along René Hardy. Representing LIBERATION-SUD was a PCF member named Raymond Aubrac.

The dentist's house was already staked out before they arrived and the meeting had no sooner begun than Gestapo agents burst in and handcuffed everyone, including genuine patients awaiting treatment. As they were all being herded into closed vans, Hardy made a run for it. Despite several Gestapo men turning automatic weapons in his direction, he escaped with only a slight leg wound – a remarkable achievement for a man running with his wrists cuffed behind the back.

The job of eliciting information from those arrested fell to the infamous SS Obersturmführer Klaus Barbie, the Gestapo boss in Lyon, who earned the title 'The Butcher of Lyon'. In his torture chambers at the Ecole de Santé Militaire, Moulin claimed he was Jacques Martel, an art dealer from Nice, and gave the address of a genuine art gallery there, of which he was the legal owner. Barbie brushed this alibi aside, calling him by his Resistance code name, 'Max'. What happened in the following thirty hours is best left to the imagination. The local French police noted the arrest routinely, between reports of ID cards stolen from a town hall and an increase in thefts of vegetables from private gardens. On the evening of 23 June the 'trusty' prison barber in Montluc prison was ordered to shave an unconscious man, who had obviously been severely tortured and whose flesh was cold to his touch. Moulin mumbled something in English and asked for water. The guard rinsed out a shaving mug and the barber held it to Moulin's mouth, but he could only swallow a few drops before losing consciousness again.

Driven to Paris, he was lodged for two weeks in a cell at No. 40 Boulevard Victor Hugo, a suburban villa in Neuilly used by the Gestapo as an interrogation centre. Delestraint and another prisoner were brought there from Fresnes prison to be shown Moulin lying on a stretcher. Noting that his skin had turned yellow and his respiration was hardly noticeable, the dignified Delestraint, who could speak German, replied coldly to the guards' questions with, 'How do you expect me to identify a man in that condition?'

Officially, Jean Moulin died in a train taking him to Germany on 8 July 1943, aged 44. General Delestraint was transferred to the concentration camp at Natzwiller[9] in Alsace and from there in September to Dachau, where he was shot and cremated on the morning of 19 April 1945, aged 64. In one successful operation the Gestapo had neutralised both the military and the political leaders of the Gaullist Resistance.

Just occasionally, Klaus Barbie seems to have been cheated of a victim. Arrested with Jean Moulin was Raymond Aubrac, whose Jewish wife Lucie was also a member of the PCF. The mother of a young child by Raymond, she devised a plan to rescue her husband, based on a huge gamble: that his false identity as 'Claude Ermulin' had not been broken under torture. Two days after the arrests, she arrived asking to see Barbie at the Ecole de Santé Militaire. Smartly dressed and visibly pregnant, she called herself Ghislaine de Barbantine. Most French people avoided the sadistic Gestapo officer and his colleagues like the plague, so Barbie was intrigued and agreed to see her. He was smartly dressed, she afterwards recalled, in a light summer suit and pink shirt, and had an attractive woman with him, as usual – he enjoyed fondling a woman while watching his victims being tortured.

Lucie's first request to see 'Ermulin' was rejected, but she returned on 21 October and succeeded in meeting Barbie again by dint of bribes to French staff working for the Gestapo. When he asked what she wanted, Lucie cried hysterically that she was ashamed to be carrying a child by a criminal like 'Ermulin' and wanted to tell him just what she thought of him. As she had astutely deduced, the idea of a wronged woman tongue-lashing a tortured detainee so appealed to Barbie's perverted sense of humour that he sent for prisoner 'Ermulin' to be brought to the Ecole de Santé Militaire.

Apparently unmoved by his pitiful state after four months in the Gestapo cells of Montluc prison, Lucie raved at 'Ermulin' that whatever was happening served him right as far as she was concerned, but she needed a name for her child and expected him to 'do the decent thing' and marry her. 'Ermulin' was hardly in a condition to marry anyone. The whole point of the dangerous pantomime was to have him brought to the medical school for the confrontation. As the police van was returning him and Barbie's other victims of the day to Montluc prison after interrogation, two cars closed in on it and automatic fire from silenced weapons killed the men in the driver's cab and mowed down the guards who jumped out, save one who escaped. The prisoners were unharmed in the attack. By risking her own life, Lucie Aubrac had saved that of her husband.[10]

Was that the truth? Accused of being the traitor who betrayed Jean Moulin and the others in Dr Dugoujon's house on 27 May 1943, René Hardy was tried by a civil court in 1947 and a military tribunal in 1950, but narrowly escaped conviction on both occasions for lack of proof. When Barbie was eventually extradited from Bolivia in 1983, he was held in Montluc prison at Lyon, where so many of his victims had suffered atrociously. Throughout his detention, he repeatedly threatened to 'tell the truth' about some scandals of the Resistance. The following year Maître Jacques Vergès, Barbie's lawyer, claimed that Raymond Aubrac was a double agent, working for Barbie.

On 11 May 1987 Barbie's first trial for crimes against humanity – the only possible charge still legally valid after so many years – opened in Lyon. After two months of hearings, he was found guilty and sentenced to life imprisonment. In October a second trial opened, with Vergès determined to discredit the Resistance by proving his allegation of 1984 that its great heroine Lucie Aubrac was a liar and that her husband was the traitor who had betrayed Moulin, having agreed, when arrested in March 1943, to act as Barbie's secret informer within the Resistance. According to Barbie's testimony, he had personally arranged Raymond Aubrac's seemingly miraculous rescue by his wife in return for this collaboration. On 25 September 1991 Barbie died, still unrepentant for his actions during the occupation of France, and the investigation was officially closed.

Two days after his death, a sixty-three-page document called *Le testament de Klaus Barbie*, but allegedly written by Vergès, circulated in French media circles. It included this allegation. Vergès, a shadowy Francophobe French-Thai-Algerian figure, who professed to be both a communist and a Muslim, was a personal friend of the insane Cambodian dictator Pol Pot and was best known to the general public for his high-profile cases defending extremely unpopular clients like the assassin Ilich Ramírez Sánchez, nicknamed 'the Jackal'.

In April 1997 the Lyonnais reporter Gérard Chauvy published *Aubrac, Lyon 1943* repeating the accusations against Lucie and Raymond Aubrac, who sued for slander and demanded the withdrawal of the book. The Aubrac couple assembled a number of eyewitnesses to the events of 1943, including the man who organised the raid on the prison van, all of whom testified that Chauvy had never bothered to interview them. The tribunal imposed fines of 60,000F on him and 100,000F on the publisher. Their appeal being rejected, the fines were raised to a global sum of 400,000F.

Lucie Aubrac wrote several books about the Resistance and naturally did everything to refute Barbie's story, but some people in France choose to believe Barbie rather than credit her with the rescue of her husband. Which account is the truth? After the liberation, de Gaulle's priority was to restore the shattered morale of the French nation, so many heroes and heroines were created to bolster 'the legend of the Resistance'. Lucie Aubrac was one. It is hard to credit the account of a sadistic torturer and murderer like Barbie, as manipulated by the Francophobe Vergès, but was he telling the truth or simply attempting to besmirch the record of real French heroes and heroines?

The Resistance numbered many women in its ranks. Some, like Aubrac, Marie-Madeleine Fourcade, who ran the Gaullist HERISSON network, the feminist Bertie Albrecht and Danielle Casanova, who died in Auschwitz, are famous. There were also thousands of other women who played their parts, exploiting the advantages of their sex. This became increasingly important as time passed and controls tightened up in both zones, since women per se were not perceived as being dangerous by the predominantly male German security forces. Women's potential for resistance activity was likewise underestimated by the Vichy Milice, whose members had grown up in the ultra-chauvinist pre-war Third Republic, under which women had no rights to sign contracts, own property, vote or hold public office – rights that would not be granted to Frenchwomen until after the liberation.

2

PUTTING THE DIRT IN 'DIRTY WAR'

The concept of SOE stems from the very first days after the invasion of France in May 1940, when the Chiefs of Staff minuted the British War Cabinet that, should the French army and Lord Gort's British Expeditionary Force be defeated, Germany might in turn be brought down in the long run by economic pressure and a campaign of industrial unrest in the conquered territories. This was followed by Anthony Eden, then War Minister, forwarding a proposal for an organisation to train agents and execute irregular warfare in German-occupied Europe with special emphasis on France, where any re-invasion of the Continent was almost bound to take place.

The new prime minister, Winston Churchill, was delighted and decided that the enterprise should be independent of the three services. The new organisation was, in the words of Hugh Dalton, Minister for Economic Warfare, to be free of:

> … the British Civil Service [and] the British military machine. [It must] coordinate, inspire, control and assist the nationals of the oppressed countries, who must themselves be the direct participants. We need absolute secrecy, a certain fanatical enthusiasm, willingness to work with people of different nationalities, and complete political reliability. Some of these qualities are to be found in some military officers and, if such men are available, they should undoubtedly be used. But the organisation should, in my view, be entirely independent of the War Office machine.[1]

As indeed it was, except for borrowing of training personnel for instruction in unarmed combat, wireless transmissions and use of weapons – and for use of RAF aircraft to drop supplies and land and recover agents from the field. SOE was tasked, in the prime minister's words, 'to set Europe ablaze'. His private nickname for it was 'the Ministry of Ungentlemanly Warfare'. Within certain limits, it did set parts of Europe ablaze, at the cost of burning also many innocent people, including citizens in the occupied countries who thought they were working with London to liberate their homelands, but were in fact being used as pawns, sacrificed in games of which they were unaware.

Section F of SOE, with responsibility for espionage and sabotage in France, was headed from September 1941 by Maurice Buckmaster, an Old Etonian who had been employed pre-war as a manager for the Ford Motor Company in France. His permanent staff numbered no more than seven, based in a flat in Orchard Court, off Portman Square in London's West End. Buckmaster's chief assistant was Nicholas Bodington, a pre-war Paris correspondent for the *Daily Express*, thought to have moonlighted there for British Intelligence. During that time, he met an extrovert French air force pilot named Henri Déricourt, who made friends wherever he flew, including in Nazi Germany. In charge of welfare and 'prepping' agents for their missions was an astonishingly cool and competent civilian, Ms Vera Atkins, who hid her exotic Romanian-Jewish origins under her very English manners. Recruitment and supervision of training was the responsibility of Major Selwyn Jepson, who used the alias 'Mr Potter' when interviewing prospective agents in English and French, of which his knowledge was so good that he could tell in what region of France they had picked up the language.

All this had to be done without the prospective agents knowing for what or by whom they were being interviewed. As one of them afterwards recalled:

> I met [Jepson] in a bare office at the Northumberland Hotel and we talked together in French for three-quarters of an hour. He didn't say anything at all about the actual set-up and at the end he said, 'All right, I think we've got a job for you. You start your training on 1 August.' And that was it. I still had no idea what I was actually signing up for.[2]

The training course was so tough that a failure rate of twelve out of a course of fifteen recruits was not unusual. It included field craft such as recognising when one was being followed and techniques of losing a tail, and the use not only of British weapons but also of American and enemy small arms, which had to be stripped down and reassembled in the dark by feel alone. Target shooting was made more difficult by taking place at the end of an exhausting obstacle course. The course ended with parachute training at Ringway airport near Manchester.

In 1942 Buckmaster decided to set up a totally new network to be run by Francis Anthony Suttill, a 33-year-old lawyer qualified in both Britain and France. He may have been a good lawyer but, like Delestraint and Moulin, lacked the paranoia necessary for clandestine work in an occupied country. Déricourt afterwards summed up Suttill as 'more suited to be an officer in a gung-ho cavalry regiment than for clandestine warfare'. In retrospect, that may have been a powerful reason for selecting Suttill.

He christened the new network PROSPER, after a fifth-century theologian named Prosper of Aquitaine. On 24 September 1942 PROSPER's courier Andrée Borrel was parachuted into France in preparation for Suttill's arrival. In the early hours of 2 October 1942 a signal flashed from a field near Vendôme, midway between Orleans and Le Mans, was spotted by the pilot of an RAF Hudson whose passenger was Francis Suttill. Once on the ground, Suttill immediately set about recruiting agents throughout northern France with very poor security until several thousand people were involved directly or indirectly, many of them knowing the identities of far too many other members of the network.

At Norfolk House in St James's Square in London was the office of Chief of Staff to the (yet to be appointed) Supreme Allied Commander (COSSAC). This was also the umbrella beneath which several shadowy sub-organisations lurked – in particular, the London

Controlling Section run by Colonel John Bevan, among whose creative brains was Wing Commander Dennis Wheatley, later to be a world-famous author. Bevan's predecessor, Colonel Oliver Stanley, had resigned rather than deliberately misinform Resistance agents regarding the Dieppe raid. This was done with a view to letting them be caught in order to reveal under torture their false information so as to convince Hitler that the disastrous raid which cost 906 deaths in the invasion force and saw 2,195 men taken prisoner was a prelude to a full-scale invasion. Bevan, in civilian life a stockbroker, was made of sterner stuff.

It is against that background of cynical deceit that the PROSPER network must be assessed. Suttill's first wireless operator Gilbert Norman arrived in November, followed a few weeks later by a second radio operator of Armenian origin named Jack Agazarian. Bodington brought in his old pal Déricourt to select and supervise landing grounds for Section F agents.

On 22 January 1943, Déricourt returned to France, tasked with organising reception parties and safe houses for new arrivals and agents returning to Britain. At first, everything seemed to be working out surprisingly well. During April and May PROSPER received 1,006 Stens, 1,877 incendiary devices and 4,489 grenades; in June it took delivery of another 190 man-sized containers of materiel on thirty-three landing grounds spread over twelve *départements*. Within a few months, Déricourt also safely brought in no fewer than sixty-seven agents, but his amazing confidence and success rate was beginning to worry Agazarian so much that when next recalled to London, he passed on his suspicions to Bodington and Buckmaster.

Agazarian was right. Déricourt's successes were due to his pre-war friendship with SS-Sturmbannführer Karl Boemelburg, the senior German spy-catcher in France. Listed in the Paris Gestapo files as Agent BOE/48,[3] Déricourt fed the details of the clandestine flights to Boemelburg, who then ordered anti-aircraft batteries along the flight path of the aircraft not to fire at them. What Boemelburg did not know is that his double agent was in fact a triple agent acting under instructions from SIS that overrode his duties for Section F. This was the real dirt of the deception operation: Suttill's vast network was to be sacrificed in order to feed false information about the date of the planned Allied invasion of Europe when its members were tortured after capture by the Gestapo.

However, Buckmaster remained unconvinced by Agazarian and sent Bodington into France to check out the situation. Even when Suttill, Borrel and Norman were arrested by the Gestapo on 23 June and the PROSPER network wound up, Buckmaster never lost his faith in Déricourt and even put in writing as late as December 1945 that he was innocent of any collaboration with the Germans, and 'had the finest record of operations completed of any member of SOE'.[4]

One essential requirement for a spy is to have the appearance and demeanour of a grey person who does not stand out in a crowd, which could certainly not be said of Noor Inayat Khan, a head-turningly beautiful courier whose looks would cost her her life. She was now the only member of the PROSPER network still at liberty, apart from Déricourt. Khan reported to London that she could no longer contact any members of the network. One can imagine the loneliness and fear she must have felt, stranded in an enemy-occupied country, knowing that so many people had been betrayed, and that some of them must have given her description, under torture or otherwise, to Gestapo officers. Déricourt tried unsuccessfully to persuade her to return to Britain. Was her refusal to go because she suspected he would hand her over to the Germans after bringing her to the landing field? We shall never know because she was betrayed and arrested on 13 October. Thereafter, the only concrete record of her existence is a sad little plaque at Dachau concentration camp, recording the deaths of Khan and three other SOE women agents on 13 September 1944, allegedly after a near-lethal beating meted out for his personal pleasure by the sadistic Allgemeine-SS officer Friedrich Wilhelm Rupert, later executed for this and other crimes.

That date was over two months after the deaths of Andrée Borrel and three other women agents at Natzwiller concentration camp in Alsace, as recorded on an equally sad plaque that was affixed to the camp crematorium there and is now in the memorial museum. Why the delay? Presumably because the women at Dachau were being interrogated for longer than the other four.

As *Nacht und Nebel* prisoners were destined to vanish without trace, the women at Natzwiller ceased administratively to exist. It was later discovered that they were taken individually to the sick bay on the evening of 6 July 1944, told to undress on the pretence that it was for an inoculation against typhus and then given what should have been an instantly lethal injection of phenol by the camp medical officer SS Untersturmführer Dr Werner Röhde or his assistant. Within minutes their bodies were shoved into the four-body camp crematorium by Hauptscharführer Peter Schraub. At least one of the women recovered consciousness sufficiently to scar Schraub's face with her fingernails before being forced inside and the door slammed, so that she was burned alive. When Buckmaster's assistant Vera Atkins, who made it her personal mission after the war to trace what had happened to the lost women agents, interviewed Schraub three months later, his face still bore the scars.[5]

After the Gestapo wound up PROSPER with the exception of Déricourt and Khan, London continued to receive radio transmissions from Norman. Although the 'hand' of the sender was his, the SOE officer responsible for codes and ciphers was convinced that these messages were being sent under German control. Refusing to share this view, Bodington volunteered to go to France and check out the situation on the ground. Given his knowledge of all the Section F networks, this was an incredible lapse of security. Although equipped with his cyanide pill, who could be sure he would use it on capture? Or, did he know of Déricourt's deal with Boemelburg, which made him as safe in France as he would have been in London?

Parachuted from an RAF Hudson on the night of 23 July, he was welcomed by Déricourt in a field near Soucelles, between Angers and Le Mans. According to his debriefing on return to Britain by Lysander on 17 August, he and Agazarian tossed a coin to decide which of them should go to an address Norman had given as his safe house in Paris. The coin-tossing was an unnecessary embroidery since, given the risk that it was a trap, it was logical for Bodington, as the senior officer, to order the less well-informed Agazarian to go. He was arrested at the house and tortured over a six-month period in the Gestapo wing of Fresnes prison before being deported to Flossenburg concentration camp in Bavaria. Although not designated an extermination camp, one in three prisoners died there.

At this stage the account of an episode in the Great Game descends into the shadowy world of a spy novel: who was the traitor? Soon after returning to Britain, Bodington was accused of being a double agent, as though he had betrayed Agazarian. Sacked from SOE, he was relegated to a non-sensitive post, lecturing servicemen on French politics. Suttill, Norman, Agazarian and several hundred of the PROSPECT agents died in captivity. Post-war interrogations of German counter-espionage officers revealed Déricourt's relationship with Boemelburg.

In April 1946 Déricourt was arrested at Croydon airport when about to fly to France with a considerable quantity of gold and platinum, for which he had no export licence. In view of his ostensibly excellent war record, the magistrate let him off with a £300 fine, which was paid by a mystery man, never formally connected with any government organisation. In November 1946 Déricourt was arrested in France and eventually tried in June 1948 for causing the deaths of the PROSPER agents. At the trial Bodington admitted that Déricourt had told him about his contacts with the Germans shortly after he landed in France on 23 July 1943. Largely on the evidence provided by Bodington, Déricourt was acquitted for lack of proof that he divulged any important information or betrayed any specific individual. He continued flying until meeting his death in a crash somewhere in Laos in November 1962.

Interviewed by author Rita Kramer, another SOE agent who worked successfully in France named Francis Cammaerts told her that he believed Bodington and Déricourt became double agents for the thrill of fooling their comrades, but a shrewd locally recruited radio operator working for PROSPER argued that the winding up of the network was deliberately arranged by MI6. Suttill and the others, he argued, had been given to understand that the planned Allied invasion was scheduled for Autumn 1943 – this in the knowledge that one or more of them would divulge this under torture, causing the German High Command Oberkommando der Wehrmacht (OKW) to keep in the north of France forces that could have been deployed elsewhere.

According to the alternative explanation of the PROSPER fiasco, Colonel Claude Dansey, deputy director of SIS, was using Déricourt as a triple agent inside Section F. In the context of the campaign of deception operations to confuse the Germans about the true date and whereabouts of the Normandy invasion, Déricourt was ordered by Dansey, without Section F having any suspicion of the darker game that was being played out right under its nose, to betray Suttill's network. Giving the enemy the PROSPER transmitters enabled them to mount a *Funkspiel* against London, as had been done in Holland with notable success. But that was only a sideshow. The real purpose of the triple agent betrayal was much darker: to sacrifice hundreds of Suttill's recruits in order to convince the Gestapo of the false information they divulged under torture.

This version, if true, is typical of Dansey's cynical worldview. He was a frigid, unlikeable man, known to dislike the French and mistrust all women, especially women agents. Unfortunately for history and historians, he gave orders for his widow to destroy all his confidential papers, secure in the knowledge that she would never dare to disobey him even after his death. And Nicholas Bodington died in Plymouth on 3 July 1974, taking with him, as did many intelligence officers, his secrets – in this case, the truth about the PROSPER betrayal.

It is against this background of deceit and betrayal that one has to assess what follows.

3

THE MAKING OF THE MAQUIS

Whatever their differences, and whenever they were founded, all the Resistance movements were formed for action, whether this was dissemination of news from the BBC or neutral sources, fly-posting anti-German tracts during the hours of darkness when curfew-breakers were liable to be shot on sight, or the collection of intelligence to be passed to de Gaulle's BCRA or Section F in London. In contrast, the Maquis arose not from any patriotism or political motivation, but was inadvertently created by the collaborationist French government based in the spa town of Vichy, headed by Marshal Philippe Pétain, the head of state, and his prime minister Pierre Laval, the manipulative Auvergnat lawyer who had single-handedly engineered the end of the Third Republic and the installation of the marshal as dictator, answerable to no one.

Laval had been hailed on the front cover of *Time* magazine, dated 4 January 1932, as 'The Man of the Year'. Yet, Pétain's dislike for the manipulative lawyer who had made him dictator was such that he fired Laval, but could not govern without his political acumen and was forced to reinstate him at German insistence. In one, possibly apocryphal, exchange between them at the time of Laval's return to power, he won back the premiership by saying: '*Monsieur le Maréchal, nous sommes dans la merde. Laissez-moi être votre éboueur*' – 'We're in the shit, marshal. So let me do the digging to get us out.'[1]

After Hitler's Minister for Armaments, Albert Speer, complained that the manpower shortage in the Reich was critical as losses on the Eastern Front sucked almost every fit adult German male into uniform, on 21 March 1942 Fritz Sauckel was appointed plenipotentiary labour boss empowered to drain the occupied territories of able-bodied workers and transport them into the Reich as a replacement labour force. Hanged at Nuremburg in October 1946 for the brutality of the German slave labour programme,[2] Sauckel was a physically insignificant man who grew a Hitler moustache to give him what he thought was an air of authority. Meeting Prime Minister Laval on 16 June 1942, he demanded 2,060,000 workers from France in addition to the 1.6 million Frenchmen locked away as POWs under the terms of the armistice of June 1940 and used since then as cheap labour in the Reich.

A week later Laval announced to the French people that he had done a deal under which, for every three volunteer workers heading east, one POW would be released to return home. Called La Relève, or 'the relief shift', the scheme was a dismal failure, enabling him to twist the facts at his post-war trial – he was a lawyer by profession – and claim that it was thanks to him only 341,500 French workers actually left, earning the release of 110,000 POWs. Of these, 10,000 were wounded and disabled men who should have been released without any *quid pro quo*.

On 8 November 1942 the Allies opened the 'second front' by invading French-occupied North Africa, where they met such brief resistance from the Vichy troops confronting them that on 10 November Admiral Darlan, as senior French officer in North Africa, ordered all French forces to cease fire. Effectively occupying all strategically relevant parts of Morocco and Algeria, the Allied forces prepared to move eastwards into Tunisia, threatening the rear of the Axis forces south of the Mediterranean, which were being pushed back westwards by the British forces based in Egypt.

Even on a map in Berlin, it was obvious that the sick Desert Fox, General Erwin Rommel, commanding the German and Italian forces in North Africa, could not win the war on two fronts which had now overtaken him. Given the problems of re-supply and shipping reinforcements across an increasingly Allied-dominated Mediterranean, it was only a question of time before the Allies would occupy the entire North African littoral from Morocco to Egypt. The German High Command was thus obliged to secure the Mediterranean coast of France against an amphibious invasion from North Africa by driving into the Free Zone on 11 November, after which the whole of France was occupied. The former Occupied Zone was now designated 'the northern zone' and the former Free Zone became 'the southern zone'.

The next step was Operation Lilac, which came on 17 November: the disarmament and demobilisation of the units in mainland France of Vichy's puny Armée de l'Armistice. Ordered by their own government to comply with German demands, many individual officers and men decided to act according to their own consciences and formed the disciplined Organisation Armée Secrète (OAS), separate from the political factions of the Resistance. Typical of these officers was Colonel Schlesser at Auch. Demobilising his 2nd Dragoons there, he told each man to keep in touch with comrades and hold himself ready for the call. Some demobilised men slipped away from their homes in darkness; others made gestures of open defiance, like Lieutenant Narcisse Geyer la Thivollet who rode out of 2nd Cuirassiers barracks in Lyon on horseback in full uniform and kept riding until contacting a Maquis unit in the bleak limestone uplands of the Vercors.

At the time of the armistice, Minister of War General Colson had penned a personal letter to the commander of each military region, ordering materiel and stores to be spirited away against the day when they could be used again, rather than tamely handed over to the Germans. The results were sometimes surprising. Within a few months, 65,000 rifles, 9,500 machine guns and automatic rifles, 200 mortars, fifty-five 75mm cannons and anti-tank guns had been administratively 'lost'. Several thousand trucks were 'leased' to civilian transport contractors who agreed to maintain them ready for return to the army at six hours' notice. The owner of one small trucking company in the south of France thus saw his fleet rise from five vehicles to 687! Sadly, when the Wehrmacht invaded the Free Zone in November 1942, all the secret arms dumps were useless to stop it. Based in Pau, Captain André Pommiès now created a network of arms dumps throughout the south-west. Yet, within a week of Operation Lilac many dumps had been betrayed by local informers.

The OAS reasoned that the Germans could not possibly afford sufficient manpower to police the whole of France, but would secure the Mediterranean littoral with a military presence and then rely on collaborators and informers to help them keep control of the rest of the southern zone. All it took to neutralise one of these traitors was a bullet, and there were plenty of those hidden away. Vichy's reply to this 'terrorism' and that of the PCF hit squads was the formation on 31 January 1943 of a paramilitary anti-terrorist force called La Milice under its infamous hard-line secretary general, Joseph Darnand. The *miliciens* – as its members were called – were charged with rooting out, arresting, imprisoning, deporting and killing Jews and members of Resistance movements, especially the various PCF groups. The brutal methods and lack of scruple they used, especially torture and blackmail, soon earned them the hatred of most of the population, even those who still supported Pétain politically.

In February 1943 Sauckel's unsated hunger for French labour forced Laval to introduce compulsory conscription of men of military age for labour service in the Reich. This was initially called Le Service Obligatoire du Travail until someone in Vichy with the vestige of a sense of humour pointed out that the initials SOT spelled the word *sot*, meaning 'stupid'. The hastily re-baptised Service de Travail Obligatoire (STO) applied both to men and to women aged 18 to 45 with no children. In practice, although 200,000 Frenchwomen did volunteer to go and work in Germany for money while their children were looked after in specially established residential homes, there was no forcible conscription for females because the Catholic Church refused to sanction this and Pétain could not afford to alienate the French cardinals and bishops who were among his most influential supporters.

It is estimated that only 785,000 men actually left France under the STO, half of them deserting on their first home leave.[3] Even before British bombs started falling regularly on industrial targets all over the Reich, it was impossible to keep secret that the conditions of work in Germany were far from what had been promised. The French STO conscripts lived in poorly heated dormitories often adjacent to factories which had become strategic targets for the RAF; they worked alongside prisoners and forced labourers from a score of conquered territories with no common language; few German women would have anything to do with sex-hungry foreign men because that was a criminal offence; there was little wine and meals were *Eintopf* – a single dish of unidentifiable stew instead of the traditional five-course French meal of soup, entrée, meat course, cheese and dessert.

The summons from the STO arrived couched in elegant officialese:

> I have the honour to inform you that the joint Franco-German Commission … has selected you for work with the Todt Organisation (or) to work in Germany. I invite you to present yourself at the German Labour Office on … to learn the date and time of your departure. Failure to comply with this posting is punishable under the provisions of the law.

On 15 February 1943 men who had reached their eighteenth birthdays in 1940, 1941 and 1942 received their STO call-up papers. However, Resistance tracts posted on walls and blowing along the streets of towns proclaimed that leaving France to go and work in Germany was treachery. Briefly, the communists and the Church were on the same side. On 21 March Cardinal Liénart defied the posters threatening 'pitiless sanctions' for those who did not present themselves at the recruitment centres and railway stations to catch their trains by announcing in Lyon that reporting for duty under the STO was not a duty of conscience for Catholics.

There were some legal alternatives to going to work in Germany. The Todt Organisation, charged with major construction projects like the bombproof submarine pens along the Channel and Atlantic coasts and the Westwall of anti-invasion fortifications that stretched from Norway to the Spanish border, was the biggest single employer in Europe with 2 million workers at its peak, including thousands of locally conscripted French labourers, who were paid a reasonable wage, and 3,000 men recruited as uniformed armed guards for construction sites. Working for it in France gained exemption from STO, as did employment in any French factory working for the Germans, which also paid twice the going rate elsewhere. The STO legislation caused severe rifts between the business community and Vichy because the only factories that could keep their labour forces intact were those fulfilling German orders.

The national police, Gendarmerie, Milice, fire services, railways and civil defence all offered shelter from the STO, and saw a rush of volunteers. A friend of the author signed up with Le Service de Surveillance des Voies. Wearing a blue-and-white armband, equipped with a torch and whistle and a bilingual *Ausweis*, he and a friend patrolled the rail tracks near his home town at night, ostensibly to prevent sabotage. In the event, when encountering saboteurs, they asked to be hit a few times in the face and then tied up, as their alibi for doing nothing.[4]

Another legitimate escape from the STO was to find a job with one of the many German organisations in France, so 2,000 young men went to work as fitters on German navy ships in French ports and as armed guards of the port installations. Another 1,982 donned German uniform as drivers in NSKK Motorgruppe, freeing Germans for more military tasks. On 7 October that year, Laval did another deal with Speer, under which 10,000 factories were designated 'S' and their workers exempted from the STO.

It was one thing to enact a law, quite another to enforce it. The response to the STO summons was feeble. As one example of what increasingly happened, three neighbours of the author set out for their STO train in a *gazogène* wood-burning car driven by the owner of the local garage that conveniently 'broke down' in front of the village gendarme. The gas produced in the generator bolted on to the rear bumper being notoriously unreliable, he obligingly issued a signed and stamped *procès verbal* confirming the breakdown. They continued their journey to the railway station, being careful to arrive after the departure of their train. The *procès verbal* stamped a second time by the STO representatives there, the three young men returned home and were not called again, their names having slipped through some administrative loophole.

At Vesoul in Franche-Comté only three of 400 conscripts reported for duty; in the Jura twenty-five out of 850; in Seine-et-Loire only thirty-one from 3,700.[5] The attitude of many police officers towards arresting defaulters was summed up by Lieutenant

Theret, head of the detachment at the Gare d'Orsay mainline station in Paris. He warned his men on 9 March 1943 that he 'would not find a single STO dodger and counted on them to do likewise as good Frenchmen'.[6] The Milice, however, made the tracking down of STO no-shows one of its main priorities.

It was thus, and with no political intent, that tens of thousands of young men went on the run after receiving their STO call-up. The majority decided to live rough in wild country. Meaning 'scrubland' or wild country, *maquis* is the only Corsican word to make it into the French language. Thus these young men were said to *prendre le maquis*. The report by Gendarmerie *chef d'escadron* Calvayrac in Haute-Savoie dated 22 March 1943 said, 'No-shows for STO are so numerous that only fifty of 340 reported in. Many men have abandoned their homes, their work and their family to take to the *maquis* instead'.[7] From there, the noun Maquis came to mean collectively 'those hiding in rough country' and *maquisard* was coined to mean a man hiding out on the run.

On 5 June 1943 Laval announced the departure of another 220,000 young men including agricultural labourers to Germany, resulting in widespread comments that the Germans were going to bleed France white by taking all its young men. One German administrator retorted to protesters that, whereas so far Germany had limited itself to taking only half of French production, it would in future take all. If a Frenchman wanted to eat well, his best plan would be to work in, or for, Germany. However, even Laval's new move did not pacify Fritz Sauckel, who reported to Hitler on 9 August:

> I have completely lost belief in the honest goodwill of the French Prime Minister. His refusal … to execute a further programme for recruiting 500,000 French workers to go to Germany before the end of 1943 … amounts to downright sabotage of the German struggle for life against Bolshevism.[8]

Life was tough for the young men hiding out far from a town, or even a village, where someone might betray them or inadvertently give them away. In Maquis groups with a semblance of discipline, reveille was at 6.30 a.m., followed by ablutions and breakfast. The salute to the flag, if observed, was accompanied rarely by a bugle call, more often by accordion or mouth-organ. Cleaning camp and other chores occupied the rest of the morning; obtaining food took up much of the afternoon. Often, foraging turned to robbery. Another neighbour of the author recalls answering a knock on the door in the middle of the night, to find three young men outside. One waved a pistol at him and demanded clothes and food against a scribbled receipt which he alleged de Gaulle would redeem after the liberation. More enterprising *maquisards* in the Ardennes hijacked mail bags containing several villages' food tickets and stole 150kg of government tobacco the next day.

The daily routine described by one *maquisard* with a band at La Plagne in the Alps, only 18 miles as the crow flies from the Italian frontier, was similar, but he mentioned the after-breakfast chore of packing up all personal belongings in case of need to evacuate the camp at a few minutes' notice. Morning drill was conducted in squads of six, without weapons because the only weapon in the camp was one pistol. After lunch there was a forced march in mountainous terrain to toughen up those recruits who were unfit city-dwellers. In his camp, 'lights out' was at 10 p.m., with everyone fully dressed in case of need to decamp during night. Sleep was interrupted by guard duty in two-man shifts of two hours each. The diet in his camp consisted of plenty of locally produced cow and sheep cheese, but little bread. When the weather was bad in winter, it was impossible for the foraging parties to make it down to the valley to replenish the stores, so the band had to subsist on boiled beef for a week at a time. Interestingly, he noted that it was easy to tell who was there intending to fight when weapons were available, and who was simply on the run from the STO.

He also described a night-time arms drop after SOE Major H.H.A. Thackthwaite, a headmaster in civilian life, had paid a visit to select suitable dropping zones where the surrounding mountainous terrain would not oblige the pilots to drop from too high an altitude. On hearing the right phrase on the BBC French Service announcing a drop for that same evening, they had to await confirmation at 1900hrs that a flight of thirteen Flying Fortresses would make the drop – but at the wrong place, higher up the mountain in deep snow. Even at the lower site there was between 1.5m and 2m of snow. Beacon fires were lit where they wanted the drop lower down the mountain, in the hope that the pilots would see them and simply adjust course. This worked well, except for one aircraft, which dropped its load several kilometres away, where it was recovered by the Germans. That served as a useful distraction, since they could hardly fail to hear the huge bombers flying overhead and the Maquis needed as long as possible to stash the arms and explosives in a nearby mine. Everything had to be back-packed to the mine by men on skis or snowshoes. Later, the men from this and other local Maquis groups came to the mine for weapons training in the galleries, transformed into firing ranges.

Although exempt from the STO because he was employed as a Paris fireman, Raymond Bredèche decided to go absent without leave while he still had the chance, despite this making him technically a deserter from the armed forces.[9] Prudently prepared with a compass and rucksack filled with warm clothing and food, he took a train to Grenoble and simply walked out of the town heading south-east into the wild country of what is now the Ecrins National Park until challenged by a sentinel at the approach to a Maquis camp. For him, it was as simple as that.

Whatever his dreams of glory, the reality was hard. The group had no weapons at all until an Italian army unit negotiating the 8,000ft high Col de la Muzelle in September lightened its load by dumping three crates of ammunition, handkerchiefs, socks and two rifles. Only then could Bredèche's band of young men pretend that they were fighters. There was little aggression involved; most were more concerned that they could now defend themselves if attacked by the Milice.[10] Their diet mainly consisted of potatoes bought under threat from local peasants, who would have preferred to sell their surplus on the black market at higher prices. It was a feast when Bredèche killed a metre-long *couleuvre* grass snake and roasted it over a fire.

Maquis 'wages' did not run to restaurant meals: camp leaders received 20F a day; 'NCOs' had from 9F to 15F; the rank and file received 5F only. Even these slender funds had to be stolen in raids on railway stations, post offices or houses of suspected collaborators and black marketeers. In January 1944 – only five months before D-Day – one Maquis band in Dordogne had a total of three Sten guns with ninety-two rounds

of ammunition, seven revolvers and twenty-three rifles. Another group further north
had three Sten guns, six grenades, thirty-five revolvers and thirteen rifles to be shared
between 100 men.

By the beginning of 1944, from a total of 670,000 French workers drafted to work
in the Reich, only 400,000 remained there, the missing quarter-million having failed
to return from home leave. Of them, it was estimated that about 40,000 were with one
or other of the Maquis bands.[11] The others took the risk of living in the towns under
assumed names with false papers. One of the luckiest was singer Yves Montand, who
came to Paris that spring to seek his fortune while on the run from the STO and being
technically Jewish. On the night after his first engagement in a night club, he was saved
from arrest by the proprietor of his hotel distracting a German military police NCO
from checking Montand's obviously false ID. Having lost his first pay packets playing
poker, Montand had a second stroke of luck when Edith Piaf sacked her male singer.
Supporting her on stage, Montand detested Piaf as heartily as she sneered at what she
called his 'poor singing', but when she insisted that he dress on stage like her – all in
black – he decided to make this his trademark style for the rest of his career.

Since there was no command structure linking the many Maquis bands, and even
those in the same locality kept contact with each other to a minimum for security
reasons, the Milice dealt with them piecemeal, usually by infiltrating informers. Each
new recruit had thus to be carefully vetted. When a Belgian walked into a camp of
maquisards near Thônes in the Rhône-Alpes region, full of plausible details of his family
being massacred by the SS, a search of his belongings revealed a hidden SS identity
card. Since he would not talk, there was no alternative but to kill him.

None of the group had any military training, but they all used *noms de guerre*, to
protect their families if caught. The one called Blanc-Blanc was chosen to do the deed
because he had already 'killed his first German', as the saying went. He picked up the
group's single Sten gun and begged the Belgian to pardon him. They embraced, after
which Blanc-Blanc could not press the trigger. With everyone looking embarrassed,
the Belgian said, 'You can't expect me to give you the balls to do it, so please get a
move on.'

The leader took the Sten from Blanc-Blanc and fired a single shot at close range, his
hands shaking so much that the Belgian was only wounded in the shoulder. Staunching
the blood with his handkerchief, he begged them to send it back to his mother
unwashed. The next bullet pierced his heart.[12]

4

THE LONELINESS OF THE
LONG-DISTANCE AGENT

In late 1943, as Allied planning for the invasion of Normandy advanced day by day, SOE stepped up its operations to cause the maximum amount of disruption and distraction for the German occupation forces all over France. Part of the aim was to delude OKW into thinking that Normandy was not the only area of France at risk of invasion and therefore keep its available manpower and weaponry spread out more widely across the country than was justified by the real risk. After the invasion, SOE's function was to be the tying down elsewhere of as many as possible of the Wehrmacht, Waffen-SS and Luftwaffe units that could otherwise be moved to the Normandy bridgehead.

One way to do this was somehow to weld the thousands of *maquisards* hiding out in wild country into a number of guerrilla armies that the Germans would have to deal with far from the beaches. SOE's French counterpart BCRA was now based near Algiers, as was an outpost of Section F code-named Massingham at Guyotville, west of Algiers. Both had the same idea, but for different reasons. In the case of BCRA, it was de Gaulle's desire that history should show how French people had liberated their own country, albeit with Allied help, so that it should not be thought by future generations that their forebears had sat passively at home waiting for the Anglo-American forces to drive the Germans out of France.

On the night of 21 September 1943 Major Richard Heslop of SOE was flown in to a landing ground near Tournus in Burgundy with cavalry officer Captain Jean Rosenthal of BCRA, a high-class jeweller and furrier in civilian life. Operation Musc was Heslop's second mission inside occupied France. He and Rosenthal were tasked with liaising with Maquis units in Resistance zone R1, concentrating on the valley of the River Ain north-east of Lyon and on the Glières plateau, lying to the south-east of Geneva, near the Italian frontier. The valley of the Ain had already been the scene for a sustained campaign of sabotage and guerrilla attacks on Vichy and German forces.

The purpose of Musc was to ascertain the numerical strength of the various Maquis bands, their level of training and combat readiness and need for airdrops of weapons and ammunition. Flown back to London on the night of 16 October, Heslop and Rosenthal reported conversations with Resistance leaders who had convinced them that a force of 2,350 *maquisards* could be assembled on the plateau of Glières

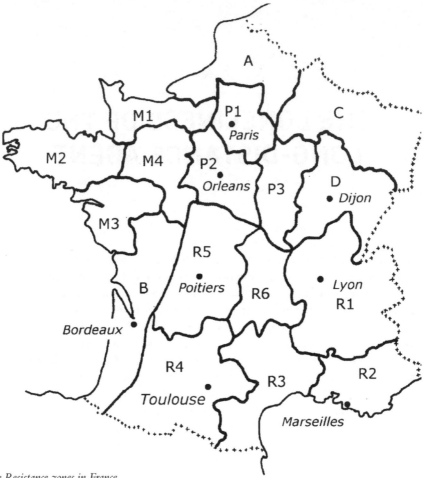

The Resistance zones in France.

as a self-contained army needing only to be supplied with arms and ammunition by air across the Mediterranean. This, it was thought, would enable them to hold off any German attack in this wild upland area while building up their strength to the point where they could harass the Germans in the rear after the coming Allied invasion.

Less than forty-eight hours later, Heslop was back in south-eastern France commanding the Marksman mission, with radio operator OSS Captain Owen D. Johnson and a wild card, American citizen Elizabeth Devereaux-Rochester, as courier. SOE had a penchant for well-educated girl agents and she certainly fulfilled this requirement, having been educated at Roedean school, lived with her British mother in Paris before the war and attended two Swiss finishing schools. However, she was untrained and undisciplined. Ordered back to Britain in the spring of 1944, she refused to comply and made her own way to Paris, where she was arrested at her mother's house in March. She managed to convince her interrogator that she had been wandering around France for months as a homeless refugee in order to avoid being locked up with all the other

American civilians in an internment camp. Imprisoned in the same camp at Vittel as her mother, she was eventually liberated in September.

Arriving with the Marksmen officers, but acting independently for BCRA, Rosenthal also returned to prepare both Maquis and Resistance groups for concerted action in conjunction with the coming Allied invasion. In January 1944 the inter-Allied mission code-named Union arrived in the area under the Gaullist Pierre Fourcaud. With him were SOE's Colonel Thackthwaite and a US Marine Corps officer seconded to OSS, Captain Peter Ortiz. He was a flamboyant character who had served five tough years in the French Foreign Legion pre-war, enlisting under the name of his Polish girlfriend in an effort to prevent his influential French father curbing his youthful urge for adventure by buying him out. Stationed in North Africa, he rose from *engagé volontaire* to acting lieutenant in his five-year term and would have been promoted to full lieutenant if he had signed on for a further five-year term. Instead, he left the Legion in 1937, but re-enlisted in October 1939 at the beginning of the phoney war, gaining a battlefield commission in May 1940.

He was wounded in northern France in June 1940 while driving a motorcycle through the German lines to blow up a fuel dump that should have been destroyed as a routine measure during the French retreat. Mission accomplished, Ortiz was returning through the lines when shot and left paralysed with a bullet-chipped spine. He recovered in a POW camp but, after fifteen months that included several escape attempts, he made his way to Lisbon in December 1941, whence he was repatriated to the United States.

Having an American mother, he was bilingual even before his service with the Legion and also had reasonable German, Spanish and Arabic, which earned him a promise of a commission in American intelligence. Ortiz, however, grew impatient to get back into the war and enlisted in the US Marine Corps Reserve, to be recommended for an officer's commission by the commanding officer of the training camp on Parris Island. On 1 August 1942, Ortiz was commissioned and then – in the way of the military – this ex-legionnaire who had made more than 100 jumps in North Africa was posted to Camp Lejeune for parachute training.

His second spell in the war began in Tangier after the Allied invasion of North Africa. With the rank of captain, he commanded a band of Tunisian nomads who could, as neutrals, move freely through the desert collecting intelligence on German dispositions. Accompanying them on a mission, he was wounded a second time during an encounter with a German patrol. No less a person than Major Gen. William J. Donovan, director of OSS, wrote of this exploit:

> While on reconnaissance on the Tunisian front, Captain Peter Ortiz U.S.M.C.R. was severely wounded in the right hand while engaged in a personal encounter with a German patrol. He dispersed the patrol with grenades. Captain Ortiz is making good recovery in hospital at Algiers. The P[urple] H[eart] was awarded to him.[1]

After a spell of convalescent leave, in July 1943 Ortiz was posted to London and parachuted by OSS into France with Thackthwaite's party on 6 January 1944. Once on the ground, Ortiz donned his USMC uniform and became the first Allied officer to be seen openly wearing a uniform in south-east France since 1940.[2] Thackthwaite once said, 'Ortiz knew no fear.' The allegation was denied by the man himself, who insisted that he carried out this display of bravado to raise the locals' morale. It also enabled informers to track the mission's movements and relay them to the Germans and Milice.

The Union mission spent four months visiting Maquis groups, conferring with Resistance leaders and prospecting suitable sites for airdrops, not only of arms and ammunition but also blankets, clothes and food. Like other Allied missions, they swiftly picked up the friction between the Resistance networks of different political persuasions, and passed warnings of this to London. On completion of the mission in late May 1944, Thackthwaite and Ortiz returned safely to Britain, but Fourcaud was arrested and held for two months by the Gestapo before being released.

Ortiz's citation for his award of the OBE included the words:

> For four months this officer assisted in the organisation of the Maquis in a most difficult département where members were in constant danger of attack … He ran great risks in looking after four RAF officers who had been brought down in the neighbourhood, and accompanied them to the Spanish border. In the course of his efforts to obtain the release of these officers, he raided a German military garage and took ten Gestapo motors which he used frequently. He also procured a Gestapo pass for his own use in spite of the fact that he was well known to the enemy.[3]

Back in Britain, Ortiz was decorated with the first of two Navy Crosses he was to earn. The citation read in part:

> For extraordinary heroism … in connection with military operations … in enemy-occupied territory. Operating in civilian clothes and aware that he would be subject to execution in the event of his capture, Major Ortiz parachuted from an airplane with two other officers of an Inter-Allied mission to reorganise existing Maquis groups and organise additional groups in the region of Rhone [sic]. Although his identity had become known to the Gestapo with the resultant increase in personal hazard, he voluntarily conducted to the Spanish border four Royal Air Force officers who had been shot down in his region, and later returned to resume his duties. Repeatedly leading successful raids during the period of this assignment, Major Ortiz inflicted heavy casualties on enemy forces greatly superior in number (and) upheld the highest traditions of the United States Naval Service.[4]

In the confusion of missions on the ground, with some officers taking orders from SOE, some from OSS and some from the Gaullist BCRA, Section F's most important agent in south-east France was Francis Cammaerts, son of a Belgian father and a British mother. His height of 6ft 4in earned him the local nickname 'Big Feet' and made him embarrassingly tall when trying to lose himself in a crowd of much shorter southern French people. Uniquely among those who had the sheer unrelenting courage to volunteer as an agent in occupied France, he had started the war by registering as a conscientious objector. He later explained this:

My generation grew up in the shadow of the horror of the trenches, millions of men killed pointlessly trying to gain two or three hundred yards of ground. Like many of my peers, I thought, this must not happen again. There was only one thing we could do: not take part. If everyone did that, we reasoned, there would be no one to go to war.

There were many people in Britain equally innocent in 1939. Working as a teacher in London at the time of Dunkirk, Cammaerts saw his pupils taking drinks and food to wounded soldiers whose trains were halted in sidings near the school. Realising that the parents must disapprove of their children being taught by a man who refused to fight, he then took work as a farm labourer, as approved by the Conscientious Objection Tribunals. After getting married, he came gradually to understand that his moral stance was dubious when his country was involved in a total war. The final straw came when, three weeks after the wedding, his brother was killed flying with the RAF, after which Cammaerts called an old classmate from Rugby school who was known to be 'something to do with intelligence' and asked what he could do to help the war effort, stressing at the time and afterwards that he would refuse to obey orders to kill anyone.

Speaking French as fluently as English, he was rapidly put in uniform and posted to Scotland for commando training. On the moonlit night of 22 March 1943 he was one of two passengers in an RAF Lysander, camouflaged green and grey to make it difficult to spot from above against a background of low cloud, and with a long-range tank slung like a huge bomb below the fuselage. Trying not to think about the dangers that awaited him on the ground, Cammaerts found it an unreal experience, keeping a keen eye out for any attack from astern in the pilot's blind spot:

> As we flew I could see night fighters – friend or foe I could not tell – swishing past so fast whereas the Lysander moved so slowly. This strangely was an advantage – fighters move fast but take miles to turn around and by then we'd gone elsewhere.[5]

But not always. The pilot of the Lysander recalled that they were pursued by a night fighter and shot at with tracer bullets. Taking evading action, he executed a series of very violent steep turns, at the end of which he had lost his bearings, but later found them again, landing to deposit his two passengers in a field near the major German concentration camp at Compiègne. The drill after the aircraft had turned, ready for take-off, was for one passenger to remain aboard to heave the baggage out of the cramped rear compartment of the little aircraft and load that of the passengers for the return trip.

The initial intention of Section F was for Cammaerts to replace the flamboyant Peter Churchill, head of the network code-named CARTE in southern France, which had got badly out of control. Churchill's only briefing as they brushed past each other beside the Lysander was, 'Be careful to take some newspaper in with you when you go to the toilet. They're very short of toilet rolls.'

Driven through the night to Paris and along the grim darkened streets of the capital under curfew, Cammaerts was horrified by the over-confidence of his guides and the

general poor security in the DONKEYMAN network. Cutting all contact with it, he travelled south to Provence, where Peter Churchill had been living openly in a luxury hotel
with his lover, fellow agent Odette Sansom, in flagrant defiance of their training, in which
it was stressed that an agent should have no permanent 'home' or even regular movements,
by which French or German counter-intelligence could home in on him or her.

To Cammaerts' mind, Peter Churchill's permanent headquarters for the CARTE
network was a fatal error, as indeed it proved to be. Each day, numerous members of
the network came and went quite openly, without precautions. Worst of all, he learned
from Sansom that Churchill and she were in negotiations with an Abwehr officer who
called himself 'Colonel Henri' – real name Sergeant Hugo Bleicher. Both she and her
lover seemed to think they could arrange for Bleicher to be flown to London, where
he would shortly end the war by serving as a direct link between OKW and the British
Cabinet. Cammaerts was horrified to hear this. He had already been distressed at the
lax security of some of Section F's officers in London:

> … who allowed their agents, who were supposed to be kept apart, to bump into each
> other and learn each other's real names, while files were left on desks as the officer
> dealing with the agent left the room for whatever reason.[6]

Such sloppiness was dangerous even in the relative safety of London, but the lack of
security procedures of the CARTE network on the ground in France was far more
reprehensible – as was proven after Peter Churchill's return, when Bleicher pounced
and arrested him, Odette and many of their agents.

Deciding to have nothing to do with any of the existing networks, Cammaerts
relocated to the Rhône valley, passing himself off as a refugee schoolteacher from the
north, where people were generally taller than the locals. His reason for coming south
was given, to those who needed to know, as to convalesce from an attack of jaundice.
Like all the best cover stories, this was as close to the truth as could be, since he had suffered from jaundice shortly before Christmas. Using whatever identities seemed most
plausible to justify his constant travelling throughout Resistance zones R1 and R2,
usually on a motorbike, he set up his own sabotage and espionage network.

London gave it the code name JOCKEY. It stretched 300 miles from St Etienne in
central France to Marseille and Nice in the south. With not a single member recruited
before Cammaerts had kept him or her under surveillance for several days, JOCKEY
was organised in watertight cells of less than fifteen people, so that any one member
could betray under torture only the others in his or her cell. When 40-year-old Irish
yachtswoman Cecily Lefort, who had been acting as his courier, was arrested in
Montélimar and tortured by the Gestapo, this damage control system ensured that she
could give away no one except Cammaerts, for whom the Gestapo was already searching all over France.

Starting from scratch, after six months' hard work by Cammaerts, JOCKEY comprised fifty cells, which he visited at irregular intervals, never telling anyone where he
was going or when they would see him again. He refused to stay in hotels because
they were under routine surveillance and made a point of never spending more than a
couple of consecutive nights in any of the safe houses recommended and checked out

in advance by a trusted member of his network. These hideaways ranged from mountain refuges to farms, middle-class town houses and luxurious châteaux. After the war,
one of his typically modest understatements was:

> Individual agents were dependent for every meal and every night's rest on people
> whose small children, aged parents, property and livelihood were continually put at
> risk by our presence. Their contributions involved a much greater sacrifice than ours.[7]

Their houses could be burned down or blown up, fields of crops set afire and whole
families subjected to torture and transported to concentration or death camps, never to
return – and the helpers were well aware of this.

For security, Cammaerts never made a phone call or wrote a letter all the time he
was in occupied France. Learning of the birth of his second daughter from a BBC
message, '*Joséphine ressemble à son grand-père*' – Josephine looks like her grandfather –
Cammaerts gave way for once to the loneliness of his clandestine existence with no
home and no one to confide in or share the news with. 'For the first and only time in
my life,' he said, 'I sat down on my own and got drunk.'

How close he came to disaster time after time is illustrated by the night when the car
in which he was travelling was stopped at a roadblock near Senas manned by Waffen-SS
troops. Getting out of the car, he realised that it was heavily overloaded and visibly
weighted down on the rear suspension by all the weapons and ammunition hidden
in the boot. His travelling companion was a German-speaker, who overheard that the
roadblock was part of a hunt for the crew of an American bomber shot down nearby.
When one of the SS men started sticking his bayonet through the rear seat cushions,
he made a joke: 'You surely don't think we've sewn the crew of a bomber into the
seats, do you?' He laughed, the SS men laughed and sent them on their way, the boot
unsearched. 'It was,' said Cammaerts, 'my closest piece of luck.'[8]

That sounds very swashbuckling, but Cammaerts usually avoided obvious risks. He
was also very sanguine about the tensions between his own people working for SOE,
other networks owing allegiance to BCRA and those with their own agenda, like the
communists, who acknowledged neither. The stress of the clandestine life was such that
agents were flown back to Britain at intervals for debriefing but also for a short period
of home leave. In November 1943 it was Cammaerts' turn after nine months in the
field. As he remembered:

> Virtually every day was a working day, catching the tube from South Harrow to the
> blacked-out offices in Baker Street. There were frequent debriefings. I talked to a few
> future agents about rationing, identity permits. I went on a course for S-phone use,[9]
> which proved useless. I was invited to meet about a hundred aircrew who were going
> to be used on special operations. They needed to hear someone who had been there to
> tell them what it means to be down on the ground as opposed to being in the aircraft.

Time and again, he pressed home the dire need of deliveries to JOCKEY's carefully
selected seventy drop zones of arms and ammunition, but also soap, winter clothes,
bicycle tyres and a host of other mundane things impossible to obtain in France.

If the days during his time in London were put to good use, the dream of spending time with his wife, their small daughter and the new baby turned rapidly sour. His wife Nan knew she could not ask him any questions and he could not tell her anything about what he had been doing. There was thus between them no bond of trust, natural between a couple:

> All we could do was cling to each other wordlessly, as one does to relatives at a funeral. Our lovemaking was entirely desperate, due not only to the fact that I was physically incompetent, virtually impotent – partly the reward from hundreds of bruising miles on a racing saddle – but also, I think, mentally.[10]

The anniversary on 11 November 1943 of the armistice that ended the First World War, which was the only armistice of which French patriots could feel proud, was celebrated in Oyonnax – a town in eastern France only 25 miles from the Swiss frontier at Geneva – by 150 men of the local Maquis parading openly, led by their commander Captain Henri Romans-Petit, with weapons carried openly and tricolor flags bearing the Cross of Lorraine. With the silent consent of the local gendarmes, they marched to the war memorial and laid a wreath bearing the legend 'From the victors of tomorrow to those of 1914–18'. A drummer beat the step for the marching men led by their officers in uniform, and a bugler played the fanfare, after which the whole population joined in singing *La Marseillaise*, with many people weeping openly.

A short 8mm black-and-white home movie was even shot to record the occasion for posterity.[11] It shows the small convoy of trucks, some crudely re-painted in camouflage colours to look more military, arriving in the town and the men deploying from them with the population watching. The parade had been planned by Romans-Petit partly out of bravado and partly to show the people that they were not outlaws as portrayed by Vichy propaganda, but disciplined soldiers. De Gaulle said afterwards that this one show of open resistance to the Germans was an eye-opener for the Allied command, seeming, as it did, to demonstrate at least a local superiority in arms.

The occupation forces could hardly let that go unpunished. According to the official report of the prefect, on 14 December at 0730hrs German Security Police and SS troops arrived in the station of Nantua (9 miles south of Oyonnax) in a special train. Part of this force immediately set off for Oyonnax, while the others stayed in Nantua, occupying the post office and throwing a cordon round the town, inside which a house-to-house search was conducted. Denounced by informers, the mayor – a doctor who looked after wounded and sick *maquisards* – and the Gendarmerie captain were locked up in the railway station and later shot with two others.

All able-bodied men aged between 18 and 40 found in the streets or in their homes were arrested, as also were twenty-one teachers and pupils from the town's secondary school.

They were joined by men arrested in Oyonnax until eventually 150 men and youths were forced into an unscheduled train that left at 1300hrs for Bourg and the German-run concentration camp at Compiègne.

A number of the hostages jumped from the train and escaped. The only able-bodied men left in Nantua and Oyonnax were those who had slipped through the German dragnet or had been away from home on 14 December. The prefect of the *département* of Ain noted:

> The population of Nantua and Oyonnax is deeply troubled and subversive elements in the arrondissement are likely to provoke incidents. I have therefore demanded police reinforcements to keep order during the funerals of the victims and on following days.

The official announcement posted outside the Kommandantur confirmed that 150 men from Nantua between the ages of 18 and 40 had been taken for the duration of the war to a work camp in Germany. Some work camp! Of the 116 hostages still on board the train when it arrived at Compiègne only eleven lived to return home.

Oyonnax was not the only town where patriotic feelings anticipated the liberation on 11 November 1943. A smaller wreath-laying took place at Montélimar in Burgundy. Three days afterwards fourteen *maquisards* were arrested by German troops. Twelve were imprisoned at the Fort Montluc in Lyon. Given a summary trial by a German military tribunal on 15 January, they were executed on 1 February at a suburban firing range near Villeurbanne. One of them, 23-year-old Georges Bernard, wrote a last letter to his family:

> My dear parents, brothers and sisters,
>
> I am writing you these few words to give you my last news. My morale is good, right up to the last minute. Dear Papa, dear Mama, please give a big kiss to my brothers and sisters for me. I shall love them always. You can put my photo on the sideboard. We are going to be shot at 4 p.m., but that has not stopped my appetite. I've just eaten a good soup and some bread. Thank you, Mama, for the parcel I received at Christmas. It was very kind. Please keep this letter as a souvenir for my dearest Monique and give her a big hug. I am leaving you for ever but my heart will always be with you. I leave you with a big kiss, dear Papa and Mama. A thousand kisses for you all.

The letter is signed 'Lili', his family nickname.[12]

PART 2

FIGHTING TO
THE DEATH

5

LIVE FREE OR DIE!

After the Teheran Conference in November 1943, Prime Minister Winston Churchill needed to convalesce from pneumonia brought on partly by the stress of being humiliated by Roosevelt, who had excluded him from some discussions with Stalin, partly by physical exhaustion and partly by an excessive fondness for cigars. During the time he spent recovering in the mild winter climate of Morocco, he was approached by de Gaulle and other important figures in the Free French forces, who persuaded him that equipping the thousands of *maquisards* inside France with arms and ammunition could render Operation Anvil, the planned amphibious invasion of southern France, unnecessary.

Their argument fitted in with the British prime minister's strategic view. Although having a limited talent as a military commander, he fatally over-rated this on occasion. In this case, he thought it would be better to keep the troops allocated for Anvil in Italy, pressing General 'Smiling Albert' Kesselring's well-managed forces further and further northwards. It was a view not compatible with the strategic vision of President Roosevelt, General George Marshall or the Anglo-American Combined Chiefs of Staff, who planned to relax the pressure on the Allied troops in Italy by opening a bridgehead in southern France, from which Allied troops could fight their way north up the Rhône valley and rendezvous somewhere in north-eastern France with troops landed in Normandy. This pincer manoeuvre would cut off hundreds of thousands of German soldiers in central, western and southern France, denying them any possibility of retreating into the Reich and 'living to fight another day'.

To push his alternative strategy, on return to London Churchill summoned a representative of de Gaulle's Free French forces to a meeting with Lord Selbourne, Minister for Economic Warfare, and representatives of SOE. The message that emerged from Downing Street was for SOE to step up by all means possible arms deliveries to Maquis groups in south-eastern France. It took Selbourne two weeks to provide a cautious report on the possibilities and a promise of six sorties to be flown in the following week. Churchill replied, 'I want March deliveries to double those planned for February.'

That would have sounded hollowly in the ears of Captain Henri Romans-Petit, now commanding all Maquis bands in Region R1, who had been pestering Heslop and the other Allied liaison officers for drops – of which none were received in his zone of activity between August 1943 and February 1944. Even before the stepping up of these airdrops, Vichy's forces of law and order in the region were increasingly uneasy about the number of 'bandits', as they were officially termed, hiding out in the hilly country and forests – and whose activities ranged from hold-ups to stealing funds, ration cards and identity documents, often with the complicity of the officials concerned, to the assassination of informers and collaborators.

On 30 January 1944 a Gendarmerie colonel named Georges Lelong was posted to Grenoble as overall boss of Vichy's police and anti-terrorist forces in the Haute Savoie *département*. One of his first acts was to publish a warning that anyone found in possession of arms or explosives would be tried by court martial without right of appeal and shot within twenty-four hours, also that anyone harbouring a fugitive would be severely dealt with.

How difficult it was for many French people in and out of uniform to determine where their allegiance lay was clear when OAS officers Clair and Anjot went to visit Lelong and sound him out. Their meeting at his headquarters in the Villa Mary at Annecy lasted for a full hour, at the end of which they decided that although he was an honest Gendarmerie officer, he had never questioned an order in his life and could not make the moral judgement that this was exactly the time to take that course. On the contrary, he told the two OAS officers that they were still under military discipline and their duty was to obey the orders of their legitimate government in Vichy.

Lelong explained that he was a French patriot and bitterly anti-German, but had been given a mission to wipe out the Maquis in Haute Savoie, which he was determined to fulfil. Clair and Anjot suggested as a compromise that their men could help him to track down the bands of real bandits in the area who lived by robbery and extortion, if he would leave the patriotic Maquis alone. Lelong made a counter-offer, proposing that they deliver to him the FTP and other communists on the plateau, in return for which he would take no immediate action against the non-political *maquisards*. They took their leave in an atmosphere of icy truce.

Heslop and Rosenthal had already approved the plateau of Glières as being suitable for airdrops. It offered a number of drop zones that were (a) not too dangerous for aircraft to use and (b) difficult for German or Vichy ground forces to reach in time to prevent collection of the supplies dropped. At a meeting in Annecy early in February, Rosenthal ordered captains Clair and Anjot to take command of an operation that would prove to London how well-led Maquis groups on the plateau of Glières could mount a major operation against the German occupation forces. The regional MUR chief Jean Guidollet later summed this discussion up as follows:

[Rosenthal] kept hammering away at the idea of concentrating our forces. 'Actions such as sabotage are not sufficient,' he said. 'We have to give London the proof that the Resistance is not just talk, but a considerable force, which the Germans will have to reckon with.' With misgivings, we adopted [Rosenthal's] position. For my part, with the advantage of hindsight, I realise that this fateful decision was indeed the only way to force the Allies to admit that the Resistance inside France was capable of fighting. Contrary to what some people think, it was not a decision lightly taken, nor was it inspired by personal ambition, rather by a realistic appreciation of the difficulties our representatives had to overcome in London.[1]

Clair and Anjot then enlisted the help of other officers and NCOs from the disbanded 27th Battalion of Chasseurs Alpins, the elite mountain warfare troops formerly headquartered in Annecy, which lay only a few miles south-east of the plateau. Their undisciplined and untrained rank and file numbered about 467 men from assorted political and social backgrounds, of whom the most likely to be useful were eighty-eight men of mixed ages from the communist FTP and fifty-six Spanish republican refugees who had joined the Maquis because they had no wish to be handed over to the Germans and sent to the gas chambers, as had happened to thousands of other Spaniards who had fought for the communist brigades in the republican army during the civil war and had since been held in French concentration camps.

Wishing to demonstrate to the Germans that it was capable of dealing with the anti-government forces in Haute Savoie, the government in Vichy charged Lelong

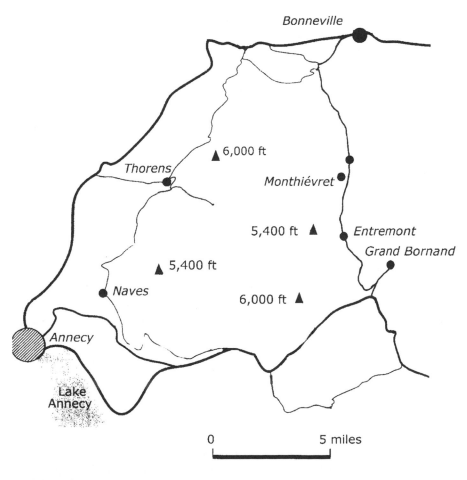

The Glières plateau.

with wiping out the growing number of Maquis bands. For this purpose, he attempted to seal off the plateau with 125 gendarmes, 700 men of the specialist anti-terrorist units known as Gardes Mobiles and 650 of the Groupes Mobiles de Réserve (GMR), plus 700 ordinary *miliciens*. Attempting reconnaissance in force up on to the plateau on 12 February and 8 March, Gardes Mobiles forces fell into an ambush that cost them three dead, six wounded and three men taken prisoner – with no losses on the defenders' side.

Charismatic OAS officer Lieutenant Theodore 'Tom' Morel was in charge of organising rudimentary military training on the Glières plateau and attempting to weld his disparate force into something like a military formation under his morale-raising slogan 'Live free or die!' On the night of 13 February Morel's men received their first airdrop, consisting of fifty-four containers of ammunition and weapons: Sten guns, some Bren light machine guns, hand grenades and explosives for sabotage, but no heavier weapons that would stop a tank, or even an armoured car. Further drops were received on 5 and 10 March.

After four men who had been given a safe conduct by the GMR were arrested below the plateau and medical student Michel Fournier was also apprehended on 1 March while seeking medical supplies in Grand Bornand, Morel decided to act. On the evening of 9 March he led half his force in an attack on the village of Entremont, lying below the plateau, which was held by sixty GMR men. That night 150 *maquisards* encircled the village. A squad leader named Roger Cerri described the action in his log book thus:

> With some other guys I made a detour to cover the high ground above the village. Just as we reached the outskirts of the village, a sentry saw us and began firing a light machine gun in our direction. We returned fire straight away. The tracers formed a rainbow [sic] and we took cover behind some piles of firewood. After about an hour the GMR, who were getting worried, stopped fighting. Leading his section of Chasseurs Alpins, Lieutenant Morel captured the Hôtel de France, which was the GMR HQ. There was a violent argument between him and their commanding officer Major Lefebvre, who had only taken over on 7 March. We disarmed the prisoners, but Lefebvre took a small revolver from a pocket and shot Morel down with one bullet through the heart at point-blank range. Lefebvre was immediately shot and killed, but the loss of Lieutenant Morel, who was a very motivating man, left us with a big problem. We rounded up our prisoners with their arms and materiel on the road, and made off back up to the plateau.[2]

After receiving Lelong's promise to liberate Michel Fournier – a promise that was not kept – the prisoners were released, not just as a goodwill gesture but also to avoid having to share rations with them. Their release was to cost many lives in the coming weeks. The attack on Entremont proved a pyrrhic victory for the Maquis forces. Three days after the killing of Morel, another large arms drop attracted savage reprisal by the Luftwaffe, in which the upland farms and isolated chalets where the Maquis were hiding were bombed and strafed. With this softening up came several skirmishes and losses on both sides.

On 18 March 1944 Captain Anjot took command on the plateau at what could not have been a worse time. Colonel Lelong's masters in Vichy were looking for heroic action on the part of the anti-terrorist units in Haute Savoie, to prove to the Germans that they could be an effective fighting force when up against a determined resistance, as against arresting a few dissidents and Jews here and there. Those expectations were not to be fulfilled: on 20 March the Milice launched a number of attacks on the plateau, each one easily driven off by the defenders. On 24 March another Milice attack was driven off by the Spanish republicans, who lost two of their men.

In Annecy's Imperial Hotel a council of war was chaired by General Julius Oberg, commanding 12,000 men in the 157th Alpine Division, with Luftwaffe General Knochen, who promised ground support missions, and two representatives of the Gestapo. Officers of the Vichy anti-terrorist forces were also present. It had already been agreed that, if they could not eliminate the Maquis on the plateau, Lieutenant General Karl Pflaum's 157th Reserve Division would take over. The division was a heterogeneous force formed for training purposes and currently tasked with eradicating the concentrations of *maquisards* in the wild country near France's eastern borders.

Ground forces totalling 3,000-plus of Pflaum's men now moved in to encircle the plateau in an operation code-named Aktion Hoch-Savoyen. For the defenders, the most dangerous were the trained mountain warfare troops of Reserve-Gebirgsjäger-Regiment 1, organised in four battalions, plus two battalions of security police. Their armament included heavy machine guns, mortars, mountain artillery, anti-tank weapons and armoured cars, with Luftwaffe ground-support missions available on call. Backing up the German forces were some 1,200 Vichy anti-terrorist troops who might not have been great shakes in the firing line, but had knowledge of the terrain and could therefore act as guides.

On 25 March all hell broke loose on Anjot's men, their positions on the plateau bombed by three Heinkel 111 medium bombers and strafed by four Focke-Wulf 190 fighters. The main ammunition dump was destroyed. They were also shelled by 75mm mountain artillery and, in many places, locked in close combat with their attackers. Although Pflaum's force managed to occupy less than a quarter of the plateau, Captain Anjot rightly decided that the odds were impossible and that the only sane course was to exfiltrate his men while there were still some gaps in the cordon. However, Captain Rosenthal again used his standing as the officer representing BCRA to veto this move. His motive was of the sort that has led to so many military disasters: he wanted a heroic stand to be made in the name of the Free French forces, with all that this implies. Anjot gave way, still hoping to save as many of his men's lives as possible.

Then began an all-out confrontation between lightly armed French irregulars and a trained German force as three of Pflaum's four battalions of mountain troops on skis wearing white camouflage overalls advanced on to the plateau. After aerial reconnaissance and photography by a Fieseler Storch, Luftwaffe ground-support missions pummelled the Maquis bases again while two battalions of the Gebirgsjäger probed the defences. In the first attack at Lavouillan, they were driven back. The second attack targeted Monthiévret[3] on the easiest route up to the plateau. Although at an altitude of 3,000ft, the hamlet stood only 1,200ft above the jumping-off point in the valley of the Borne River. The previous afternoon, Roger Cerri recorded in his diary:

Saturday 25 March – heavy shelling on our positions at Monthiévret. The shells whistled over us and exploded everywhere for two hours, releasing a strong smell of gunpowder. The chalets (in which we were quartered) were all set on fire.

First contact with ground forces was a probing attack by a single section of the Gebirgsjäger. The main assault had been planned for 28 March but was brought forward, according to a telex sent immediately afterwards from Lyon by SS-Obersturmbannführer Dr Knab:

The earlier attack took place, as reported in a personal interview with Lt Gen Pflaum [commanding 157th Division] as a result of a decision taken by Col Schwehr without referring to Gen Pflaum or warning the Milice. His three battalions [one was kept in reserve] had already been en route [to their jumping-off position] for two hours before the Security Police were informed. Col Schwehr took this decision after receiving definite intelligence that the terrorists had been ordered to evacuate the plateau in small groups. According to the interrogation of terrorists taken prisoner, the artillery bombardment of 26 March and the attack of an assault section the same day had convinced the terrorist commanders that the main attack was beginning. They therefore planned to evacuate the plateau during the night of 26–27 March.[4]

After a first contact that morning at Lavouillan, the name of a place too small to be shown even on local maps, towards dusk a second section of fifty men with four MG34 or MG42 machine guns and a 50mm mortar managed to outflank the Maquis at Monthiévret.

Roger Cerri's diary continues:

About 1700hrs[5] firing broke out behind us. The alert was given, but we could see nothing. One of my guys did a circuit and came back to tell us that a lot of Boches had managed to get behind us. The situation was serious. There were only eighteen of us on the level ground, spread out in three positions. The Boches advanced silently between the trees. We heard nothing. Suddenly they emerged, automatic weapons firing and grenades exploding everywhere. Several comrades were wounded. We lost touch with the first section that had advanced. After outflanking us, the Boches were throwing grenades down from the rocks above. We could not hold. The order was given to disengage. We slipped away and took refuge in a cave.

Another eyewitness account relates how the Bavarian mountain troops used a difficult route up to Monthiévret, which the Maquis had thought impassable. This explains how they got behind the Maquis positions unnoticed. All accounts of the fighting are confused, as is understandably the case with many accounts of conflict, especially in bad light, but they do agree that there were moments of intense firing and some lulls between. In one of these, a six-man squad under Second Lieutenant Baratier, which was stationed further up the road to Petit Bornand, made a counter-attack on the Germans. This was greeted by a hail of fire that wounded one man and killed another immediately. Some grenades were thrown by the attackers at close range, but they were also using a light portable mortar with a range of 50 yards. The counter-attack failing after one Bren gun seized up, Baratier wrote afterwards to another survivor:

> You remember that your Bren did not work and I took the Belgian's Bren and kept firing alone for fifteen minutes. More importantly, do you remember that I kept calling my men by name and no one replied?

A runner was sent along the road to where some of the Spaniards were positioned. He was unable to make himself understood, but they had in any case received orders not to get involved. Calling his men to retreat, Baratier heard no reply and disengaged, successfully making his way down into the valley. The rearguard had travelled no more than 200 yards through the darkness and thick snow when they heard a chorus of shouts in German and sustained firing as their abandoned positions were overrun. Emerging from the cave after dawn, some of Cerri's comrades also succeeded in slipping between the German positions and escaping into the valley of the Borne. Three only made their escape up on to the snowbound plateau. The defenders had suffered eighteen casualties and lost several men taken prisoner and facing torture to extract information about the defenders' numbers and dispositions.

At 2200hrs Anjot decided that his men had done all that honour required and ordered a complete exfiltration, so that when the German forces pressed home their attack after dawn they found no resistance, and had to content themselves with unearthing and destroying the hidden dumps of airdropped weaponry. However, the end was not in sight for the *maquisards*, many of whom were tracked down by the Milice or denounced by collaborators.

On the Western Front in the Second World War, Wehrmacht forces generally respected the rules of war when taking prisoners in uniform, but on the Glières Pflaum's men were fighting guerrillas. Many having seen service on the Eastern Front, they meted out to *maquisards* taken prisoner the same treatment they had given captured Soviet partisans. Twenty wounded men were shot where they lay; other prisoners died under torture, were shot by firing squad or were deported to death camps in Germany.

According to Obersturmführer Dr Knab the assault 'had not obtained the desired result in numbers of killed and prisoners' because it had been thwarted by Anjot's decision to exfiltrate. A manhunt was therefore launched to track down those who had escaped, in which a significant part was played by the GMR men who had been taken prisoner and released unharmed, and were therefore able to identify many of their erstwhile captors. Knab's role – and indeed the role of the Sicherheitspolizei (Sipo-SD) detachments in the anti-Maquis operations – was made clear in a telex he sent, of which a copy was found after the German withdrawal. An officer or NCO of the Sipo-SD security troops always accompanied Wehrmacht units on these operations. Prisoners were handed over by the Wehrmacht to the Sipo-SD, in this case at Annecy, for interrogation, torture and disposal. The Sipo-SD also conducted reprisals on people and property in the area of operations. Of Anjot's force, 140-plus were killed in combat or shot after capture or died in German concentration camps. He himself was shot and killed on 27 March at Nâves while attempting to escape; it was to take seven months before he could be given a proper burial. The enemy losses were minimal: twenty of the Vichy anti-terrorist forces were killed, plus three Germans, with seven Germans wounded – and five of those were injured in an accident.

A moving tribute to Morel was composed by the Jesuit father André Ravier, who had been one of his secondary school teachers:

> Let us imagine for a moment that Tom was not shamefully struck down by a French officer, that the airdrops had not been so unfortunately delayed, and that Tom had found himself on the plateau facing the German attack with 1,000 men instead of 450, with fifty or sixty officers instead of five ... all would have turned out differently.[6]

Ravier's tribute is interesting because it places blame not only on the Allies' failure to provide any heavy weapons but also raises one issue deliberately ignored in hagiographic accounts of the Glières campaign and the Resistance generally. Before the German attack, Morel had appealed to the officer cadets of the Charles de Foucauld *promotion* at St Cyr military academy (relocated to Aix-en-Provence), whose instructor he had been, to join his force of *maquisards*. Of all the people in France, they were least likely to have been ardent supporters of Vichy, so their failure to respond indicates that a reasoned consideration of the military possibilities decided them in advance that it was a lost cause, with which it was better not to get involved.

Since the decision to concentrate forces on the plateau had been political and not military, it was predictable that a propaganda war would be unleashed. On Radio Paris, Pétain's Catholic supporter Philippe Henriot managed not to mention the German intervention in order to laud the achievement of Vichy forces over 'the ragtag army of cowardly foreign and Communist terrorists, who chose to surrender rather than fight'. Over the BBC French Service de Gaulle's spokesman Maurice Schumann hailed the pointless Battle of Glières as a repeat of the Free French forces' heroic stand against German and Italian air and ground forces after being surrounded and cut off at Bir Hakeim in Libya during May and June 1942. Radio Algiers praised 'the patriots who had held out for two weeks against a full Alpine division of the Wehrmacht with artillery and Luftwaffe ground-support missions'[7] and the BCRA exploited the heroic nature of Anjot's struggle to create a legend of valour that attracted fresh groups of *maquisards* on to the Glières plateau.

Bolstered by a massive airdrop of arms on 1 August 1944, this second Maquis force emerged from the plateau after the Franco-American landings of Operation Dragoon[8] between Toulon and Cannes on 15 August. Units of the US forces driving up the Rhône valley were guided by some of the surviving *maquisards* from Glières, who also harassed some German forces before the American arrival and prevented the retreat of others. This greatly accelerated the process of liberating the *département* of Haute Savoie. The town of Grenoble was liberated on 19 August, only four days after the Franco-American landings of Operation Anvil and eighty-six days ahead of the planners' schedule. This enabled de Gaulle to claim that it had been liberated by French force of arms. Of the sad adventure on the plateau of Glières, he said, 'Their example will live on, I can assure you, as testimony to the whole world of the resolution shown by France in the most terrible war of her history.'[9]

Also dropped on 1 August was the Allied mission designated Union II. Unlike earlier missions whose task had been to unite the Maquis, encourage and equip Resistance saboteurs and get involved in espionage, this was an operations group of heavily armed men in uniform with their own transport, whose function was to attack German forces, disrupt their communications after the landings in southern France and prevent destruction of German arms and fuel dumps that could be useful to the Allies.

Union II was composed of Ortiz, now promoted to major, an Army Air Corps captain, five USMC sergeants and a Free French officer. The mission's first casualty never even made it to the ground: Sergeant Charles Perry's static line broke and his parachute failed to open. He was buried on the field near Les Saisies, some 60 miles north-east of Grenoble. The ceremony, held where he fell, was conducted with full military honours, which impressed the reception party. Perry's uniform and papers were then given to Free French officer Joseph Arcelin, in the hope that this would be some protection for him, if taken prisoner.

Ortiz was itching for action, but the first priority was to train the local *maquisards* in handling the arms dropped in the 864 man-size containers dropped with the mission and their jeeps. On 14 August, the small convoy of jeeps was in the village of Montgirod when it came under fire from German artillery, making the point that the enemy was well aware of their presence. On the following day, with German troops everywhere jittery following the news of the nearby Allied landings of Operation Dragoon earlier that morning, Union II bumped into a convoy of a dozen trucks transporting troops of the 15th Alpine Reserve battalion in the neighbouring village of Centron. Spotting the American jeeps, the convoy promptly disgorged several hundred troops to give battle.

The Americans split up into two parties, to facilitate exfiltration under fire. The Air Corps captain and the French officer were wounded; two others managed to escape by swimming across the ice-cold River Isère against a strong current. Ortiz ordered the two sergeants with him to make a run for it, leaving him to cover their getaway. They refused to leave him.

With the inhabitants of Centron pleading with him to surrender because Montgirod had been burned to the ground in reprisals after the mission's confrontation there the previous day, Ortiz made a difficult decision. In his own words:

> Since [our] activities were well-known to the Germans, there was no reason to hope that we would be treated as ordinary POWs. I had been involved in dangerous activities for many years and was ready for my number to turn up. Sergeant Bodnar was next to me and I explained to him what I intended to do. He looked me in the eye and said, 'Major, we are marines. What you think is right goes for me too.'[10]

Ortiz called out in German several times that he wanted to surrender and then walked towards the encircling forces with machine-gun rounds hitting the ground by his feet until he was face to face with the commanding major, who agreed to accept the surrender and not take reprisals on the villagers. When only two more marines and the wounded men appeared from cover, he could not believe that so few men had held off a battalion and ordered every house in the village to be searched from cellar to loft before finally accepting that there were no more Americans in Centron. Ortiz seized the psychological advantage as the two uninjured sergeants were being disarmed by calling them to attention and ordering them to divulge only names, ranks and serial numbers as required under the Geneva Convention. Impressed by this show of discipline at a moment that should have been demoralising for the marines, their captors showed more respect.

Locked up in Marlag/Milag Nord POW camp for officers at Westertimke near Bremen, Ortiz was ordered by the senior naval officer, a Royal Navy captain, to desist from trying to escape because of the problems his attempts caused for the other prisoners. The troublesome Marine Corps major then constituted himself the senior American POW, announcing that he would set his own rules for escape and everything else. On 10 April 1945 orders were given to evacuate the camp and move the prisoners farther away from the approaching Allied spearheads. Ortiz and three others took advantage of the confusion when the marching column of prisoners was strafed by a marauding RAF Spitfire to escape into the woods. Ortiz later reported:

> We spent ten days hiding, roving at night, blundering into enemy positions, hoping to find our way into British lines. Luck was with us. Once we were discovered but managed to get away, and several other times we narrowly escaped detection ... By the seventh night, we had returned near our camp. I made a reconnaissance of Marlag. There seemed to be only a token guard and prisoners of war appeared to have assumed virtual control of the compounds.[11]

By then, the escapers were in bad physical shape. On the tenth day after their escape, the four men decided it was better to chance their luck inside the camp, rather than starve to death outside. They walked back through the main gate, with the guards taking no notice, and were given a rousing welcome by a reception committee that included three men from the surrender at Centron. On 29 April, the British 7th Guards Division liberated the camp and Ortiz and his men immediately volunteered to take up arms again in the drive, as they thought, to Berlin. Permission was refused. The citation for his second Navy Cross,[12] awarded in London, read:

> For extraordinary heroism ... during operations behind enemy Axis lines in the Savoie Department of France from 1 August 1944 to 27 April 1945. After parachuting into a region where his activities had made him an object of intensive search by the Gestapo, Major Ortiz valiantly continued his work in coordinating and leading resistance groups. When he and his team were attacked and surrounded during a special mission designed to immobilize enemy reinforcements stationed in that area, he disregarded the possibility of escape and, in an effort to spare villagers severe reprisals by the Gestapo, surrendered to this sadistic Geheim Staats Polizei [sic]. Subsequently imprisoned and subjected to numerous interrogations, he divulged nothing, and the story of this intrepid Marine Major and his team has become a brilliant legend in that section of France where acts of bravery were considered commonplace. By his outstanding loyalty and self-sacrificing devotion to duty, Major Ortiz contributed materially to the success of operations against a relentless enemy.[13]

Ortiz was shipped back to California, where his mother was living. There he earned a living as military advisor on several feature films directed by John Ford and acted in two that he could not bear to watch afterwards because they were typically embarrassing Hollywoodian dramatisations of his own exploits. One was *13 Rue Madeleine* with James Cagney, and the second was *Operation Secret* with Cornell Wilde.

In the 1950s, promoted to lieutenant colonel in the USMC Reserve, Ortiz volunteered to be sent as an American 'adviser' to French Indo-China, where his beloved Legion was fighting the communist Viet Minh. This was refused for political reasons. Decorated many times by US, British and French governments, Ortiz died of cancer in 1988 and was buried in Arlington National Cemetery with full military honours.[14]

6

THE TROJAN HORSE

Lying some 75 miles south-west of the Glières is another limestone outcrop of the Alps that divide France from Switzerland and Italy. The Vercors plateau is an irregularly shaped block pushed upwards 1 million years ago by tectonic pressure when the African continental plate collided with the European plate. Wind, water and glaciation combined to split it into several sub-blocks separated by spectacularly deep gorges. Approximately 30 miles wide north–south by 10 miles east–west, with the near-impenetrable eastern escarpment rising sheer to over 6,000ft above sea level, the region is today primarily known for Nordic skiing in winter and for hiking, mountain cycling, rock climbing and other outdoor sports in summer. The casual visitor with an eye for natural beauty will marvel at the savage bleakness of the bare higher slopes, the forests and alpine meadows leading from them down to the valleys, the rugged gorges dropping vertiginously 1,800ft to darkness at noon and rushing water, and at the peacefully cultivated valleys with their villages and small towns seemingly untouched by time.

The tourist need never be troubled by the appalling history of the plateau, on which the locals seem – understandably – to have turned their backs. One could easily visit the sleepy village of Vassieux without seeing any sign indicating the way to the museum that tells the story of the total destruction of the village and massacre of its inhabitants in 1944. Inside, the modest display was the work of one man swimming against the tide, for the authorities preferred to ignore his documentation of a horrifying episode of military incompetence and political vacillation.

The son of poor Italian immigrants who was sent out to work as a shepherd at the age of 7, Joseph la Picirella was determined to preserve the memory of the horrors he lived through and saw with his own eyes. Although now administered by the Département de la Drôme, as museums go, Picirella's is not large, although the exhibited photographs, weapons and other memorabilia are an impressive personal collection.

On a typical midsummer day at the height of the tourist season only a handful of people wander round the crudely fashioned showcases. A German mother in her forties translates the captions – which are in French only – for her three blonde sons. Elderly French couples wander round silently, perhaps lost in their own memories. The men tend to concentrate on the weapons, especially those they recognise and possibly used in France's conflicts after 1945. Some bored young children play tag between the showcases. At the reception desk, a member of staff who speaks reasonable German shares a joke with another visitor from Germany who has just been photographing the carcase of a DFS-230 assault glider displayed outside, in which Waffen-SS men brought death from the sky to this peaceful place on the morning of 21 July 1944.

In addition to the usual village cemetery, there is a military one just outside Vassieux. In precise rows of identically marked graves lie 192 people who died here in the summer of 1944. It is called *Le Necropole de la Résistance* and some headstones mark the graves of officers and soldiers of the FFI with their rank at time of death, as one would expect in a war cemetery. Two of these stones display, instead of the Christian cross, the crescent of Islam. The visitor who takes the trouble to scan every headstone will swiftly notice that one-third of the markers are simply designated 'Unknown' because the body buried beneath was too badly damaged by torture and/or explosions and/or fire to be identifiable, or even sexed, with the means available in 1944. Most surprising of all, in a military cemetery, is that one-third of the headstones bear female names.

Marie Blanc was a 91-year-old great-grandmother when she was killed on 14 July 1944. Jacqueline Blanc was 7 when she was killed on 21 July, the same day as her 4-year-old sister Danielle and 18-month-old brother Maurice. Suzanne Blanc was 20 when she died on 31 July, the same day as her sister Arlette, aged 12. The spread of dates tells its own story: this was no isolated air raid, no single skirmish that resulted in the deaths of defenceless civilians, but a sustained three-week campaign of terror and torture that began with bombing and strafing civilian targets on 14 July 1944 and escalated to sheer barbarity after the German gliders landed just outside the village limits one week later. The skeleton of one DFS-230 is still airborne just outside the cemetery, supported by a steel girder as mute evidence of what happened. Still in place is the single row of ten metal passenger seat frames, one behind the other, on which sat the killers of Jacqueline, Danielle and Maurice.

To begin the sequence of events that led to their deaths, it is necessary to turn the pages back four years exactly – to June 1940, when a refugee Parisian architect named Pierre Dalloz came to live in the small town of Sassenage at the foot of the north-eastern escarpment. Being a keen mountaineer, he explored the Vercors, which seemed to him, with its few access routes between unscalable cliffs and its generally hostile terrain, such a remote area that it could become what he likened to a Trojan horse.

Rather carried away by his simile, he was convinced that a small force of irregulars installed on the heights could easily block the steep and twisting access roads which the German forces based in Grenoble, standing literally in the shadow of the eastern escarpment, would use in any attack. The irregulars could then convert the plateau into an inland bridgehead, so Dalloz thought, where Allied airborne troops could safely be landed, and from where they could sally out to cut off German forces retreating along the Rhône valley after an eventual invasion of southern France.

The idea was simple, but the term 'plateau' is misleading because the Vercors has very little level terrain, even in the inhabited parts which lie generally at 3,000ft-plus above sea level. In addition, a deep gorge running south-west–north-east divides the massif in two, making it difficult if not impossible for defenders on one part of the plateau to come rapidly to the support of comrades under threat on the other part.

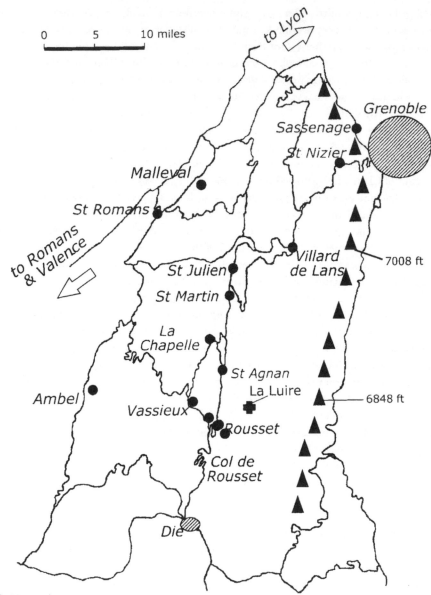

The Vercors plateau.

After the Germans occupied the Free Zone in November 1942 Dalloz and his friend Jean Prévost persuaded the Lyonnais journalist Yves Farge, whom they knew to be active in the Resistance, to put this somewhat sketchy 'plan' to Jean Moulin. Moulin, who had no military experience, gave it the seal of his approval in January 1943. In keeping with de Gaulle's wishes that the liberation of France be seen to have been accomplished at least partially by French forces, General Delestraint also approved the Dalloz plan and 'sold' it to BCRA in London.

The first Maquis band established itself in 1942 at a remote farm on the western side of the plateau named Ambel, where they were joined by thirty Polish-Jewish refugees and a Jewish doctor from Alsace. At an altitude of over 3,000ft, winter conditions were harsh. By the end of April 1943 there were nine or ten bands installed separately on the plateau, mostly commanded by professional army officers from Vichy's disbanded Armée de l'Armistice, who insisted on a semblance of military discipline: a morning parade with saluting of the French flag and some drilling with weapons.

By November 1943 there were an estimated 30,000 *maquisards* spread out all over France, but only 250 were in the Vercors. On 13 November 1943 came the first arms drop, enabling each group to have a few Sten guns to add to a collection of outdated firearms, relics of the First World War.

An observant volunteer with an enquiring mind was Gilbert Joseph, who had fled Paris aged 17 to avoid the STO and took a job overseeing the boarders in a small school at Villard de Lans, a winter sports resort in the Vercors, whose normal population was swollen by people with reason to feel insecure in the Vichy state but relatively safe up there. Hotels, chalets and apartments in Villard and the neighbouring communes were temporarily home to an assortment of refugees with money and some poorer ones like Joseph who had to work. Those with money spent it fast, as though living on the edge of the abyss. The black market flourished. The local Gendarmerie officers ranged from some positively helpful to the refugees and *maquisards* to the majority who simply turned a blind eye.

The golden youth, as Joseph called it, paraded in fashionable clothes after rising late, visited the cinema and attended dances while their elders played interminable games of bridge and exchanged wild rumours about the war. From time to time a German column drove up from Grenoble, usually at night, but failed to dent the sense of security for long because their approach was signalled by the ringing of church bells in Villard. A loudspeaker truck toured the streets, warning all the young men to leave town until the danger was past and the game of *dolce far niente* could re-start.[1]

After contacting a local woman known to have links with the Resistance in the autumn of 1943, Joseph told the headmaster of his decision to leave and join the Maquis. The reaction was an outburst of sardonic laughter: 'War, my boy, is shit, mud and blood.' Undeterred, Joseph followed a complicated route to a *camp de triage* where would-be recruits were tested for physical endurance and questioned on their political views before finally being sent on to one Maquis band or another.

Walking through Grenoble on his way to catch a bus back up to Villard, he noticed that people no longer looked each other in the eyes. There were no other young men in the streets. Anyone young enough and physically fit for STO conscription, especially if wearing weather-proof clothing or stout boots or carrying a rucksack of provisions, risked being stopped at any moment by police auxiliaries called *physionomistes* who ordered their victims to lower their trousers in search of a circumcised penis. Among their prey were also STO no-shows like Joseph.[2]

In November 1943 Dalloz made his way through Spain to French North Africa, from where he was flown to London to explain in detail his plan for the Vercors, which BCRA code-named Operation Montagnards. Dalloz was quite explicit that there could be no question of using the Vercors as a base from which the Maquis could attack German regular forces, nor turn it into an entrenched fortress. Its purpose, he repeated, was to provide a safe landing ground for Allied airborne troops or paratroops when the German forces in the area were already in disarray. Taking advantage of this, local *maquisards* could guide Allied incomers to where they could inflict the maximum damage on the enemy.[3] In other words, the military purpose of the redoubt was to be fulfilled after the invasion and in conjunction with trained Allied troops.

On being demobilised from the Armée de l'Armistice on 4 December 1943, Joseph la Picirella told his mother that he had decided to join the Maquis. She was distraught, having seen her younger son deported to Germany shortly before. He arrived on the plateau in the depths of winter, to find himself one of the few volunteers with any military experience. The difference between talk and action is illustrated by a mention in Picirella's diary saying that he was meant to have gone to the Vercors in a group of eighteen, of whom only two actually turned up there. Their arrival at the foot of the plateau was greeted with disbelief by a postman of whom the two young men asked the way to Maquis HQ.

'You're going to St-Martin?' he asked them incredulously. 'You're crazy. There's more than a metre of snow on the road and the mail hasn't got through these last three days.'

Defying the weather, which grew crueller as they climbed, the two volunteers were eventually challenged by a sentry and directed, with a Sten poking them in the back, to the HQ where Major Thivollet made a point of telling them how bad conditions were and what their lives would be like on the plateau. As a foretaste of this, one of their first tasks the following day was to melt masses of snow to be used for cooking and drinking, the farm in which they were staying having no other water supply in winter.[4]

The growing numbers of *maquisards* in the Vercors attracted the first reprisals on 22 January after a band based near the village of Baraques in the south of the plateau kidnapped two German military policemen and a Dutch journalist, thus provoking a rescue mission by a column of thirty trucks towing mountain artillery. Picirella describes it thus:

> The road being open again, a column of 300 Germans in trucks and armoured cars gained the plateau by the pass of Grands Goulets. Maj Thivollet sent several men armed with sub-machine guns under Lt François, who set an ambush near Echevis. Hidden in the rocks, our men laid down a harassing fire until their ammunition was running out, when they slipped away. Having lost 25 men in the operation, the Germans took their revenge by burning down the village of Baraques-en-Vercors.[5]

Malleval is a tiny hamlet situated at 3,000ft above sea level in the north-west of the plateau and accessible by a single road, difficult in summer and impassable for much of the winter. Officers, NCOs and men from 6th Battalion of the Chasseurs Alpins came to Malleval as a suitable base from which to harass the German enemy, recreating there military discipline, with smartness of dress, saluting and daily fatigues taking priority. The considerable quantity of arms and ammunition they had brought with them was not shared with local Maquis bands, despised by these regular soldiers as ignorant amateurs. The commanding officer Lieutenant Eysseric decided that the Germans could attack only by coming up the single road from the plain below, so that there was no need for security apart from two sentries at an outpost overlooking the road.

On 29 January 1944, just one week after the attack on Baraques, German troops, guided there by Vichy paramilitaries who knew the country, succeeded in ascending the road unobserved. They killed the two sentries and cut the field telephone line. On a routine check, Eysseric noted the cutting of the line and sounded the alarm. It was too late. By then, the main German force had encircled the hamlet and heavy machine-gun fire cut down Eysseric and twenty-three of his men. Only five men escaped. To punish the civilians nearby, eight adults were thrown alive into a burning barn and seven others deported, to die in camps in Germany. The Germans also took possession of the intact arms and ammunition store.

Picirella's diary describes the occasional action. On 10 February a group of *maquisards* was sent down into the valley to 'liberate' a supply of petrol. The garage owner was expecting them and offered no resistance, but an informer had warned the local gen-darmes, loyal to Vichy. They mingled with the crowd of sympathisers before opening fire, knowing that the *maquisards* could not fire back without killing their human shield. In the brief skirmish one man was seriously wounded and had to be hospitalised.

In late February a senior officer in OAS named Didier Cambonnet sent a message to BCRA:

> … in the Vercors, two types of scenarios are possible:
> 1. Should the enemy decide to use all his resources to liquidate the [Maquis] camps, there is no doubt as to the outcome. Given the odds, it would be overwhelmingly unfavourable to us. The plateau would be cleared and its population massacred.

That analysis was to prove fatally accurate. Cambonnet continued:

> 2. Should the enemy fear a confrontation and decide to block the exits from the pla-teau, they would turn it into a sort of concentration camp. If we choose locations that are easy to defend, they will also be easy for the enemy to isolate.[6]

It seemed that no one was listening in London. On 27 February the BBC French Service transmitted the message '*Les Montagnards doivent continuer à gravir les cimes*' – 'the mountaineers must continue to climb the peaks'. This was the green light for Operation Montagnards, summoning more young and untrained *maquisards* up to the Vercors. The RAF flew night-time drops of weapons, but there were never enough to go round. Alerted by a number of daylight airdrops by American B-17s, a Fieseler Storch spy plane overflew the plateau and located the farms, shepherds' huts and hamlets where the *maquisards* were hiding by following tracks in the snow leading back to them from the drop zones.

Picirella's description of the routine was: guard duty two hours on and two hours off, plus drill, instruction on use and cleaning of weapons, practice ambushes and preparation of beacon fires for an airdrop at the village of Vassieux. Recovering the containers dropped took all day. In some were Allied battledress jackets and trousers, much coveted by the ragged men who discovered them until a formal order was given that French soldiers must not wear foreign uniforms. It was almost a relief to be sent on patrol on 18 March, when a German force attacked and blew up the base at St Julien with a savagery that was going to become worse with each raid on the plateau:

I was stationed near Mme Gauthier's farm, lying full length in the snow with orders to observe, but not open fire. Mme Gauthier was chased out of her farmhouse and forced to kneel in the snow. She was only twenty metres from me, alternately putting her hands together to pray and clutching her head, thinking she was going to be shot. I whispered to Yves, next to me, 'If they take aim at her, I'm going to fire anyway!' Side by side in the snow, we waited, but the search ended and the Germans set off past us, running. There was only a dozen of them and it was hard not to fire. Three other farms were burned down that day. Passing by our camp, I took the opportunity to destroy the address of my mother on a parcel I had received.

Twenty-four hours in the snow. Cémoi had frozen feet. We learned that Marc Leroy, who was only twenty, let himself be burned alive in a hayloft so as not to cause problems for the farmer who was sheltering him. André Couderc was killed. Hubert Levacque from Paris managed to shoot two Germans before they shot him. Furious, the Germans took their revenge on the farmer's son, but his father offered himself instead and was gunned down in front of his horrified wife.

In this enemy raid, we lost three officers and three men.[7]

Captain Jacques Bingen, one of the first French officers to answer de Gaulle's call of 18 June 1940, took over the NM (non-military) section of BCRA in London about this time, replacing Jean Moulin. He warned that the great limitation of any plan for using the Maquis as a military force was the complete dependence for arms drops on British and American aircraft. The influential Major Buckmaster of SOE supplied those groups that conformed with SOE policies and withheld arms from other groups, of whose agenda he disapproved or was uncertain. In part, Bingen's report read:

> In the southern zone (formerly the Free Zone), everything is prepared for a massive arming of the French resistance networks, but it seems as if Britain or de Gaulle does not want to arm the Resistance. We need the weapons. We are counting on the loyalty of the Allies.[8]

That same month Cammaerts returned with the acting rank of lieutenant colonel, to give him the status to deal with liaison officers of de Gaulle's Free French forces, who were to be parachuted in. SOE also placed him in nominal control of all irregular forces in Maquis zones R1 and R2, disregarding the fact that the *maquisards* owed no allegiance to Britain and several Resistance factions were openly hostile to British policy. Cammaerts radioed SOE that he believed several thousand men could be assembled on the Vercors plateau and welded into a sort of army, if supplied with Stens, automatic pistols, sniper rifles and anti-tank weapons. The request was ignored since SOE and OSS both considered that this would lead to over-confidence and the sort of disaster that occurred in Yugoslavia when 20,000 partisans under Josip Broz Tito, with 4,500 sick and wounded comrades, were trapped at the Neretva river in January–April 1943 and suffered huge casualties. BCRA's concern was simpler: de Gaulle did not want sniper rifles and bazookas falling into the hands of FTP and other communist factions, possibly to be used by them in a coup d'état against his provisional government when it was eventually installed in France.

Between 16 and 24 April the village of Vassieux was attacked by Vichy paramilitaries under Raoul Dagostini, who looted and burned down farms, torturing the inhabitants for information and afterwards deporting a number of them and shooting three people dead on the spot. It was a foretaste of what was to come.

One wonders what sort of men the *miliciens* were, to track down, torture and kill their fellow countrymen. The answer is that while some of the senior officers were politicians who had made no secret of their right-wing inclinations before the war, many of the rank and file were simply misfits, grabbing power for the first time in their frustrated lives and exercising it viciously against anyone who fell into their hands. Dagostini made a fitting commander for such men, having served as an officer in France's pre-war repression of independence fighters in Morocco, where he earned a reputation for excessive brutality and perpetration of atrocities against the civilian population in a campaign where brutality was the norm. Enlisting in Vichy's Légion des Volontaires Français to fight in German uniform on the Eastern Front, he had the unusual distinction of being sentenced to death there by a Wehrmacht court martial for massacring twenty civilians living near the scene of an ambush that cost the lives of some of his men. For political reasons, the sentence was not carried out.

After being sent back to France in disgrace, he joined the Milice, where his record of atrocities during the Vercors campaign was so gross that Milice commander Joseph Darnand relieved him of his functions. He was particularly remembered by the people of Vassieux for bringing his mistress Maude Champetier de Ribes to torture sessions, where she gloated over the victims and terrorised any children who omitted to greet her with a smile.[9]

One of Dagostini's alleged tactics in the Vercors was to infiltrate *miliciens* into the ranks of the Maquis bands. These traitors were said to have turned their weapons on the men beside them during the German attacks. Since they knew their fate if unmasked, such men must have been very brave, but it is impossible to know whether this story was true or invented like the rumour of the 'fifth column' supposed to have been responsible for the French defeat in 1940. The probable explanation is that the *miliciens* wore a tricolour armband similar to that of the Maquis. In some close combat situations, this caused fatal confusion.

In between actions, both provoked by German intrusions and Maquis raids to obtain food and petrol, Picirella recorded the stultifying boredom of his quasi-military life during and after the thaw: fatigues, long treks to obtain fresh milk from farmers, sprucing up for parades and memorial masses for the dead. The first dandelion shoots were harvested. For days on end, they were cooked and eaten without bread because the flour had run out. Water at many camps was so bad as to give stomach problems all round.

On 22 April Picirella was woken at 0400hrs with the news that another camp had been surrounded by a detachment of the GMR – the toughest of all the Vichy anti-terrorist forces. After thirteen hours of marching through difficult wooded country, avoiding several Milice patrols, his group arrived at the camp, where he was nearly shot by mistake after returning from a reconnaissance. At 0600hrs the signal was given to attack the GMR base.

Picirella's captain walked up to the old monastery where the GMR men were sleeping while the single sentry was answering a call of nature. The alarm given, the captain called out, 'Surrender. You are surrounded by 150 of my men.' In reality there were only thirty *maquisards*. The *miliciens* were convinced by the sight of Picirella with a grenade in each hand and were, in his words, 'very friendly' from then on, sharing their, by Maquis standards, excellent breakfast with their captors, who did not even bother to disarm them. To avoid having to feed their captives on the plateau, the *maquisards* freed them and returned to camp – a hard march, even in daylight, that took over six hours.

Not everybody could take the hard life on the plateau. The following day, Cémoi – the man with frozen feet – deserted, but this was not the last his comrades would see of him. The day after, three others also slipped away, hoping to return home without being arrested, followed by three more the day after that. The numbers of Picirella's squad became so depleted that it had to be merged with another squad. And still more men deserted, fed up with a diet of boiled dandelions, with neither clean water to drink nor bread to fill their empty stomachs.

On 5 May Picirella was sent down to the village of St Romans on a mission to persuade the Russian Cossack conscripts in its German garrison to desert. Narrowly missing being caught in a Milice dragnet, Picirella and a comrade stayed in the town for the best part of a week, their return to the plateau delayed by the Cossacks' refusal to leave unless provided with motor transport for themselves and their mounts! Negotiations dragged on until 19 May, when Picirella found that the Cossacks and some of the German garrison had been ordered by train to the north. A single Cossack, who had been left behind, was persuaded to accompany them back to camp, where he was warmly welcomed.

On 12 May, during Picirella's unsuccessful recruiting drive, the Resistance had suffered a grievous blow. Jacques Bingen was betrayed by a double agent and arrested by the Abwehr in Clermont-Ferrand. His major achievement, after volunteering to be parachuted into France to take Moulin's place, was to weld the OAS, ORA and FTP into the Forces Françaises de l'Intérieur (FFI). A man of action to the end, Bingen escaped by killing one of his guards. Recaptured almost immediately, he chose the only way to be certain that he would not give away any information about his work under torture, and bit on his cyanide pill.

Through over-confidence or otherwise, men and women were being arrested all over France for Resistance activities. Given a summary trial with only one possible verdict by the Milice, by the Gestapo, by the Wehrmacht and the Waffen-SS, they were shot or deported to camps in the Reich. Executed on 23 May 1944 at the military firing range of Doua outside Lyon was 21-year-old butcher René Villaret. His last letter, written on the day before his execution, began:

My dear Mama,
This letter is to let you know that in a little while the doors of Paradise will open for me. I have made my peace with God and took Communion in the greatest calm. Yes, I have been condemned to death by the German Military Tribunal and, believe me, I heard the verdict calmly and coolly, thinking of our dear Charles and dear Papa.

My life has been the suffering of a kid who strayed from the right path. It was my destiny, although I knew the pain I was causing you. I regret nothing about my life, unless it is that I cannot give you, dear Mama, a last kiss.

In my wallet that they will send you, you will find some photos. Have re-prints made and give them to my workmates, telling them that this life must end sometime and that I leave it with courage.

Dearest Mama, forgive me the pain I have caused you since I was little. You were so gentle and so good, you did not deserve it. Give a kiss from me to my brothers and sisters and all my good friends. I send you a kiss in the hope that you will be happy in the years of your life that remain. A thousand kisses from your little one.

René
P.S. I enclose a lock of my hair.[10]

On 23 May, while Dalloz was still in London, Eugène Chavant, socialist mayor of a commune on the outskirts of Grenoble, and his friend Jean Veyrat rendezvoused near St Tropez with an American fast patrol boat and landed in Algiers on 23 May, hoping to agree with the Gaullist command there when and how the volunteers on the plateau would play their part in the war. They found themselves in another world – a world with no rationing, no fear, an abundance of wealth, and thousands of men in and out of uniform. Whatever vague hopes had motivated the dangerous trip across the Med, it must have seemed to them that the strength of the Free French forces which they could see for themselves must mean that a division or so could easily land on the plateau and lead the volunteers to victory.

After a frustrating beginning, Chavant managed to reach the tripartite Special Projects Operations Centre (SPOC), where his service career stood him in good stead. The French and Allied officers who listened to him for four days pored over maps – how many foreigners even knew where the Vercors was? – and nodded in apparent agreement with the idea of the redoubt becoming the setting for an 'inland airborne invasion' in conjunction with the seaborne invasion that was shortly to be launched. What totally escaped Chavant's simple appreciation of the situation was that the Free French were riddled with political factions and the other Allies did not trust any of them.

Chavant returned to France by a night flight on 3 June, convinced that his plan had been approved, yet without a shred of evidence or confirmation of any kind from the officers with whom he had been talking. On 5 June in Lyon he met Lieutenant Colonel Descour, the 44-year-old No. 2 i/c of zone R1 and handed him two sealed envelopes. One letter appointed Descour overall commander of the forces on the plateau. The other was signed by Jacques Soustelle, nominally head of Gaullist intelligence. It read:

Algiers, 30 May 1944
The directives given in February 1943 by Gen Delestraint for the organisation of the Vercors remain in force. Their execution will be carried out within the framework of the regional and departmental organisations under the control of the military delegate of Zone R1 in liaison with the mission from London and the base in Algiers.[11]

The following day, Chavant was back in the Vercors, euphoric at the news of the Normandy invasion, but loudly complaining that no Free French officer in Algiers had

told him it had been scheduled for that morning. Indeed, de Gaulle himself was seeth-
ing with anger in London at that moment, having learned of it for the first time several
hours after it was launched. Soustelle's letter was nothing more than window dressing, but everyone who met Chavant beaming with pleasure that day at the thought
that he had at last clarified the role of the Maquis on the plateau assumed that there
were detailed plans somewhere for the integration of the Maquis with incoming Free
French or other Allied airborne troops.

Descour tasked Major François Huet, a 39-year-old career cavalry officer who
joined the Organisation Résistance Armée (ORA) when the Armée de l'Armistice
was disbanded, with the impossible job of turning the untrained and undisciplined
maquisards on the Vercors plateau into a unified fighting force that could fortify and
hold the plateau against an all-out German attack. As the *maquisards* included members
of FTP – whose previous activities had been intelligence gathering and assassination of
German soldiers in the cities – the authoritarian, Catholic and deeply patriotic Huet
found himself, probably for the only time in his life, unable to disagree with a communist – FTP national military commander Charles Tillon warned that Operation
Montagnards entirely ignored the two basic rules of irregular warfare: never concentrate your forces or risk a pitched battle. Better, Tillon argued, to keep the bands of
maquisards dispersed throughout the countryside so that they could vanish into the
population after each action, instead of being caught in a trap.

Although it is possible that no one could have been the 'right man for the job' to
unite the politically divergent leaders of the different bands including the ideologically
intransigent communists, it certainly was not Huet. Ending every written order to the
Maquis bands on the plateau with '*Vive l'Armée!*' his main concern appeared to be that
his subordinates learn to march smartly, perform arms drill like regular soldiers and
salute their officers at all times.

Huet based his HQ in St-Martin-en-Vercors with Major Costa de Beauregard
commanding the northern plateau and Geyer la Thivollet – now a captain –
commanding the southern half. Tragically, however good their previous records may
have been, few of the officers and NCOs had any experience in guerrilla warfare,
except in repressing it during France's colonial wars. Nor did Huet's decision to name
the various Maquis bands after disbanded regiments of the pre-war French army
endear him to the majority of the young volunteers, who despised the army that had
been so easily beaten by the German invasion. They were equally unimpressed by the
way Huet staffed his headquarters with fifty officers, NCOs, plus dozens of *maquisards*
compelled to act as servants and orderlies on rigid military lines. There were also two
political leaders on the plateau – in the north Dalloz's friend Jean Prévost and in the
south Dr Samuel Clément.

The stage was now set for tragedy.

7

DREAM OF VICTORY, REALITY OF DEATH

At the BCRA offices in London, Pierre Dalloz discovered that his report from the Vercors had never been forwarded to the right office. The missing file duly located, he repeated his warnings that the Maquis on the plateau could only emerge and take the initiative in conjunction with Allied regular troops. Yet, on 1 June the BBC had transmitted among the nightly Resistance messages, '*Il y a de l'eau dans le gaz*' – 'there is water in the gas'. Like all the action messages, it was nonsense except to those with the key. As far as Resistance activity in the south of France was concerned, a SHAEF directive dated 21 May restricted this to cutting north–south rail and road communications with Normandy. In this vacuum, it was not surprising that local Resistance commanders made their own uncoordinated decisions, some of which were to cause great tragedy. In addition, far from rushing to reinforce Maquis units in remote countryside, many communist groups decided to remain in the towns and cities, with a view to taking political control in the power vacuum after the collapse of the Vichy administration.

In the nationwide confusion caused by the plethora of conflicting rumours, Colonel Henri Zeller, the Gaullist officer commanding Resistance zone R1, declared the valley of the Ubaye River liberated on 5 June. When Cammaerts hurried there, he was dismayed to find a large tricolor bearing the Cross of Lorraine hanging in front of the town hall of Barcelonnette, the main town in the valley. In justification of his jumping the gun like this, Zeller told Cammaerts that Algiers had promised him 'boots on the ground' in his sector within ten days after the Normandy invasion. Knowing this to be impossible, Cammaerts was horrified. Zeller expected him to conjure arms from thin air and seemed oblivious that a public celebration was not only premature, but also invited severe German reprisals as soon as their informers told them what was happening.

A further BBC message came on 5 June: '*Le chamois des Alpes bondit*' – 'the alpine chamois is leaping'. The confusion on the plateau was compounded by the personal messages from the BBC in London mobilising all FFI units in France. This was largely to delude OKW's monitoring stations and keep Hitler guessing whether Normandy was the main invasion or simply a feint to disguise the true invasion shortly to be launched elsewhere. In the reigning uncertainty, after Colonel Descour ordered the sealing off of the Vercors plateau, to make it into the fortress where the inexistent air-borne forces could safely land, access by the nine principal routes up from the plain was blocked by small groups of *maquisards*, whose total numbers did not exceed 300 at the time. One of them was Gilbert Joseph. Watching preparations to mine the access roads, he realised that the Germans could do the same thing and bottle up any Allied forces landing on the plateau.

By 9 June 400 other men, known as *sédentaires* because they had sat at home pursuing apparently normal lives until this moment, had arrived on the plateau. There were weapons for less than half of them. Some 3,500 other *sédentaires* followed them by car, by bicycle, on foot and in coaches. They came in the belief that 4,000 Allied paras would be dropped on the plateau a few days later. If that was Descours' and Huet's understanding, it was not Eisenhower's. In his view, Resistance activities should be confined to sabotage and other actions impeding German reinforcements moving towards Normandy by road or rail.

The new recruits arrived in a mood of premature euphoria induced by the feeling that they were doing something at last and that the end of the occupation was in sight. Huet transmitted frantic pleas to Algiers for airdrops of desperately needed supplies and arms, unaware that Allied HQ had decided not to send in any heavy weapons.

If the symbolic mobilisation looked good on paper to Huet and his officers, many of the men involved like Gilbert Joseph saw clearly that with so few armed men covering the 460 square miles of the plateau, its most likely effect was to taunt the Germans into some kind of retaliation, which their slender resources would be insufficient to counter. His section was posted to the tunnel of Engins, overlooking the twisting road climbing up from Sassenage, traffic on which was out of range for any of their weapons except three light machine guns. Through binoculars they watched 500 German troops per hour negotiating the bends on trucks laden with arms and ammunition and with mortars transported on mule back.[1]

On 6 June 1944, as news of the landings in Normandy spread by word of mouth, people all over France thought that the whole country would be liberated within a few weeks at most. On the plateau the entirely unjustified euphoria reigned supreme. A 23-year-old girl who had volunteered to serve as a nurse with the Vercors Maquis wrote, 'Everyone was so happy. We had a lovely day. We thought the war was as good as won. People came out from Grenoble to the villages of the Vercors to share our joy.'

On 7 June the envoys sent to Algiers returned to the Vercors, full of enthusiasm for the role they thought they were about to play. Road signs were improvised at the top of the access routes bearing the legend '*Ici commence le pays de la liberté*' – 'Here begins the land of freedom'. It was a beautiful dream that was about to turn into a nightmare. On 9 June several hundred able-bodied men in the town of Villard de Lans volunteered to join the Maquis. They came by the coachload, having 'liberated' all the vehicles of the local transport company, whose owner was to pay a hard price, with his garage burned down, his home blown up and two sons killed in German reprisals. Even the local gendarmes volunteered. To give them an alibi and avoid reprisals on their families, a mock kidnapping was arranged, so they could be seen to be 'arrested' by armed *maquisards* and forced to get into one of the coaches. Some criminals locked up in the Gendarmerie insisted on coming along too.

With 2,000 of the new arrivals having no weapons at all, on 9 June Huet's HQ radioed Algiers:

WE HAVE RECEIVED ONLY ONE DROP, FROM WHICH WE RECOVERED ONE MACHINE GUN, ELEVEN RIFLES, TWENTY-TWO SUB-MACHINE GUNS, ONE HUNDRED AND TEN GRENADES AND EIGHTY PAIRS OF SHOES ENDS

Another signal radioed that day from Captain Robert Bennes in charge of re-supply by air, read:

REMINDING YOU OF URGENT NEED FOR AIRDROPS OF ARMS AND MEN IN THE VERCORS AREA STOP WE CAN ACCOMMODATE AT LEAST A REGIMENT OF PARATROOPS STOP MOBILISATION ACCOMPLISHED IN THE VERCORS BUT CURRENT ARMAMENT COMPLETELY INSUFFICIENT STOP WE SHALL NOT BE ABLE TO RESIST IF ATTACKED STOP LACKING LIGHT AND HEAVY WEAPONRY FOR TWO THOUSAND MEN STOP URGENT NEED TO ARM AND EQUIP THEM STOP WE ARE STANDING BY NIGHT AND DAY AT LANDING FIELD NEAR VASSIEUX AND BOTH FIELDS AT ST MARTIN ENDS

Bennes' message was reinforced by one from Lieutenant Colonel Descour:

VERCORS TWO THOUSAND VOLUNTEERS TO BE ARMED STOP INITIAL ENTHUSIASM SAGGING AS WEAPONS LACKING STOP EXTREMELY URGENT SEND MEN WEAPONS GASOLINE TOBACCO IN NEXT FORTY-EIGHT HOURS MAX STOP ENEMY ATTACK POSSIBLE STOP CURRENT CONDITIONS RENDER EFFECTIVE RESISTANCE IMPOSSIBLE STOP FAILURE WOULD MEAN PITILESS REPRISALS STOP WOULD BE DISASTER FOR REGION'S RESISTANCE ENDS

On the following day, he radioed:

NOT KEEPING PROMISE NOW WILL CREATE DRASTIC SITUATION VERCORS ENDS

On 12 June, Bennes radioed:

URGENT SEND MAXIMUM QUANTITY MACHINE GUNS AND MORTARS AND IF POSSIBLE CANNONS AND ANTITANK WEAPONS ENDS

About the same time as his message was transmitted, a signal from BCRA in London arrived that stunned everyone who read it:

SEND THE MEN HOME STOP MOBILISATION PREMATURE ENDS

The background to this is that General de Gaulle had not been told of the date of D-Day until after the first troops hit the beaches at dawn on 6 June. Messages broadcast to Europe from Supreme Allied Commander Eisenhower and Prime Minister Churchill made no mention of him as leader of the provisional government and commander of the Free French forces. After hours of tense negotiations between his HQ and Downing Street, he had been allowed access to a BBC microphone at 1730hrs. The hastily composed speech he then broadcast contained the ambiguous phrase 'the duty of the sons of France ... is to fight with all the means at their disposal.'[2]

All over France, this premature call to arms was to cause tragedy. In a desperate attempt to avert the massacre of thousands of *maquisards* and *résistants*, for whom no Allied reinforcement was possible, General Koenig, C-in-C of the FFI, broadcast on 11 June the following message: 'Since it is impossible for us to supply you with food, arms and ammunition, I repeat that all guerrilla activity should be kept to a minimum. Stay in small groups.'[3]

But it was too late to send the men home from the Vercors, the Germans having roadblocks in place on the exit routes.

An airdrop of weapons on the following day at St Nizier brought sustained artillery fire from batteries in Grenoble. On 14 June Picirella recorded a sad event. A patrol disguised as *miliciens* stopped two men in civilian clothes, one of whom tried to pull rank on the disguised *maquisards* by telling them that he was a Milice officer on his way to infiltrate a Maquis camp – in proof of which he showed them written orders hidden in a shoe. The would-be traitor was recognised as Picirella's old comrade Cémoi. Shrugging his shoulders, he admitted everything and was duly shot.

The Germans in Grenoble could hardly believe their eyes when an enormous banner was defiantly displayed on the cliffs overlooking the city, bearing a French flag and the legend 'Free Republic of Vercors'. When Lieutenant General Karl Pflaum saw it while eating breakfast on the terrace of his HQ, it was a red rag to a bull. He decided that the time had come to relegate the Milice and GMR to a secondary role and move his specialist anti-partisan troops on to the plateau.

Although the Maquis had laid booby traps and mines at the head of all the access routes, and had set ambushes, between 13 and 15 June Pflaum's forces pressed up the winding road from Grenoble to occupy St Nizier, which was the key to the northern plateau, destroying the village in the process. Code-named Operation Bettina, the neutralisation of the plateau was under way.

Also on 15 June, a German armoured column roared into Barcelonnette in the Ubaye valley. A lone British liaison officer who was present managed to destroy two tanks before being killed, together with 150 local men. Zeller and his entourage extricated themselves from the slaughter and headed for the Vercors, arriving there just in time to see the 14,081 men of Pflaum's division, guided by Vichy collaborationist paramilitaries, commence deploying on the plateau on 17 June. Pflaum's core element was again the 157th Reserve Division including the four battalions of Reserve-Gebirgsjäger-Regiment with mule-transported mortars and light mountain artillery that made them a formidable enemy for the lightly armed *maquisards*. Two of his anti-partisan formations – Sicherungsbataillon 685 based in Grenoble and II Sicherungsregiment 194 based in Digne – had recently committed atrocities against civilians when mopping up Maquis bands in the Jura region, despite Pflaum's personal disapproval. He also had Luftwaffe support, both for reconnaissance and to strafe and bomb the farms and villages where the *maquisards* were hiding.

Henri Rosencher was a medical student who arrived on the plateau on 17 June after a most un-Hippocratic day spent advising on the use of explosives at a railway tunnel near Lus-la-Croix-Haute. His military experience included service in North Africa and Italy, where he had been taken prisoner and escaped, little knowing that he would end the war in Dachau concentration camp. Surviving this, he later wrote cold-bloodedly of the sabotage mission that day:

> TNT and plastic charges were placed to collapse the mountain, sealing off the tunnel at both ends and its air shaft. We stationed our three teams and ensured they could communicate with each other. I settled down in the bushes near the tunnel's entrance. Towards 1500hrs we heard the train coming. First came an empty flatcar, to detonate any explosives that might have been laid on the tracks. Next was a wagon with repair equipment, followed by an armoured wagon. Then, the train stuffed with men in field-grey, followed by another armoured wagon. After the train had completely disappeared into the tunnel we waited a minute before setting off the charge at our end. Boulders cascaded down in a huge mass blocking the entrance. Right afterwards, we heard the other two explosions. The 500 men in field grey had no way of escape and the railway was blocked for a long time.
>
> That evening I arrived at St-Martin-en-Vercors, where two brilliant surgeons from Paris named Fischer and Ullmann had set up a well-equipped hospital in the buildings of a holiday camp outside St-Martin with a local doctor named Ganimède. He was there also, with his wife and young son. Some forty wounded men were undergoing treatment, including ten Germans, who were astonished to be cared for, after believing that 'terrorists' like us would massacre them or leave them to die since they knew and we knew that the Germans tortured and killed all our wounded whom they captured.[4]

A perpetual menace hanging over the plateau was the Fieseler Storch observation aircraft that haunted the sky day after day. Knowing that it came from the airfield at Valence-Chabeuil, Huet's HQ radioed BCRA in Algiers, begging daily for a raid on Chabeuil, where the Germans were also assembling a fleet of gliders that could be used for airborne landings on the plateau. BCRA in turn forwarded these requests to the HQ of Mediterranean Allied Air Forces (MAAF) in Naples, which allocated the missions for all Allied aircraft in the theatre.

Many individual *maquisards* were unaware of the threat building up. Typical was Paul Wolfram, a 20-year-old student from Lyon, who wrote:

> When I arrived on 25 June, life in Vassieux was comfortable. Instead of the weekly ration of 250 grams of butter that we got at home, we had huge lumps of it and as much bread as you could eat. The atmosphere was like a holiday camp and we made no preparations for defence because it seemed impossible that the Germans could attack Vassieux.

A 36-year-old nurse named France Pinhas summed up by recording that everyone on the plateau believed the Vercors was already liberated, so they thought themselves quite safe there.[5]

The fluid nature of guerrilla warfare is illustrated by an expedition mounted on 23 June, when a convoy of two empty trucks and two others transporting a Maquis task force drove all the way to Lyon and liberated fifty-three black Senegalese soldiers with their French NCO and his wife – all of whom were given a rapturous welcome on the plateau.

On Sunday 25 June there was a grand parade in St-Martin. Picirella's photograph of the event shows three impeccably uniformed officers on horseback being saluted by a sentry as they lead a column of marching men along the main street. It seemed briefly that the *maquisards'* dream of re-supply and reinforcement was coming true when American aircraft dropped 420 containers in daylight while Colonel Huet was officiating at a memorial service following the parade. The contents included seventy Bren light machine guns, 1,000-plus Stens, 648 Lee-Enfield .303 rifles and thirty-four bazookas. But where, the *maquisards* asked, were the Allied airborne troops that they were expecting?

On 29 June SPOC in Algiers sent in by parachute a fifteen-man American mission code-named Justine and a four-man US-British-French mission code-named Eucalyptus. Although the sight of these officers and men in Allied uniform was a brief morale-raiser, they could do little except provide training with the parachuted weapons. Neither they nor anyone else on the plateau had any way of knowing that the invasion of southern France was planned for mid-August, a date so far in the future that there was no way irregular forces in open insurrection against the Germans could possibly hold out that long.

On 3 July Yves Farge, who was now de Gaulle's personal representative in the Vercors, proclaimed the restoration of the Republic and the abolition of all Vichy legislation. Posters announcing this were plastered on walls in the villages and locally printed newspapers entitled *Le Vercors Libre* and *Le Petit Vercors* circulated with Farge's latest proclamations. More sobering was the text of a cable to Algiers on 6 July, summarising the forces at his disposal:

HEAD COUNT OF MEN ARMED TWO THOUSAND STOP PARTIALLY ARMED ONE THOUSAND STOP NO WEAPONS ONE THOUSAND ENDS[6]

Cammaerts' relationship with FFI officers on the ground was increasingly difficult. They were not impressed with his rank, knowing he was just a civilian who had enlisted for the duration of hostilities. He also had other duties in the 20,000 square miles of south-eastern France over which the JOCKEY network was spread out, primed to go into action in conjunction with the eventual invasion of southern France. On returning to the Vercors, he found that the Paquebot mission had parachuted in on 7 July from SPOC in Algiers, to supervise construction of a landing strip code-named Pencil Sharpener, suitable for use by DC-3 Dakotas, to the south of the village of Vassieux. Arriving with the Paquebot group was a petite and pretty 29-year-old Polish woman using the name Christine Granville, who had been sent to replace Cecily Lefort, now in the hands of the Gestapo.

Either because she weighed far less than the men, or because she was less adept at manipulating the shrouds of her parachute to control direction in the strong winds, Christine landed 3 miles from the drop zone. Burying her parachute as she had been trained to do, she started walking in what she thought was the right direction and met a search party, who asked whether she had seen any sign of a parachutist. She pretended to be just a local peasant girl out for a stroll until their chat convinced her that they were *maquisards.* Escorted by them to meet Cammaerts, she found him delighted at her arrival, but little thinking that it was to this slightly built girl he would shortly owe his life.

One of the most glamorous female agents of SOE, who was later thought to have been the inspiration for Ian Fleming's first Bond girl, she was born Countess Krystyna Skarbek of an impoverished Polish aristocratic father and his rich Jewish wife. Avoiding the usual prolonged SOE training by virtue of having already performed brilliant undercover work for Section D of SIS (the predecessor of SOE) in Poland and Hungary, she was described post-war by Vera Atkins as 'a very brave woman, but a loner and a law unto herself. She had tremendous guts.'[7]

One example of this was when she was arrested on the French Italian frontier while on a self-appointed mission to subvert Polish conscripts serving in German uniform in the Val d'Aosta. Keeping her nerve, she managed to convince her captors that she was an innocent local girl visiting relatives on the other side of the mountains. Her natural beauty belied by a total lack of make-up and a wardrobe of dull-coloured skirts and blouses, she looked and acted the part to perfection.

Two more French officers and one British officer dropped in on 10 July, to share in the good news that, two days earlier, with the cooperation of the footplate crew, a whole trainload of provisions had been 'liberated' near Crest. Hearing that 30 tons of sugar were on board, women rushed from nearby houses even before the firing ended with bowls at the ready to fill them for their hungry families. Also 'liberated' were 60,000 litres of alcohol and a whole wagonload of tobacco.

Picirella was not present, having been sent *en mission* with fourteen comrades and fourteen Americans to intercept what he described as a German division en route to the Normandy battlefront:

On a rock overlooking the road, I stretched out behind a hastily constructed wall of random stones. A few minutes afterward heard the sound of motors and saw the first vehicle appear. Opening fire on it, I heard another maquisard fire a bazooka taken from one of the Americans. With three trucks now in my field of fire, I saw the Germans returning our fire with the machine guns mounted above the drivers' cabins. Other men were leaping from the rear of the trucks and taking cover. A German bullet passed between the stones of my wall. I felt it tug back the scarf wound around my neck. Since I was the only man positioned to fire on the lead truck, I watched for the least move-ment but missed a German who leaped out and took cover beneath the truck, but I got the man who followed him – or so I thought. He lay still for a minute or so, then rolled into cover and started returning my fire. His first bullet pierced my shelter and wounded me in the hand. Since I still had 200 rounds on me I laid down a harassing fire and my comrades did the same. A German was trying to pull a wounded comrade to shelter beneath a truck. In trying to hit him, I punctured the tyres, depriving them

of a way out. Another German jumped out, was hit, fell and lay in the roadway covered in blood. The same thing happened again and again. My comrades attacking the
third truck coming under heavy fire, I laid down covering fire that enabled them to
withdraw across open ground. Moving closer to the first truck, I could see men lying
beneath it and threw two American grenades at them and managed to pick up another
from where the Americans had been. This one exploded beneath the truck. Some cries
and groans, then an awful silence.

I was alone, the others having withdrawn some time since. Hearing a burst of sub-
machine gun fire, I climbed down to the road, thinking that it came from a comrade
– and found myself face to face with a German soldier. The sling of my rifle being
caught up in some branches, I managed to get it free just in time to fire first. Before
beating a retreat, as we had been trained to do, I tried to recover Picard's body. He had
been killed by a mortar shard right in the heart, and had only come with us because
his work was in the kitchen and he desperately wanted to see some action. By a
strange coincidence, his mother sold eggs to mine at the market of St-Antoine. In the
uncanny silence, I picked my way homeward, recovering en route food and ammunition that had been thrown away by the Americans. Catching up with them, I and my
comrades helped to carry their weapons and other burdens, as they were unused to
travelling in the mountains. As nobody had eaten since the previous day, we stopped
for a snack from the food I had recovered, and eventually fell into bed, counting the
missing and the dead.[8]

Some civilians went in a car to try to collect the body of Picard and came across the
corpse of another *maquisard*, which had been hideously mutilated. Some peasants living
nearby had been forced at gunpoint to collect the bodies of dead Germans, and had
seen the whole thing. Hearing groans coming from a thicket, in which he had hidden,
the Germans had dragged the wounded man out, broken his shoulder blades and tied
his hands behind his back, then used him for bayonet practice after crushing his tes-
ticles. His forehead bore the imprint of a rifle butt, and he had been finished off with
five bullets in the head.

An affidavit sworn by a Mme Fernande Battier the following day added that
Gayvallet had been dragged by his own belt, so that his trousers came off, and then tied
to a tree where, one after another, the Germans beat him. An ambulance then came
between Mme Battier and the man being tortured. She heard five revolver shots finishing him off. A corroborative affidavit was sworn by M. Charles Zois, a local butcher.[9]

After this operation, 22-year-old Gaston Gély hid out for weeks deep in the forests.
Literally starving by then, he risked making his way surreptitiously to his uncle's house
on the plain, to be turned away with, 'What the hell are you doing here? Clear off, or
you'll get us all shot.'

8

RANSOMED FROM THE DEATH CELL

As though to welcome Christine in her mother tongue, twenty-seven pupils and teachers from the Polish Lycée in Villard de Lans arrived at Huet's HQ in St-Martin-en-Vercors to play their part. Seven were assigned as labourers to the team levelling the Vassieux landing strip under Captain Jean Tournissa, the others being spread out among combatant units. By now there was a confusion of SOE, OSS and Free French officers present, all with different assignments, but their numbers fell far short of the 4,000 paras that Huet had been expecting.

Among the SOE officers parachuted into the Vercors in August was the darkly handsome 26-year-old Major Alexander Wallace Fielding, nicknamed 'Xan'. Son of British parents, he had been brought up by his grandmother in France and spoke the language perfectly, if a little hesitantly after all the years he had been away. Meeting Christine and Cammaerts just after he landed, he found them an impressive couple – as they were in every sense of the word: after the long lonely solo months, Cammaerts was understandably finding comfort in the arms of his uninhibited courier.

Unusually for an SOE agent, Christine frequently absented herself on missions of her own choosing, although always telling Cammaerts afterwards where she had been. She was thus not present on 11 August – some say 13 August – when a bona fide Red Cross car transporting Cammaerts, Fielding and a section RF officer named Christian Sorensen was stopped at roadblock near Digne. It was a rude awakening to Fielding who had spent the day enjoying the scenery and dropping into the local bar for a drink each time Cammaerts stopped in a village to brief members of JOCKEY on the latest developments.

As to what three SOE officers were doing, travelling together along a road with frequent German security checks, no one has the answer. Unable to read French identity papers, the Central Asian SS troops manning the roadblock would probably have let them go after comparing photographs and faces, had not a Gestapo car arrived with a sharp-eyed officer in civilian clothes. He noticed that the SOE office in Algiers had, in providing Fielding's forged papers, committed two appalling errors: one document was out of date and another had never been date-stamped.

Seeing the Gestapo car approach, Fielding thought it prudent to divide the large amount of money he was carrying and gave some to Cammaerts and some to Sorensen.

The driver of the Red Cross car had told the guards at the roadblock that he did not know his three passengers, but had picked them up on the road, where they were thumbing a lift. This was a perfectly normal occurrence at the time, with motor fuel in critically short supply. His passengers, in turn, said that they had only met while hitch-hiking that morning. Unfortunately, this alibi was useless when a body search revealed that Cammaerts, Fielding and Sorensen were carrying between them a considerable sum of money in notes all numbered in the same series. This, the third grievous mistake made in Algiers, blew right out of the water their story of being strangers. Within an hour they were all thrown into a cell in the Gestapo wing of Digne prison, although the driver was allowed to go because his Red Cross papers were genuine. It was through him that news of the arrests reached Christine.

The three SOE men were still in the Gestapo cell on 15 August, when 94,000 men of the US Seventh Army and the Free French First Army landed on the beaches between Toulon and Cannes in Operation Anvil, re-named Dragoon. By nightfall, the breakout from the beachheads was moving so fast that the Gestapo in Digne were already pan-icking and preparing their escape before the spearheads arrived four days later. In such circumstances, it was normal practice for them to kill all prisoners and hostages before departing. The lives of Cammaerts and his two companions hung on a thread.

On the Italian frontier, liaising with Italian partisans, Christine heard of their pre-dicament and hastened to the rescue. Her first plan was to organise an armed attack on the prison in Digne. When this proved impossible to set up in time, she took what she later called a calculated risk. Had the three prisoners been just rank-and-file members of JOCKEY, her duty was to stay clear and not get involved, but only Cammaerts knew the details of the network's command system and how to contact the different cells. It was thus her duty to risk her life in order to save his.

After a 40-mile bicycle ride, she arrived at the prison and chatted up an elderly gendarme under the pretence of being Cammaerts' wife, saying that she wanted to leave a parcel of food and clothes for him. The gendarme introduced her to Albert Schenk, a bilingual Gestapo liaison officer from Alsace. She had learned when work-ing undercover in Poland that, when you have to bluff, you bluff big. So she told Schenk that she was General Bernard Montgomery's niece, in daily radio contact with the Dragoon forces advancing up the Rhône valley. To her request that he release the prisoners in order to save his own neck, Schenk replied that he did not have the necessary authority and introduced her to Max Waem, a more senior colleague from Belgium, whose job was to liaise between the German security organisations and the local gendarmes.

To back up her story when meeting Waem in Schenk's apartment that afternoon, Christine took the additional risk of showing him some of the crystals used to lock her transmitter on fixed frequencies for transmissions. That they were old ones which had been damaged was irrelevant because, in doing so, she had given a Sicherheitsdienst officer proof that she was an Allied spy. She also told Waem that the local Resistance planned to assassinate him shortly, unless the Americans arrived first, in which case he would either be lynched in the post-liberation frenzy or hanged by the Americans as a war criminal for having ordered the arrest and execution of what she called 'the three most important prisoners in France'.

The only chance of Schenk and Waem staying alive, she said, was for them to help get 'her' three prisoners out of the prison alive and well, in return for which she would hand over enough money for the two of them to make good their escape. Probably at no other time would her incredible story have been believed, but in the confusion generated by the invasion and rapid advance of Dragoon forces Waem and Schenk were rightly worried about their fate, if they left their departure too late.

At any point in these delicate negotiations, either of the men she was dealing with could have had her arrested and shot. Indeed, Waem repeatedly threatened her with a loaded pistol but, as the negotiations dragged on, Christine knew she had judged her adversaries correctly. After three hours' haggling, impressed by her apparent total calm – she said afterwards that she was too busy to be frightened – Waem named his price for liberating the prisoners. He wanted a handwritten note confirming that he and Schenk had saved the lives of the three SOE officers and 2 million francs in cash as getaway money.

With no time to lose, Christine hurriedly left town and made her way to where she had hidden her transmitter, to radio news of the deal to Algiers. In what must have been one of the swiftest operations mounted in the entire war, the cash was dropped that night in the hills close to Digne. Returning to the prison the following day, she handed the money over to Waem and waited for him to deliver. Nobody knows what bluff she used at that stage to stop him simply pocketing the money, arresting her and shooting her, Cammaerts and the other two SOE men.

When footsteps were heard approaching the miserable cell in which the three men were languishing, Cammaerts woke up. It may seem strange that he could sleep in a condemned cell, but his nerves were so shredded by the months of clandestine life that he could fall asleep anywhere. He and the others had just been served the best meal since their arrest. Expecting to find themselves shortly facing a firing squad in the prison courtyard, they saw Waem standing in the doorway, wearing a Wehrmacht uniform jacket over civilian clothes. He motioned them outside with his revolver. As Cammaerts walked out, Waem said, 'What a wonderful wife you have!'

Waem was saluted by the guards as he marched his prisoners out of the main gate and then turned right, instead of left towards the football pitch used as an execution ground by the Germans. A few hundred yards from the prison, Waem hustled them into the rear seat of a waiting car and got in beside the driver. His uniform jacket guaranteeing them safe passage past the checkpoint at the edge of town, Waem ordered the driver to halt at the first bend, where the slim figure of Christine was waiting. She squeezed into the front seat. Shortly afterwards, Waem got out and buried his uniform jacket as the first step in his personal getaway. With the car heading for the mountains, Cammaerts and his companions realised they were free.

A few days later, Schenk was assassinated by the Resistance during the liberation of Digne. His share of the ransom had been given to his wife, who tried to exchange the Vichy notes Christine had handed over for new currency after the war, but found the rate of exchange such that her widow's 'fortune' was all but worthless. What she did receive was thanks to Christine's and Cammaerts' personal intervention. Waem, however, was a born survivor, using Christine's safe conduct to have himself 'rescued' by British paras and handed over to British Field Security Police in Bari, a prisoner, but alive.

One always wonders how incredibly brave agents like Christine Granville settled down to peacetime living after the war. After all the danger and stress to which they had become accustomed, the answer is often tragic. Stranded in Cairo with one month's salary when SOE terminated her contract in 1945, she volunteered for the missions being sent from London into her homeland, now Soviet-occupied, but these were cancelled when the first group was betrayed and all its members arrested on arrival in the country. Since her record of wartime working for Britain debarred her from openly returning home, Christine applied for British nationality in the belief that all her work for SOE would mean a welcome with open arms for a woman holding the MBE, the George Medal and the Croix de Guerre. Not so. Her application was delayed because she could not prove the requisite five years' previous residence in Britain, as required by some nameless bureaucrat. Eventually reaching Britain as a stateless refugee after borrowing the money for her fare, she took work as a switchboard operator and sold dresses in Harrods department store before signing on as a stewardess aboard the SS *Winchester Castle* and SS *Rauhine*.

Christine had always enjoyed sexual relationships with men – sometimes more than one at a time. As SOE's Vera Atkins said of her: '[Christine] was no plaster saint. She was a vital, healthy, beautiful animal with a great appetite for love and laughter.' Atkins also said that, like so many agents who had burned up a lifetime's adrenalin, 'After the war Christine was quite unable to adapt herself to a boring day-to-day routine. She lived for action and adventure.'[1] Her free-loving lifestyle proved her undoing when a schizophrenic senior steward aboard *Rauhine* became obsessed with her. To escape him, she decided that life afloat was not for her. Her unwanted suitor followed her ashore and took a job at a London club. After persistently stalking her, on the evening of 15 July 1952 he accosted her in the lobby of her Kensington hotel and stabbed her through the heart. For this crime he was hanged two weeks after his trial that September.

Cammaerts, on the other hand, had the benefit of British nationality, but still found it hard to get a suitable job after de Gaulle was securely established as head of government of the Fourth Republic and insisted on the withdrawal of SOE, OSS and other Allied officers from France. In Cammaerts' own words, he was over-promoted, yet knew nothing of military life. Nor did he want to. Despite Buckmaster's personal recommendation, he was twice rejected for posts, being blacklisted by the Foreign Office because his father was not British by birth and the posts could not be given to someone who could thus obviously not be trusted with confidential information! Such stupidity, which Foreign Minister Anthony Eden was unwilling to correct, proved that Colonel Blimp was alive and well in London's post-war corridors of power.

A period of service in uniform with Special Allied Airborne Reconnaissance Force (SAARF), tasked with preventing massacres before liberation of concentration and death camps in Germany, included a visit to Ravensbrück, where his courier Cecily Lefort had been gassed only a few months before. On 1 July 1945 SAARF was disbanded, after which Cammaerts spent the last seven months of his military career as liaison officer between Lieutenant General Sir Brian Robertson, the Deputy Military Governor of the British zone of occupied Germany, and General Koenig, Military Governor of the French zone. His own modest assessment was that the job was a waste of time since, although he saw Koenig every day, Robertson only agreed to see him once.

Cammaerts then took the post of deputy director of the Allied Reparations Agency at the princely salary of £2,500 per annum. This eighteen-month stint based in Brussels, far from the cares of austerity Britain which was recovering from the war with agonising slowness, was a re-bonding period for him, his wife Nan and their children. When their fourth child was born, her father insisted on naming her Christine after Christine Granville. When talking about this with her eldest daughter, who thought it was an insensitive thing to do, Nan said later, 'Among the young men ... who went off to the war, the ones who allowed themselves to have affairs survived better.'[2]

Cammaerts' main contribution to the agency was a survey of staff duties which concluded that he and the other nine directors had little work to do, while drawing salaries that would globally have employed 600 lower-grade staff, all of whom were overstretched. Practising what he preached, he sacked himself and returned to his teaching career in Leicester, modestly insisting that his work as principal of the City of Leicester training college was far more important than what he had done during the war.

Talking of wartime colleagues who suffered what would now be termed 'post-traumatic stress', this extraordinarily stable man said, 'Ten of my closest friends from those days have committed suicide, some straight after the war, some thirty years later. Who knows what happens to the human mind when put under that sustained pressure?'[3]

9

FROM THE SKY CAME DEATH

On 12 July General Gabriel Cochet of the Free French informed his American contact in Algiers, General B.F. Caffey, that the Luftwaffe was carrying out intensive photo reconnaissance of the Vercors and rapidly building up German ground forces in the region. The same day, Cochet despatched one of his officers to MAAF HQ in Naples to request General Ira C. Eaker, commanding all Allied air forces in the Mediterranean, to give the situation on the Vercors priority consideration.

On 13 July, news came from Resistance sources in the Rhône valley that the German garrison at Valence had been substantially reinforced. From the town of St Romans came news that an SS general had set up his headquarters there with troops experienced in anti-partisan warfare. At Valence-Chabeuil airfield, sixty-six aircraft of various types had been counted hidden under concealment and reconnaissance flights over the plateau had been stepped up.

That day, General Cochet himself flew from Algiers to Naples to ask General Eaker, who had 3,000 aircraft conveniently based in Corsica and Sardinia, to bomb the field at Valence and remove one serious threat to Operation Montagnards. Cochet played on the fact that Eaker's bomber fleets included aircraft flown by pilots of the Forces Aériennes Françaises Libres (FAFL) – the Gaullist air force – but none of these had the range to cross the Mediterranean and reach the Vercors.[1] Passed on to Eaker's deputy, British Air Marshal John Slessor, Cochet specifically asked for a mission to hit Valence-Chabeuil and was promised that everything possible would be done.[2] It was a somewhat Delphic reply.

In fairness to Eaker and Slessor, their tactical priorities at the time were ground support missions for the Allied forces in Italy, now stalling as they came up against the reinforced Gothic Line after suffering casualties approaching 200,000 dead and wounded in the Italian campaign. Since German forces on the European fronts usually respected the status of Allied soldiers taken prisoner in uniform – with the exception of snipers, who were routinely shot on capture by both sides – there was no reason why officers at MAAF should know that the 4,000 men and women in the Vercors would be treated differently, if taken prisoner, and shot out of hand after torture. However, Cochet's persistence impressed Eaker, with terrible consequences that neither man could have dreamt of.

With half of Huet's force still without weapons, on 14 July – the national holiday commemorating the storming of the Bastille during the French Revolution – Picirella was on duty at the airstrip near Vassieux, where he was an eyewitness to a massacre. The mood early that morning was summed up by 20-year-old *maquisard* Paul Borrel: 'On 14 July we had a parade by the Chasseurs Alpins mountain troops. It was sensational.' A survivor of this terrible day said afterwards: 'We looked to the sky for our salvation, but from the sky came death.'

It came because someone on Eaker's staff with zero understanding of the situation on the ground was trying to make amends for the long delay in supplying the plateau. A fleet of B-17 bombers with a protective canopy of fighters wheeling above them was tasked to drop 1,200 canisters of arms and ammunition on the landing strip at Vassieux. To do this in daylight, in full view of the German forces surrounding the plateau, was an open invitation for them to take appropriate action.

Cammaerts and Christine were watching the celebrations below the plateau in the town of Die, and clearly saw the mass of aircraft manoeuvring throughout the drop. Shortly after the Allied aircraft had flown away, a single German fighter dived down on people dancing in the square at Die, machine guns blazing. Everyone dived for cover, except Christine, who stayed where she was, apparently unmoved by the danger. Picirella's diary tells the story on the plateau:

> By 0400hrs all was ready and the wireless operators were on standby [to talk to the incoming aircraft]. I went off to La Britière, returning to Vassieux at 0700hrs and in spite of the heavy mist covering the plateau I checked again and again every detail to ensure nothing had been overlooked. By 0900hrs everything was absolutely ready. At 0930hrs we heard the drone of engines getting louder and louder. Our planes had arrived! There were about a hundred of them flying in groups of twelve and the fighters circled around [sic] the Halifaxes and Flying Fortresses. The noise filled the whole of the plateau and must have been heard down on the plain at Valence. The Fortresses flew low over the plateau while fixing their positions and then flew off in the direction of Valence and back to us. From each of seventy-two Fortresses poured a stream of 15 to 20 (man-size) containers. It was a splendid sight. A pilot dropped a packet of Camel cigarettes wrapped in a tricolour band on which was written, 'Bravo lads! Vive la France!' The aircraft that had dropped their cargo stooged around waiting for the whole operation to be completed. It was around 1000hrs when the last Flying Fortress vanished into the clouds. A few minutes later every available truck arrived to collect the containers. While the patriots of the Vercors were helping to load the containers on the trucks two fighters suddenly flew in. Everyone thought they were British planes but, as they dived towards the landing strip the Swastika markings were plainly visible. They came in at about eight metres above ground level and opened fire at us all. This was only the beginning of the horror. Bombers appeared and bombs rained down on the landing strip and the village. An hour later, our communications were cut and we were completely isolated from any help. No vehicle could have survived the murderous fire. One maquisard did manage to get through to us. Although we appreciated his courage in taking such a risk, he had not thought to bring a weapon. Having sprayed us lavishly with bombs, the enemy planes then flew

off after dropping hundreds of grenades [sic] to tear up the strip and make it unusable. To make matters worse, one of our heavy machine guns seized up and we had to strip it down. Vassieux was on fire and so was my shelter. I installed myself with a few men in a shell hole and returned fire. Meanwhile Captain Tournissa was organising the western defences. Hardy was responsible for the eastern sector. In between each wave of bombers we dashed out to try and grab the white parachutes that made such excellent aiming points. There was no let up in the bombing and strafing. As soon as one group left, another appeared. Their base was only 18km away as the crow flies. In case the Germans invaded the village with a battalion of parachutists, it was decided to station a company of the Chasseurs Alpins in reserve in the forest, leaving Vassieux to be defended by the people there who had machine guns and other weaponry. Unfortunately, we had run out of ammunition for one of the heavy machine guns and there was no way of quickly obtaining more.

The enemy spared nobody. The [civilian] population, livestock, houses, roads and even the harvest – all were ruthlessly attacked and destroyed. By 1530hrs, the church of Vassieux was a smoking ruin. Towards 1700hrs the enemy concentrated on other targets. Yet, despite the heavy casualties, everyone went out after nightfall to gather up the containers on the plateau.[3]

The Luftwaffe fighter-bombers from Valence-Chabeuil airfield, less than ten minutes' flying time away, bombed farms and villages and strafed every person and every vehicle that moved in the open throughout the day. Incendiary bombs dropped on Vassieux and La Chapelle en Vercors turned the two villages into blazing infernos. Only after the flames in Vassieux had died down was it possible to recover some 200 undamaged containers from the 1,200 that had been dropped. None contained any of the heavy weapons that were so desperately needed.

Huet's best estimate of the strength of Pflaum's forces investing the plateau was based on the knowledge that 15,000 loaves of bread were being baked for them daily in Grenoble. Allowing two men to a loaf, he reckoned that made 30,000 enemy at the gates, while Algiers seriously underestimated their strength at 10,000. Whichever estimate one took, it was all too evident that they were armed with 45mm and 105mm cannons and heavy machine guns, with light and heavy tanks also observed standing by at Valence-Chabeuil. In what can only have been a panic move, on 15 July Huet gave an order, obeyed with reluctance, for press gangs to enter Villard and forcibly recruit every young male there. Mothers hid their sons in cellars, as they would from the Germans. With 150 youths finally embarked on their trucks, the *maquisards* drove home, wondering like Gilbert Joseph what was the point of collecting 150 more mouths to feed when 1,000 volunteers were still without weapons? Their conclusion was that Huet and his officers thought that greater numbers would mean more airdrops and perhaps promotion. There could be no other reason.[4]

The various Allied missions in the area had transmitted warnings to Algiers and London that the Luftwaffe was building up under camouflage a fleet of gliders at the Valence-Chabeuil field, but neither London nor Algiers gave any priority to destroying them on the ground until 27 July, when it was too late to save so many lives. This was despite a plea transmitted on 20 July:

MUST INSIST ON FOLLOWING STOP ONE DUE TO BUILD-UP GERMAN
FORCES REQUEST REPEATED BOMBARDMENT OF ST NIZIER SEVEN
KILOMETRES WEST OF GRENOBLE STOP TWO DROP AS MANY
PARAS INTO OUR LIBERATED AREAS AS POSSIBLE STOP THREE SEND
MONEY STOP FOUR WOULD BE VERY HAPPY TRAVEL TO ALGIERS
AND LONDON TO BRIEF YOU ON SITUATION IN MY REGION ENDS[5]

There was no reply, not even to an urgent tactical message requesting bombing of a
German armoured column. This took three days, after being decoded in Algiers, to
reach the office where action might have been taken. General Pflaum's communications had none of these problems. Every detail had been hammered out, including
instructions on how to deal with the civilian population on the plateau:

> Arrest all men from 17 to 30 years of age who do not belong, and have never belonged,
> to the Resistance (the others being shot). Burn those houses which have unquestion-
> ably been used to shelter terrorists or their stores, e.g. schools, mairies, hangars. To
> prevent the Resistance re-installing itself in the Vercors, we shall leave on the farms
> only the minimum of animals essential for feeding the inhabitants.[6]

The result was that death's second visit to Vassieux came on 21 July, a day of unseason-
able rain and low cloud, through which a flight of twenty-two Dornier DO 17 tug
aircraft towing DFS 230 gliders appeared. The 400 men labouring on the 1,050m-long
landing strip at Vassieux stopped work and stood cheering in the belief that this was
the arrival of the long-awaited Allied airborne reinforcements. The mistake was understandable, given that they were working flat out under an FAFL captain parachuted in
especially from Algiers to get the strip ready as fast as possible.

Only when they saw the Maltese crosses on the wings and fuselages of the gliders did they realise their mistake. An emergency transmission from Bennes to Algiers
reporting the landings was sent at 1111hrs. Decoded at 1150hrs, it got stuck in the
machinery like all the others and reached General Cochet by accident at 1420hrs. By
this time most of the men who had been working on the landing strip were dead. An
earlier message from the Resistance in the Rhône valley, reporting flights of Dornier
bombers towing DFS 230 gliders from Luftlandgeschwader Gruppe I en route from
Strasbourg to Lyon/Bron airport, seems not to have been evaluated in Algiers as a part
of the Vercors jigsaw.[7]

Expertly dropping tow cables and diving nearly vertically to land fast, each glider
disgorged eleven battle-hardened Waffen-SS troops with automatic weapons. It all happened so fast that most of the defenders were stunned at the vulnerable moment when
the gliders were landing and heavy losses might have been inflicted, if only Huet's men
had been prepared. One French airman with the *maquisards* named Victor Vermorel
reacted in time to throw himself behind a heavy machine gun, with which he shot
down the black-uniformed men emerging from two gliders before himself being
killed. Swiftly deploying on the ground were two companies of Legionnaire-Lehr-
Bataillon Brandenburg consisting of Russians, Ukrainians and other Eastern Europeans
conscripted into the Waffen-SS for anti-partisan warfare.

Faster thinking could have given the defenders a brief initiative, but courage was not lacking. They moved their few machine guns and light mortars from place to place in an effort to delude the attackers into thinking they were better armed than was the case. Luftwaffe ground support pressed the defenders back on all sides; the wounded could not always be rescued and there was no time to bury the dead. By nightfall the invaders had lost about twenty men and the survivors had taken cover in the still smoking ruins of Vassieux, awaiting reinforcements. A counter-attack on the village ordered by Huet failed miserably in pouring rain. By nightfall, French casualties exceeded 100 dead, including civilians, gunned down by the SS troops like game birds on a shoot.

Many sources claim that 400 men landed in that first strike, but the DFS 230 could only carry ten men and the pilot plus 250kg of equipment, and all accounts agree that only twenty-two gliders landed that morning, making a total of 232 shock troops fighting amateur volunteers for the most part. The news over the radio, passed on by word of mouth, that the attempt on the life of Hitler at Rastenburg had failed, did nothing to raise the defenders' spirits.

A desperate signal to Algiers read:

MASSIVE ATTACK BY AIRBORNE TROOPS LANDED AREA VASSIEUX IN VERCORS FROM ABOUT TWENTY AIRCRAFT EACH TOWING ONE GLIDER STOP STRONG INFANTRY AND TANK STOP [sic] OTHER ENEMY UNITS ARRIVING ON ROUTE NATIONALE 75 STOP WE HOPE TO BE ABLE TO MAINTAIN RADIO LINK ENDS

This elicited the following response:

CAN SEND THE FOLLOWING ON NIGHT OF TWENTY-THIRD STOP ONE TWO TEAMS OF FIFTEEN MEN STOP TWO FOURTEEN OFFICERS AND NCOS FOR TRAINING STOP THREE SIX BAZOOKAS WITH AMMUNITION STOP TWENTY GRENADE LAUNCHERS WITH GRENADES STOP AMMUNITION FOR AMERICAN MORTARS ALREADY SENT STOP FIFTEEN 50-CALIBRE MACHINE GUNS WITH AMMUNITION STOP FOUR NINETY BRITISH LIGHT MORTARS WITH BOMBS STOP FIVE REPLACEMENT PARTS AND TOOLS STOP SIX MEDICAL EQUIIPMENT STOP ADVISE URGENTLY WHICH OF THESE YOU CAN TAKE AND ON WHICH DROP ZONES STOP COURAGE! ENDS[8]

Another message promised that MAAF in Naples would be requested to attack the German forces on and around the plateau on the following day.

News reached Huet from the sparsely defended eastern rim of the plateau, where Pflaum's Bavarian Gebirgsjäger mountain warfare troops had brought mortars and machine guns into play to drive back the defenders in support of the airborne troops in Vassieux. At one of the eastern passes twenty-eight *maquisards* refused to surrender. When the first mortar round exploded inside the mouth of the cave where they had taken shelter, they all agreed to burn any personal papers and photographs to prevent reprisals on their families, and then joined hands singing *La Marseillaise*. Amazingly, considering that they were up against at least 100 of Pflaum's elite troops, they managed to beat off several assaults.

The Gebirgsjäger changed tactics, clambering up the rock face above the cave and letting down from there an explosive charge on a rope, swinging it backwards and forwards so as to explode inside the cave. The first charge did little damage, but inside the cave there were already six men dead and most of the others had been wounded. Now on their guard, they managed to cut the rope of a second charge and throw it outside the cave before it exploded. Later that evening, a fused 5kg block of Lyddite was let down, a defender leaped for it, but missed as it was jerked out of range, then swung inwards again with little fuse left. The explosion brought down part of the roof, burst several men's ear drums and filled the cave with choking fumes. At 2300hrs those able to run crept out of the cave and broke through the German cordon by heading away from Vassieux, and not towards it as the Germans were expecting. Their unsung victory was to have killed seventeen Germans and wounded sixty, but this would have no effect on the battle for the plateau.

Among the local commanders was Dalloz's friend Jean Prévost, a polymath in his element in a university lecture hall or on the athletics track. He was perpetually on the move from position to position, encouraging his men and leading from the front with such effortless energy that nobody could have guessed how little time he had left to live. Occupied with the defence of Valchevrière, he was not present at the emergency orders meeting at St-Martin that night. Huet began with a résumé of the situation in his habitual calm tones:

Our men are facing odds of ten to one and are surrounded or falling back everywhere. Unless a miracle happens, by tomorrow or the day after it will be impossible to continue the struggle. We must split up, leave the villages and head into the forests. Pursued by the enemy, we shall die there, if we must, weapons in hand.

This provoked a violent argument in which half of those present supported him and others accused their commanding officer of sheer stupidity in prolonging the imbecility of fighting on the plateau a battle which there was no hope of winning, and never had been. Huet's critics, including Francis Cammaerts, proposed instead a complete evacuation of the plateau. To this, Huet retorted that it was too late, since the whole Vercors massif had already been surrounded. Captain Bousquet, his severest critic, disagreed yet again:

There is one bridge across the River Drôme by a route I have ordered to be kept open at all costs until noon tomorrow. Crossing here will enable the escaping men to reach the forest of Saou, where they can easily evade pursuit. That might save the civilian population up here from a great deal of suffering. If you are not capable of exfiltrating 3,000 men in twelve hours, you're not fit to command them.

Huet refused to give way, even when Chavant and Colonel Zeller, the senior officer present, sided with his critics.

'Then colonel, you can assume my command,' said Huet.

'You know perfectly well that I have other responsibilities in the region,' Zeller retorted.

Having made no preparations, Huet pointed out that it was now impossible to contact everyone about the breakout in time and that in any case he had insufficient transport to get them all away. On that, there was general agreement, but the point was made that a fighting breakout stood the best chance of success, with some at least living to fight another day, instead of dying pointlessly on the plateau. The argument continued between those who maintained that the best course was to exfiltrate in small groups, every man for himself, and those who supported Huet's plan to take to the forests and continue the fight on the plateau. The latter plan won the day, or rather, the night. Zeller and Cammaerts dissociated themselves, saying that their other responsibilities required them to get out before that became impossible, and left immediately.

'And you?' Huet asked the most vociferous critic among his officers.

'I gave you my views,' was the reply. 'But they were rejected. *Tant pis!* But you are my superior. I shall remain here with you.'[9]

The meeting broke up after it had been agreed to evacuate at least the hospital, in case the Germans took reprisals on the wounded being cared for there. The order reached the hospital during a violin recital being given by one of the patients. By 0200hrs the evacuation was under way. Meanwhile, Huet's headquarters staff busied themselves with despatching the orders to disengage and head for the forests at 1600hrs the following day. With Huet's and Chavant's agreement, a signal was sent to Algiers reading:

LA CHAPELLE, VASSIEUX, ST-MARTIN BOMBED BY GERMAN AIR FORCE STOP ENEMY TROOPS LANDED AT VASSIEUX STOP REQUEST IMMEDIATE BOMBING RAID STOP WE PROMISED TO HOLD OUT FOR THREE WEEKS AND HAVE DONE SO ALREADY FOR SIX STOP NEED RE-SUPPLY IN FOOD MEN AND MATERIEL STOP POPULATIONS MORALE EXCELLENT BUT WILL TURN AGAINST YOU IF YOU DO NOT TAKE STEPS IMMEDIATELY AND WE SHALL AGREE WITH THOSE WHO SAY THAT LONDON AND ALGIERS UNDERSTAND NOTHING OF THE SITUATION IN WHICH WE FIND OURSELVES AND ARE CONSIDERED AS CRIMINALS AND COWARDS STOP YES REPEAT CRIMINALS AND COWARDS ENDS[10]

Of this, the rank and file were unaware. As Joseph wrote afterwards, had the *maquisards* known of this signal, they would have pointed the finger at Huet and his officers as being the true criminals.[11] Not until 1030hrs on 27 July did the signal reach General Cochet's desk. Both at the time and afterwards, considerable effort has gone into trying to unravel the tangled web of accusations and denials that surround the failure to provide air support for the beleaguered Vercors. The Minister for Air in de Gaulle's provisional government was Fernand Grenier, a communist. Accusing his non-communist colleagues of obstruction and failing to take action in order to discredit him and the PCF, on 27 July Grenier signalled de Gaulle:

I CANNOT BE ASSOCIATED WITH A CRIMINAL POLICY WHICH
CONSISTS OF HAVING FORCES AT YOUR DISPOSAL AND NOT USING
THEM WHEN OUR BROTHERS IN FRANCE APPEAL FOR HELP ENDS[12]

In reply, de Gaulle ordered Grenier to apologise in writing or resign. Grenier's personal preference was resignation, but the PCF Central Committee insisted he apologise in order not to lose his position in the provisional government. When it moved to Paris after the liberation of the capital on 25 August, Grenier left the Cabinet and was replaced by Charles Tillon, a communist more acceptable to de Gaulle.

Meanwhile, Cammaerts, Zeller, Christine and a few others found transport to take them to the Col de Rousset, the only way off the plateau still open. Cammaerts' account gives the feeling of this escape while the noise of battle was still raging nearby:

> Trying to make no noise whatsoever, we stumbled down through the undergrowth, which was not easy because it was very steep and 3,000 feet down and we had to carry very heavy gear, radios and all our own personal equipment with us. Finally we reached the valley and then we had about 4 miles to the road and the Drôme river. We were at a point just west of Die. We crossed fields very slowly because we were aware that German troops were using that axis. We never saw them and reached the river and forded it up to our knees, climbed up to the railway, crossed it and the N93 road was another 100 yards away. It wasn't a large arterial road, just wide enough for two lanes of traffic and it wound through the valley with very steep sides, every step you took with great care and we darted across it one at a time. Coming down towards Die we met the ambulance convoy with the badly wounded making its way back towards the Vercors. They'd tried to transfer their worst cases to the hospital at Die, but a totally hysterical matron had waved them away: 'The Germans are coming. You'd better go back'. And that was what they were doing. Unfortunately, it was a tragic mistake because eventually they used the Grotte de la Luire as a hospital. If they'd gone south, as we were doing, they would have been all right. But they went the wrong way.[13]

The matron had been right. When German troops invaded the hospital, the nursing staff of nuns could only watch impotently as every wounded man in the building was killed with a burst from a sub-machine gun where he lay in his bed.

On 22 July meteorological conditions improved sufficiently to allow several flights by Fieseler Storch observation planes transmitting weather reports and identifying Maquis positions, which were then strafed with machine guns and 20mm cannons by Focke-Wulf 109s. It is a testimony to the determination of the *maquisards* that the airborne assault force holed up in Vassieux was to lose 60 per cent of its strength before reinforcements arrived on 23 July, when breaks in the cloud cover enabled a further twenty-one DFS 230s and two larger Gotha GO 242 gliders to take off from Valence-Chabeuil airfield, destination Vassieux. One glider broke its cable in turbulence; the tugs of two others got lost after being swept 25km off course by the strong mistral wind blowing down the Rhône valley. The turbulence was so strong that one of these gliders had a wing torn off by the wind and crashed, killing all on board.

However, the remaining gliders disgorged another 232 Waffen-SS to reinforce the survivors of the first landing. The newcomers were Central Asian conscripts, whom the defenders nicknamed 'the Mongols', not only because of their physical appearance but also because of the sadism with which they tortured uninvolved civilians. In Picirella's words: 'The Mongols raped every female from thirteen to sixty-five years old.' The supreme irony was that the landing strip at Vassieux was used to bring in several of the GO 242 gliders carrying arms and ammunition for the attackers.

In addition, by now Pflaum had 700 men who had crossed the 'insuperable' barrier of the eastern escarpment, 3,000 advancing from the south, 3,000 advancing from the west and 4,000 driving down from the north. In addition to all these combat troops were the thousands more in support units and the girdle blockading the massif, making odds of over 10:1 against the armed *maquisards* continuing the fight. By the time the last shot was fired, the last artillery round exploded, the last agonised victim tortured to death, more than 650 *maquisards* and 200 civilians had died, 100-plus people had been deported and uncounted wounded were being cared for in the forests, in homes and hospitals, many to die later.[14]

In Algiers, General Cochet was still working away at the system, bogged down by the in-fighting between various political factions. De Gaulle being absent at the time and since General Koenig insisted that the Vercors was London's operation and not Algiers' responsibility, it was to Koenig that Cochet sent a signal requesting latest details of German dispositions on the plateau, so that MAAF could be requested to organise a raid on the Sunday evening or Monday morning. Koenig replied:

ALL INTELLIGENCE SITUATION VERCORS PASSED TO SPOC IMMEDIATELY AFTER RECEPTION STOP EFFECT MAXIMUM DROPS ST MARTIN CODENAMED PAPER KNIFE ... AND ARRANGE MAXIMUM SUPPORT MISSION VERCORS AND RAIDS AIRFIELDS AMBERIEU AND ST RAMBERT AND CHABEUIL ENDS[15]

A book could be written about each day of the Battle of Vercors, but one uneven confrontation reads very like another, one more massacre like the previous ones, the agony of one tortured prisoner shamefully like the agony of any other although the details of the torture may vary for a myriad reasons, including the sex of the victim.

In a cave near the precipitous Pas de l'Aiguille twenty-three *maquisards* managed to hold out against considerable odds for thirty hours on 22 July. Realising that their position was hopeless, the able-bodied slipped away under cover of night, leaving eight comrades dead and three badly wounded men who could not be moved. They chose to shoot themselves rather than surrender.

Considering that the long-awaited Allied reinforcements had never arrived and that there was a general shortage of weapons and ammunition, there was remarkably little panic at most of the Maquis positions, manned by young and inexperienced amateurs facing what must have looked by now as though the whole German army and air force were arrayed against them. On 23 July word was passed from Huet that it was time to disengage. Some groups decided to seek refuge in the forests; others tried their luck in making it through the German cordon at the foot of the plateau, where many were arrested and summarily shot.

General Cochet was doing his best. Returning to Italy, but unaware that it was now too late to have any effect on the defence of the plateau, he saw a mission scheduled for 24 July, in which a squadron of Marauders flown by FAFL pilots would target the field at Chabeuil. The following day, the flight took off but missed Chabeuil due to cloud cover and attacked targets of opportunity instead.

At Vassieux, the landing strip prepared for Allied airborne troops was repeatedly pressed into use for Luftwaffe flights bringing in weapons and evacuating German wounded aboard Junkers Ju 52 transport aircraft. On 24 July another Gotha brought in a GebflaK38 20mm howitzer, which rained death on the Maquis positions. Despite a suicidal rearguard action on the belvedere above Valchevrière hamlet by Lieutenant Chabal and his men, who all died weapon in hand, every house was burned to the ground.

After the fighting died down, a brief silence was rent by screams and shots as civilians of all ages were dragged out of hiding and executed, in the case of females usually after rape. In addition to ninety-one *maquisards* who died at Vassieux, seventy-three of the 430 civilian inhabitants were summarily executed in this way. Most of the men were hanged with hands tied behind their backs and their outstretched toes just touching the ground, so that they died slowly of exhaustion and prolonged strangulation. In the surrounding fields, dozens of corpses lay unburied for weeks.

By the time the German ground troops who had fought their way up on to the plateau linked up with their airborne contingent on 25 July, the Maquis of Vercors was a spent shadow, but individual feats of courage still claimed German lives. The zigzag road leading up to the Col de Rousset did not actually reach the pass itself, but cut through the mountain below it by a tunnel 700ft long. This had been used on Huet's orders to store much of the materiel recovered from the drop on 14 July and a substantial part of the food reserves. As his critics later said, storing the ammunition in centralised dumps denied it to men in desperate need.

A couple of hundred men who had chosen this way off the plateau stormed into the tunnel and broke open crates of food to gorge themselves and fill their pockets with provisions after days of being cold, soaked to the skin and ravenously hungry. After all the others left, two men remained in the tunnel mouth, watching a German convoy creeping slowly and cautiously up the twisting road towards them. Instead of slipping away while there was time, they calmly affixed a fuse to two lumps of plastic explosive and placed these in a gallery near the entrance that was filled with ammunition and other explosives. Waiting until the last minute, they lit the fuse and ran desperately for the other end of the tunnel, hoping to reach it before the charge went off.

Gasping in the open air, they waited. No explosion, but they could hear the engine noises of the convoy approaching the far end of the tunnel. Just before the first vehicles reached the entrance, a colossal explosion brought the roof down, blocking vehicular access to the plateau by that route.

On 24 July – two days too late – American aircraft bombed the airfield at Valence. On the following day, 23-year-old Paul Borrel watched from a distance as German troops rounded up the entire population of his home town, La Chapelle en Vercors. Nearly all the houses had already been burned down but after the Germans departed the inhabitants crept out of the woods and huddled together in those houses still habitable, after trying to save what was salvageable of their possessions. When the Germans returned and arrested the men, the village priest courageously protested that they were innocent, and was told there was nothing to worry about. In the end, sixteen young men were kept hostage. That evening the soldiers got drunk and the terrified villagers could hear them singing marching songs. At about 2200hrs the priest heard a fusillade near the village square. Running to the scene, he found sixteen dead bodies in a farm-yard, which is now a memorial shrine. They included comrades of Paul Borrel, who had disregarded instructions not to go back to their homes. Borrel said afterwards: 'If they had been as scared as I was, they would be alive today.'

On 25 July Pflaum congratulated himself that his ground troops had met up with the airborne contingents more or less on schedule. From all sides, his forces were con-verging on the centre of the plateau with the Luftwaffe continuing to harass the fleeing *maquisards*. Confirmed in his original assessment of Operation Montagnards, Tillon gave orders to his FTP men to disperse and fall back on the southern side of the pla-teau, thence to exfiltrate in small groups by night to avoid the daylight strafing by the Focke Wulf 109s that were attacking everything that moved.

The Justine mission split up after seeing surrendering and wounded *maquisards* shot out of hand, although the American uniform of Lieutenant Chester Meyers, recover-ing from an emergency appendix operation, was respected. He was taken prisoner and ended the war in a POW camp in Poland. Other members of the Allied mission spent weeks avoiding German ground patrols and air searches under great privation before finding safety with the Resistance. On the plateau, to quote Rosencher's account:

> The civilian population served as target practice for the [Germans]. Women, old and young, and little girls too, were raped. Old men and children were shot down … others locked inside their burning houses. The SS shot anything that moved, massa-cred man and beast, looted anything that could be taken by the cartload, blew up and set fire to entire villages. Any maquisard who was caught, was tortured before being killed. Men working in the fields, shepherds and old folk were mowed down, and their animals too. The SS blew up and burned any isolated farm and house.[16]

10

THEY GOT WHAT THEY DESERVED

On 26 July Resistance teams along the Rhône valley sabotaged all railway communications with Grenoble and also cut all telephone and telegraph lines in preparation for Operation Anvil/Dragoon, but these measures to make life difficult for the German forces came too late to help the men marooned on the plateau. That day, Algiers received this final message from the shrinking perimeter, within which the survivors were holding out:

ABANDONED AND WITHOUT SUPPORT EVERY MAN HAS DONE HIS DUTY AND SADLY HAS TO CEASE THIS HOPELESS FIGHT AGAINST ODDS ENDS

The unhelpful reply from Algiers was:

YOUR SADNESS IS UNDERSTANDABLE ENDS

Surgeons Ferrier and Ganimède decided as a last resort to hide the wounded in a deep cave known as La Luire, whose entrance was 60ft wide and 90ft high, but surrounded by thick woodland and half a mile from the nearest road. Volunteer stretcher bearers staggered through the woods along barely discernible pathways, carrying the wounded unable to walk to this natural haven, where the stretchers were placed in rows. Other injured were laid on blankets on the bare earth. A Red Cross flag was pinned outside the cave mouth, just in case.

Among Huet's HQ staff the argument continued between those who said the plateau should have been evacuated to give everyone a chance to get away after the fighting of 15 July and those who insisted that Huet had to hold on in obedience to the orders to await the reinforcements promised by Algiers. The most anger was shown by those who had seen the prepared landing strips used by the Germans to bring in weapons and reinforcements. Rosencher had encoded some of the daily messages pleading for the weapons:

IT IS IMPOSSIBLE THAT THE ALLIED FORCES … COULD NOT
TEMPORARILY SPARE FROM THEIR IMMENSE RESOURCES A FEW
HUNDRED HEAVY MACHINE GUNS A FEW HUNDRED MORTARS A FEW
DOZEN MOUNTAIN CANNONS AND ANTI-TANK ARTILLERY … AND
THE FIFTY PLANES THAT COULD HAVE DROPPED THESE TO US ENDS[1]

Rosencher was unaware of Zeller's last signal sent through Cammaerts to Algiers after
their escape from the plateau:

HAVE LEFT VERCORS VIOLENTLY ATTACKED BY GREATLY SUPERIOR
FORCE OF ABOUT TWO DIVISIONS SUPPORTED BY AIRCRAFT AND
ARTILLERY STOP FOLLOWING THE ATTACK LANDING OF GLIDERS
AND CAPTURE OF [THE TOWN OF] DIE SITUATION EXTREMELY
DANGEROUS STOP MANY OFFICERS HAVE DISAPPEARED BELIEVED
KILLED STOP AM TRYING TO JOIN [ANOTHER NETWORK] WHOSE
WHEREABOUTS I DO NOT KNOW STOP TROOPS AND COMMANDERS
CURSE FAILURE TO PROVIDE AIR SUPPORT STOP HOPE FOR EARLY
LANDING IN SOUTH STOP SEND NEWS ENDS

The reply from Algiers read:

FULLY UNDERSTAND YOUR SADNESS AND YOUR FEELING OF
ISOLATION STOP THE AIRCRAFT EARMARKED FOR DROPPING TO
YOUR MEN HEAVY ARMS AND AMMUNITION HAVE BEEN READY
FOR THE LAST SIX DAYS STOP THIS MATERIEL AND MEN WILL
NOW BE DROPPED INTO AREAS OF DRÔME AND HAUTES-ALPES
DÉPARTEMENTS STOP AM CONFIDENT THAT VERCORS TROOPS
DESPITE DISPERSAL WILL HAVE SUCCESS AND REVENGE THROUGH
ACTION AS GUERRILLAS ENDS[2]

Rosencher and other orderlies in the cave at La Luire were ordered to leave with the
walking wounded, and make a final desperate attempt to escape through the ring of
steel around the plateau. More days of waiting followed for those left behind. Two
maquisards died, leaving twenty-one badly wounded patients, three doctors, nine nurses,
a civilian priest and a chaplain. Sounds of firing and explosions were coming from all
directions as their comrades were hunted down. The medical staff tried to maintain a
semblance of hospital routine, with meals and changing of dressing, etc., at fixed times.
Some peasants carried half a veal carcase up to La Luire, where it was stored in a cool
part of the network of tunnels below the cave. The meat was jointed with scalpels and
cooked in a converted instrument steriliser run on bottled gas. The bread supply soon
ran out. The only liquid available for drinking or cleaning wounds was moisture drip-
ping from the roof of the cave.

On Thursday 27 July an aircraft overflew the cave several times. This was not necessarily because of any specialised knowledge of the plateau. La Luire was a major
geological feature mentioned in all the guide books. At 1630hrs bullets sprayed the

Red Cross flag at the entrance and twenty green-camouflaged figures could be seen outside. The four wounded Germans were released as spokesmen and explained that they had been correctly treated during their captivity, and also that there were women and wounded men in the cave. It was a waste of breath, as was the invocation of the Geneva Convention by doctors Ferrier and Ganimède.

The Germans divided the patients into two groups. Fourteen badly wounded men were unable to leave their stretchers. Nurse Anita Winter volunteered to stay with them. The other group consisted of eleven walking wounded, the three doctors, eight nurses, the wife and son of Dr Ganimède, two wounded female civilians, the Jesuit chaplain and one wounded American officer. Roughly handled by their escort, this group was harried down the path to the nearest road. Before they reached it, a black Senegalese soldier who stumbled and accidentally fell against an SS man was beaten to death by the escort.

Arriving at the village of Rousset, the prisoners were locked in a filthy barn to await their fate. At about 2300hrs Anita Winter was shoved in with them, weeping. Hardly able to speak, she recounted the story of what had happened at the cave:

> After you all left, the Germans continued to search the cave, taking what remained of our food stored there. I was busy looking after the wounded and got permission to distribute some food to them. They thought this was a good sign. At the end of the afternoon, the Germans carried the stretcher cases out of the cave, saying that a truck was waiting for them, down on the road. After an order was countermanded [sic], the stretchers were lined up all together on the ground in the field below the cave. The wounded who could still stand were herded into a wagon. I was hurried away, down toward the road, not wanting to guess what was happening. Then I heard burst after burst of sub-machine gun fire.[3]

One injured man survived the massacre at La Luire, having found his way deeper into the warren of tunnels beneath the cave, where he stayed without food or water for forty-eight hours before daring to come out. All this was watched by four other wounded men who had taken refuge with two civilian helpers from the hospital at St-Martin in another cave less than a third of a mile away on the other side of the valley. Seeing the Waffen-SS arrive in Indian file by the footpath from the road, everyone hid in the scrub, from where they observed the massacre of La Luire through binoculars.

Towards midday on 28 July the people locked in the barn at Rousset were divided into two groups by their captors. When the three doctors were being herded into a truck with the nurses, the two wounded women and Dr Ganimède's wife and son, one of the doctors asked what was going to happen to the wounded. He was told by a German officer that they would shortly be following in another truck. Instead, they were driven out into a field, where eight of them were machine-gunned to death. Another black North African soldier was taken behind the village cemetery and hanged. The tenth man, Second Lieutenant François Billon of the Free French forces, who had recently been parachuted in wearing uniform, was taken to a German military hospital, but afterwards shot. Only the American officer was correctly treated as a POW and placed in a truck with two of the German wounded from the cave and several civilians.

After the truck's arrival in Grenoble, the driver told one of the civilian women to make herself scarce. Ganimède's wife and son were also released. After being interrogated by the Gestapo, Ganimède managed to escape during the panic among his captors caused by an air raid.[4] Ferrier and a civilian doctor were shot with the chaplain Yves Moreau. The seven female nurses were deported to Ravensbrück concentration camp in Germany, where one of them was to die. Left in Grenoble were the two surgeons and the Jesuit. In the evening of 10 August they were taken out of their cell and marched to a disused firing range behind the main station. There, looking up at the moonlit massif of the Vercors, they too were shot, after which, General Pflaum issued more explicit orders for the clean-up operation as follows:

1. Enemy Resistance fighters in the Vercors have been dispersed and are attempting to escape through our lines.

2. It is now necessary to root out the bands hiding out up there and eliminate them completely, to unearth their stores of munitions and food and destroy their hiding places so that they cannot re-install themselves there.

3. The Vercors must be tightly controlled from the encircling lines to the upper slopes. On the high plateau, the Gebirgsjäger will wipe out any enemies.

4. A period of seven days will be allowed for this operation.

5. The male population of the Vercors between ages of 17 and 30 who have neither been in, nor supported, the French Resistance are to be arrested and formed into labour teams under strict military control for removal of mines, reconstruction of bridges and removal of booty into our safekeeping. Their future fate will be communicated by the Commanding General for Southern France. Houses used by the Maquis must be burned, the only exception at the discretion of local commanders being where the inhabitants were forced to shelter Resistance fighters. To prevent a return of the French Resistance to the Vercors, you will leave in each farm only enough animals, cows and pigs, etc., as is necessary for the survival of the legitimate inhabitants. After slaughtering sufficient for their needs, the units involved will ensure all other livestock is rounded up by the local population and driven into marshalling areas.

6. Orders for transporting war booty, treatment of civilian prisoners and the transporting of livestock will be given later.[5]

In enthusiastic compliance with these orders, from 28 July to 3 August Pflaum's troops, especially the Central Asian SS units, took an unholy pleasure in plundering the entire plateau. Records show that, in addition to personal looting, 2,763 cows, 305 horses and 1,301 pigs were driven off for slaughter by Pflaum's men. Animals not seized as booty were killed, so denying any food to the remaining *maquisards* hiding deep in the forests, where the German patrols were wary of setting foot for fear of ambushes.

On 30 July a signal from General Koenig was passed from man to man in the Maquis groups spread out in the forests:

THE RESISTANCE FORCES IN THE VERCORS HAVE RENDERED GREAT SERVICE TO THE ONGOING BATTLE OF FRANCE BY TYING DOWN LARGE GERMAN FORCES.

Was this any consolation for the men still on the plateau? The diary of one of these hunted groups tells the story of the privations they endured:

31 July – Corn flour brought back by a patrol cooked in bad water in a washing boiler. Those who managed to eat the mess are ill.

1 August – Several comrades poisoned by eating leaves. A little milk taken from an abandoned cow.

2 August – Found several chickens, cooked on a spit in the forest.

10 August – Have been eating raw carrots found in a field, also some apples we found.

11 August – We stripped a cherry tree.

Hearing that many corpses lay unburied after the Germans had left the plateau, a sometime chief scout of France named Maurice Rouchy headed for Vassieux with a team of volunteers from the youth leaders' school near Die, of which he was the director. His notes made on the spot give a grim immediacy to the scene:

Several kilometres before arriving at the village the smell of decomposing corpses made it hard to breathe. The farms we passed had all been looted and burned. Everywhere lay the bloated carcasses of animals. Many others had been tied up in their barns before the farm was set alight. It was a terrible sight. The first human corpse was of a farmer machine-gunned and left in a drinking trough. A couple in their seventies were lying together, the man's arm around his wife, as though to protect her. Further on, the bodies of several youngsters lay where they had been shot in the entrance to a farm. The smell grew even worse 500 metres from the pile of ruins that had been the village. An old woman of maybe ninety lay on her back with her arms out, as if on a cross, seeming to forbid us to enter Vassieux. The odour of death was by now so terrible that we could only approach by soaking handkerchiefs in lavender eau de cologne and using them as masks. Bodies lay everywhere, killed by bursts from sub-machine guns. We found them in the streets, in the ruins, in the cellars. Everywhere was death.[6]

Photographs included in the published version of Picirella's diary bear out this list of atrocities: dead bodies were dismembered and rearranged as obscene sculptures; heads had the eyes gouged out and the top of the skull sliced off to allow the brains to fall out.

Rouchy's volunteers prepared to spend the night in one of the least damaged buildings. It was a night made hideous by the stench of putrefaction and the howling of
starving dogs gorging on the corpses all around. Counting the next morning, they
reached a toll of sixty-six in the village alone, many of whom had been sexually mutilated before death. Others had been bludgeoned to death, with their skulls smashed
in by rifle butts. The bodies of two children were found under a rock, where General
Pflaum's men had thrown a hand grenade, killing them and injuring another girl. A
woman of 70 had left her hiding place to plead for their lives and been gunned down.
The wounded girl was the daughter of the Mayor of Vassieux, who seized a moment
when the soldiers' attention was elsewhere to get her and his wife into a nearby cave.
The barking of their dog gave them away to the Germans, who returned to shoot him
dead in front of his wife and child.

Bodies were discovered of men hanged upside down, so that they died slowly of
congestive heart failure. Some had been suspended like this with their heads in an ants'
nest; others in pairs so that each man's long agony was an additional torture for the
other, as shown by the trenches gouged in the ground by the frenzied banging of their
heads as they tried to kill themselves. One man's body was found thrown on a manure
heap after the head had been hacked off with an axe lying nearby. Hands had large nails
driven through them.

Men had been shot down in groups while their wives were forced at gunpoint
to watch. Seven bodies were found burned to carbon in a pigsty into which the
Germans had thrown a phosphorous grenade. A group of fifteen youths had been
killed by having their skulls bashed in, some after their eyes were gouged out. A
young woman – the first of many who had suffered the same fate – was found in the
open lying on a mattress soiled by the gang rape she had suffered before being shot.
More bodies were found of men who had been hanged after their eyes were gouged
out and tongues cut off for sheer sadistic pleasure. Rouchy's list of horrors went on
and on:

> Each day we discovered in the woods around Vassieux corpses of young and old,
> some shot down from behind after being used as 'mules' or porters carrying the loot
> away for the Germans. In the immediate vicinity of Vassieux we buried 148 bodies.
> Every day brought new discoveries of single bodies or groups of victims. As for the
> animals that could not be driven off, and had been shot on the spot to deny the survi-
> vors food, they numbered hundreds.[7]

At St Agnan several *maquisards* trying to pass as civilians were executed. A *milicien* with
local knowledge betrayed the teacher of the little school at Chabotte, in whose cellars weapons had been stored. The 35-year-old mother of a little girl, she was taken
out of the village at gunpoint and shot after refusing to say who had placed the arms
there. Houses that were alleged to have sheltered 'terrorists' were blown up or burned
down. In larger villages, the Germans arrested all the young men and trucked them
into prison in Grenoble. Their ultimate destination was to have been concentration
camps in Germany, but communications by rail were continually being disrupted by
the Resistance, so some were fortunate.

French president Philippe Pétain, who signed the armistice in June 1940.

German chancellor Adolf Hitler, who intended to bleed France dry of resources and manpower under the armistice.

Above: Signed on 23 August 1939 in Moscow, the Nazi-Soviet Non-Aggression Pact made the French Communist Party pro-German before and after the invasion.

Left: Standing with Pétain, his devious prime minister Pierre Laval pursued a policy of collaboration.

Unarmed German occupation troops relaxing. When Hitler invaded the USSR in June 1941, Stalin ordered French communists to assassinate these soft targets, causing reprisals costing thousands of French lives.

The Maquis: young Frenchmen hiding in the forests and mountains after Laval introduced compulsory conscription for labour service in German factories.

General Charles de Gaulle, commanding the Free French forces, fighting on the Allied side.

De Gaulle's military representative in France, General Charles Delestraint was caught and shot at Dachau.

*De Gaulle's political representative in occupied France,
Jean Moulin, was betrayed to the Gestapo.*

*Fort Montluc, the prison in Lyon where Resistance
prisoners including Moulin were interrogated under torture.*

Klaus Barbie, who tortured Moulin to death.

Maquisards *in the mountains. In the winter, finding food was their main problem.*

The murderous paramilitary troops of the Vichy Milice.

Milice commander Joseph Darnand was a decorated war hero who ordered his men to eliminate the Maquis.

Elite Bavarian mountain warfare troops, brought in to do the job when the Milice failed.

The concentration camp at Natzwiller in Alsace, where captured maquisards *were starved, beaten and worked to death in the stone quarry.*

The double fences at Natzwiller, between which ran Alsatian dogs trained to kill.

The camp gallows, on which public hangings were a daily event.

A captured résistant faces a German firing squad.

On 6 June 1944 160,000 Allied soldiers headed for the beaches of Normandy, where 2,500 of them died before nightfall.

Supreme Allied Commander US General 'Ike' Eisenhower.

British General Bernard Montgomery, commanding all land forces. Neither he nor Eisenhower told de Gaulle the date for D-Day. That mistrust cost many French lives.

The simple pre-war life on the high plateau of the Vercors before the war. The locals had no idea that Allied liaison officers would make them a target for Waffen-SS anti-partisan troops.

The village of Vassieux-en-Vercors. The flat area in centre of the photo was the landing strip cleared by the Allied officers.

On the Vercors Major François Huet (leaning over map) commanded 4,000 maquisards, but he had no real plan and many of them had no weapons.

Rarely photographed, Lieutenant General Pflaum commanded the 10,000 troops who assaulted the plateau.

On 14 July 1944 1,000 of these containers, stuffed with guns and ammunition, were dropped at Vassieux, after which the Luftwaffe bombed and strafed Maquis positions.

The carcase of one of the twenty-two DFS 230 assault gliders that landed there one week later, disgorging the first Waffen-SS shock troops attacking the Maquis on the plateau.

On the Vercors, Central Asian conscripts, like these captured in Normandy, tortured and raped their female prisoners before killing them.

The men taken prisoner were brutally tortured and then hanged.

The village of Valchevrières was left with only the walls still standing.

The military cemetery of Vassieux. One-third of the graves are marked 'Unknown' because the bodies were unrecognisable. Another third bear names of women, girls and infants.

Illicitly taken photographs of Waffen-SS and Wehrmacht troops hunting down maquisards on Mount Mouchet in central France. They also exacted brutal reprisals on civilians living there.

For every one of their own casualties, they exacted brutal reprisals on uninvolved civilians living there.

Schoolteacher Georges Guingouin saved hundreds of lives at Limoges by arranging a peaceful surrender of the German garrison in August 1944. For this, the French Communist Party sentenced him to death.

Right: French Gestapo interpreter Pierre-Marie Paoli, who tortured Resistance suspects in Bourges prison.

Below: French stamp commemorating Wehrmacht Corporal Alfred Stanke, in civilian life a Franciscan monk, who nursed tortured Gestapo prisoners in Bourges prison.

The lock-keeper's cottage outside St-Amand-Montrond, where parachuted weapons were distributed on the evening of D-Day. The town was then prematurely liberated for a few hours, triggering terrible reprisals.

One of the deep wells near Bourges into which Paoli's men pushed living men and women hostages head-first during the reprisals. When brought out weeks after the real liberation, the bodies were unrecognisable.

During the liberation, thousands of women guilty of la collaboration horizontale *had their heads shaven, like these publicly humiliated at Bergerac.*

Marked with swastikas on face and breasts, sometimes stark naked, they were forced to run the gauntlet between jeering crowds.

But not all. After two German soldiers were assassinated in Grenoble on 14 August, twenty of the youngsters were driven to a waste ground and there executed in groups of four, so that the later groups had to watch their predecessors being killed before taking their place. After the coup de grâce had been given to those still breathing, the soldiers returned to barracks. This was done in full view of horrified passers-by.

An eyewitness account of the 'campaign' in the Vercors, as seen from the German side, comes from a letter home, written by a wounded soldier identified only as Rudolph X, a farmer's son in civilian life. It was found, left behind after he was evacuated. In part, it reads:

> You couldn't believe what it is like in the region around Grenoble and Lyon, where a whole division is dealing with these terrorists. The day after I arrived in Grenoble, I was in a convoy of wounded being taken to the hospital in Aix-les-Bains when we were attacked without warning. I was lucky, receiving only another slight wound in the right arm and being left deaf for half an hour from a round that just missed my right ear. During the fighting on the plateau there were some terrible moments. You should have seen us gunning down those people! They got what they deserved. We killed everybody in a partisan hospital, about forty of them, including doctors and nurses. In one village there were two companies of us [Germans] and a company of Russians. Men, women and children were shot down. We were on the move every day from dawn to dusk and left not even a mouse alive where we had been. I was invalided out just after my section had 'liberated' three mares and their foals. Dear Father, those mares were a lot better than ours. I was thinking, if only I could have sent them home to you ...[8]

The records of births and deaths kept by the mayors of each village made it easy to calculate the numbers of French dead and deported. German losses are harder to add up, but were in the order of forty-five killed at Vassieux and fifty-five elsewhere on the plateau, with another fifty-six dying later in Grenoble or other hospitals.

General Pflaum was afterwards reported as regretting the excesses of his men, especially the Sipo-SD detachments. Arrested in 1945, he was released for health reasons in 1951 and died in 1959 while due to answer charges before a French court in Lyon.

11

FAILURE IS AN ORPHAN

Pierre Dalloz had returned to Algiers on 20 May but, as a civilian, was unable to make any worthwhile contact until some influential Gaullists arranged an interview for him at SPOC. There, an uncooperative lieutenant colonel denied ever having heard of his reports on the Vercors.

It seemed that some progress was being made when General Antoine Béthouart, the senior Free French officer in North Africa, who would command the French contingent in Anvil, was charged directly by de Gaulle to sort out the mess. In today's parlance, Béthouart 'kicked ass' and was informed that 400 Free French commandos were on standby at nearby Sidi Ferruch and could be dropped into the Vercors to stiffen the defence. The complication was that, equipped with only their standard-issue carbines, they would need forty-eight hours to collect the other necessary weapons and ammunition. The final count of men who could immediately be dropped on the Vercors was three detachments of fifteen paras with eleven heavy machine guns, two 60mm mortars and the ammunition for these. At 1900hrs a message was received, forwarded from London:

REQUEST DROP AT ST MARTIN WHERE WE CAN STILL RECEIVE IT STOP HELP US FAST ENDS

On 1 August a German patrol gunned down five men trying to escape from the plateau. One of them was Dalloz's friend Jean Prévost. Now that Operation Montagnards was so patently a ghastly failure, everyone involved wanted to dissociate himself from the operation. With Prévost dead, Dalloz was the obvious scapegoat. Depressed by this news and the death of another friend, the aviator and author of *The Little Prince*, Antoine de St-Exupéry – and feeling guilty for the failure and futility of Operation Montagnards – he was summoned to the Algiers office of French counter-espionage, the Direction de la Surveillance du Territoire. There, a junior officer attempted to browbeat him into some kind of confession that it was all his fault. Extricating himself by mentioning the names of several generals and high officials who had backed him, Dalloz escaped that trap.

When the Germans came for the second time to Villard de Lans, Denise Noaro – a woman with two children whose husband was with the Maquis – took the risk of asking an officer eating looted food in her house whether it was true that there had been an attempt on Hitler's life. A furious argument then ensued between the Germans present, resulting in an order to bring all radios to the empty Gendarmerie, where they would be confiscated, along with bicycles and any petrol. Left alone with her, one officer who spoke French well told her not to take any notice, so she wrapped her radio in paper and hid it inside a burial vault in the cemetery. Everything precious had already been buried in the garden.

When asked where all the men of the village were, the standard reply was that they were POWs in Germany. When an officer asked how many *maquisards* were on the plateau, Denise replied, 'As many men as you have', but was horrified to be told in return that 35,000 troops were surrounding or on the plateau. It became routine for German soldiers to force housewives to open doors – even a cupboard door – in case they had been booby-trapped. With soldiers billeted in every house, it was difficult to sleep. Women were conscripted to prepare and cook food and the few remaining men also forced to work on repairing the bridge on the road to Valchevrière, which the Maquis had blown up.

Denise Noaro's husband sneaked back into the village after the massacres and was hiding in a large wine cask in the cellar. Hearing that a curfew had been imposed, starting at 2000hrs, she feared that everyone in the village was going to be arrested when a cordon of soldiers was posted around Villard, one armed man every 10m. All the adults packed a suitcase with essentials for themselves and their children. Nobody could eat that evening. Soldiers knocked on every door with a list of all the inhabitants registered at that address. The immediate penalty for not opening up was to see the door kicked in. Every young man they found was arrested and the parents of all absentees were told to ensure they reported to the Gestapo office in the Hotel Splendide the next morning. A few parents did so, and never saw their sons alive again. Their bodies were found after the soldiers left at dawn on the Saturday, lying where they had been shot in the street.[1]

For his part in the failure to make Montagnards work, Huet was among the small number of military commanders in the FFI who were not given the honorific 'Compagnon de le Libération'. Gilbert Joseph wrote a scathing indictment of him for pitting 'hundreds of young men up there simply to avoid the STO and with no desire to fight' against elite German troops. Joseph also argued that the idea of the Vercors redoubt was a lunatic fantasy, as irrelevant to modern warfare as the Maginot Line. During his time on the plateau he had not spoken up because Huet had a prison camp at La Chapelle where not only suspect strangers and *collabos* of both sexes were locked up, but also defeatists – a term that included anyone who openly criticised his leadership.

Joseph's criticism of Huet and his officers was simple. They were, he says, of that generation of French army officers who had led the country into defeat in 1940. Instead of adopting guerrilla tactics and keeping their forces dispersed for occasional sorties to ambush Germans below the plateau, they were more intent on rifle drill and irrelevancies such as training the young men under their orders to defend fixed points – which guerrillas must never do. As to the weapons that were dropped on to the plateau, he accused Huet of concentrating them in a few inaccessible centralised dumps, like the tunnel at the Col de Rousset – much of which were recovered unused by the Germans – instead of dispersing them on mule-back to smaller dumps, where desperate men could have replenished their exhausted supplies.

After the liberation, the Vercors campaign was hailed as a heroic battle against odds and the men who died on the plateau have been made heroes of the liberation, as indeed they were. Yet, Joseph was not alone in treating Operation Montagnards as a pointless waste of human lives, property and materiel, with 639 *maquisards* and 201 civilians shot, many after torture, and forty-one others deported to camps in Germany – all this for German losses of 100 killed and another fifty dying later of wounds. The plateau was devastated, with 573 homes destroyed and over 4,000 head of livestock and large stocks of grain and potatoes carted and driven away as spoils of war by the German forces.

Joseph contrasts this sad record with the achievements of the group of fifty men with whom he escaped from the plateau under the command of Captain Costa de Beauregard. With a few rifles and one machine gun, they managed without suffering a single casualty subsequently to account for more than 100 Germans in a series of ambushes and skirmishes in south-eastern France. Using proven guerrilla tactics of conducting ambushes far from their camp, so as not to give away its location, and never continuing the action for more than a few minutes before disengaging and slipping away via prepared escape routes, they caused almost as many enemy losses as all the 4,000 men who suffered up there on the plateau.[2]

It is hard to disagree with Joseph's analysis that everything was wrong with Operation Montagnards, from its initial conception onwards. Whether the conflicts on the plateau from January to July 1944 made any difference to the success of the Allied invasions in Normandy on 6 June and in southern France in 15 August is an open question, except for the families of those who died.

Because of the near impossibility of escaping from the plateau through the cordon of Pflaum's troops, it is estimated that more than 2,000 men were hiding in the forests as the Vercors 'campaign' drew to a close. After Dragoon forces swept up the Rhône valley and liberated the area, roughly half of them chose to accept de Gaulle's offer to don French uniform and continue the drive to get the Germans out of their country, while the others were urgently needed back home to deal with the coming harvest, rebuild their homes or simply to get the machinery of local government working again.

Picirella was not one of them. After a series of skirmishes, sometimes with American support, sometimes not, and sweeps to round up and kill *miliciens* firing on the joyous crowds celebrating their liberation, he was among the FFI who marched into his home town of Lyon on 3 September. They had been told that the Germans had evacuated the city, but were held up by excited crowds, with all the women wanting to embrace these tattered veterans. After shots rang out from last-ditch *miliciens*, who knew their fate if taken alive, the Senegalese sharpshooters who had been rescued on 23 June took them out one by one.

Picirella's diary includes a plaintive note to the effect that he and his comrades had not received any pay for the previous six weeks. What especially nauseated them were the *napthalinards*, army officers who had done nothing, yet put on their uniforms smelling strongly of mothballs and paraded about wearing white gloves and expecting to be saluted by the men who had done the fighting.

Two years later, on 26 July 1946, France's senior serving general, Jean de Lattre de Tassigny, made a speech at Vassieux, in which he said:

> It was the character of the men who live here that made this region one of the strong points of our Resistance. It served for months as a strongpoint where the enemy could not come. And when they decided to destroy it, they had to devote the forces required in a large-scale combined operation. To those who denigrate the merits of our Maquis forces, I say that here it was not a little war, it was *the* war.

There were many speeches like that, understandably paying respect to the memory of those who died in the Resistance and the Maquis, but an objective examination of Dalloz's Trojan horse initiative suggests rather the reaction of another French general to the pointless charge of the Light Brigade at Balaclava. Witnessing it caused General Pierre Bosquet to comment: '*C'est magnifique, mais ce n'est pas la guerre. C'est de la folie*' – 'It's magnificent, yet it's not war, but madness'.

12

ATROCITIES ON BOTH SIDES

At the time of the Normandy invasion, 2nd SS Panzer Division Das Reich was refitting in south-west France after suffering enormous losses of men and materiel on the Eastern Front. Under the command of Gruppenführer Heinz Bernhardt Lammerding – his rank was equivalent to a Wehrmacht major general – were 18,000 men with armoured cars and tanks, many in the process of being repaired. The refitting was badly behind schedule due to the sabotage of railway lines over which spare parts were being transported from the Reich.

According to historian Dr Peter Lieb, 2nd Das Reich possessed all the characteristics of a unit likely to perpetrate atrocities: its command chain was fanatically Nazi; it had been carrying out brutal anti-partisan reprisals on the Eastern Front; and its men regarded themselves as being a military elite. Shortly before the invasion, Lammerding received orders to move the division to the area of Tulle and Limoges and suppress the terrorist attacks and sabotage by Resistance groups, mainly communist dominated, in that region.

Under the Sperrle-Erlass anti-terrorist ordinance issued in February 1944 by Luftwaffe Generalfeldmarschal Hugo Sperrle, commanding all German forces on the Western Front, local commanders were given permission to take any measures they considered necessary to eliminate 'terrorists'. Commanders who used too little force were to be punished for having put the lives of their men at risk. The Sperrle ordinance was thus a carte blanche for escalating reprisals, under which it became routine for German troops to open fire immediately upon being attacked, regardless of civilians present, their deaths to be blamed on the Resistance; areas where attacks occurred were to be cordoned off, all inhabitants arrested and houses that had been used by 'terrorists' were to be burnt down; for each German soldier killed, ten terrorists or hostages were to be hanged. Hanging was not a usual form of execution in France, and was chosen to signify that the executed men and women no longer belonged to the French people. Use of these tactics was intended to achieve the reverse of the PCF's aim when launching its campaign of assassinations in autumn 1941 – in other words, to make the population withdraw support for the Resistance fighters who brought such misery upon them.

The *département* of Corrèze in central France had already been the scene of severe reprisals in April, when Vichy anti-terrorist units, German Sipo-SD personnel from Limoges and the Brehmer Division of anti-terrorist troops mounted a concerted campaign against local Maquis bands. Pierre Trouillé, prefect of the Corrèze *département*, noted privately: 'The wolves of the Security Police and the vultures of the French Gestapo have joined forces.'

The Brehmer Division was another composite put together expressly for anti-partisan operations. It comprised both German Security Police and a Georgian infantry battalion recruited among POWs who had been captured serving in the Red Army on the Eastern Front. In the first week of April, the division arrested 3,000 people in the town of Le Lonzac, 18 miles north of Tulle, 300 of whom were deported to concentration camps in Germany. At Brive-la-Gaillarde seventeen people were killed and thirty-four houses burned down. By the time the division left Corrèze in May, it had also killed 200 Jews without apparently ever making contact with a major Maquis force.

At the beginning of May a 35-year-old communist assistant schoolteacher known as 'Colonel Kléber', real name Jean-Jacques Chapou, was in command of the FTP groups in the *département* of Corrèze and already planning to 'liberate' the town of Tulle without waiting for the Allied invasion, of which the date was then unknown.

This was in obedience to a PCF disinformation that the coming Allied invasion would 'incite the German army to make mass arrests and massacre millions of French people'.[1] The impossible claim was intended to dissimulate a PCF initiative to cause such civil unrest during the liberation that the party would be able to seize political power while all other parties were still too disorganised to prevent it.

Chapou's plan for Tulle called for the disarming and killing of the garrison of approximately 280 German security troops[2] and 600-plus men of the GMR and Milice who were stationed in the town. To carry out his plan, Chapou reckoned he would have 1,350 men under his orders. As soon as the local representatives of OAS heard of this, they were horrified and refused to sanction such a criminally stupid idea, forcing Chapou to put his plan on the back burner.

After hearing of the Allied landings on 6 June, when the Allied forces were still clinging desperately to the first few miles of beachhead, he hastily resurrected the plan. General Bernard Montgomery's schedule was for the town of Caen to be taken by the British 3rd Infantry Division on the evening of D-Day but, as his reading of Count Helmuth von Moltke's *Militärische Werke*, Vol. 2 ought to have told him, no plan of operations extends with certainty beyond the first contact with the enemy's main strength. Normally abridged to 'No plan survives contact with the enemy', the maxim certainly applied to D-Day. The first Allied troops in Operation Goodwood – the liberation of Caen – broke in five weeks behind schedule on 9 July, and the last Germans were not driven out of the town until 19 July.

Thus, with the nearest Allied troops fighting for their lives over 300 miles distant, never mind advancing, it must have been glaringly obvious even to Chapou that Tulle could not be held and that attacking the garrison was an invitation for reprisal massacres.

At 0500hrs on 7 June, Prefect Trouillé was awoken in Tulle by a fusillade of small arms fire directed at the Champ de Mars barracks and the explosion of a bazooka rocket. These were the opening rounds of what Chapou called the battle for Tulle. At this time, his forces amounted to some 400 men – far short of his original estimate. An hour later, with the element of surprise in their favour, they were in command of the post office and town hall, and all buildings occupied by the German garrison were surrounded. Shortly afterwards, the railway station was also 'liberated'. The eighteen *gardes-voies* and one railway employee found there were invited to join Chapou's forces, but politely declined and stayed – as they thought, safely uninvolved – inside the waiting room.

At 1130hrs the GMR and Milice contingents hoisted a white flag over the Champ de Mars barracks. After more than four hours' negotiation, they were allowed to leave the town, taking with them all their weapons and ammunition. Chapou had counted on acquiring their materiel to replace his own losses, but had insufficient men to impose an unconditional surrender on the Vichy forces and subdue the German garrison, which had taken advantage of the negotiations to recapture the railway station and there shoot dead all but one of the *gardes-voies* – some say because their blue-and-white duty armbands resembled the FFI armbands of Chapou's men.

During the night, still short of 400 men who had not arrived in Tulle, he withdrew to the heights above the town, allowing the Germans to re-occupy two schools and the Manufacture d'Armes de Tulle, known as the MAT arms factory. At 0600hrs on 8 June the insurgents attacked with automatic weapons and hand grenades, forcing surrender. Nine members of the Sicherheitsdienst having been identified by liberated *maquisards*, they were taken to the cemetery and shot without trial. Chapou called a ceasefire, leaving enough men in place to contain the Germans in one of the schools and the arms factory, in the hope of reducing these strong points the following day, by which time he expected substantial reinforcements to arrive.

Considering the town as good as liberated, Chapou allowed the French and German wounded to be taken to the hospital while he called on Prefect Trouillé and asked him to continue in office. Unbeknown to Trouillé, the first atrocity was about to be perpetrated. Estimates of German survivors and dead at this point vary between thirty-seven and fifty dead, twenty-three to thirty-seven wounded and between thirty-five and sixty missing in action – probably taken prisoner. The disparity between the various estimates is an indication of the confusion and lack of control inevitable in such an operation. What is certain is that the girls' school was set on fire, forcing the Germans inside to emerge, whereupon they were shot down to a man. Some, it seems, had intended to surrender, but others were alleged to have had primed grenades in their hands, which exploded when they were shot, causing hideous wounds to their bodies.

With the exception of some Polish conscripts in German uniform who chose to change sides, the rest of the prisoners were now killed. At 2100hrs the first tanks of 2nd Das Reich entered the town from three directions, having eliminated the advance posts of the FTP that were supposed to have given the alarm. The insurgents immediately fled to the high ground again. Their first intention was to use bazookas on the German tanks below, but it was wisely decided not to do this because of the civilian casualties that would have been inevitable and because the tanks had vastly superior fire power.

Serving as an interpreter with the Das Reich sappers was a young Alsatian named Charles Buch. He was one of the young men forcibly conscripted into the German armed forces when the provinces of Alsace and Lorraine were annexed into the

Reich in 1940. In private, they called themselves *les malgré nous* – meaning, we don't want to go, but we have no choice. His recollection from the German side of events was as follows:

> We in the HQ unit arrived outside Tulle and parked with a number of other vehicles on either side of the road. I heard many shots being fired by the Maquis and even saw them running away through the gardens on a hill to the left of the town. This was while the armour of the Aufklärungsabteiling – reconnaissance battalion – commanded by Major Wulf was driving off the FTP and securing the town. Wulf discovered the bodies of forty German soldiers assassinated and badly mutilated. In the afternoon of 10 June twenty more German bodies were found in the cemetery. In all, about 140 German soldiers were either killed or kidnapped. Apart from the sixty dead, the others were never found.

Inside Tulle that first night was another Alsatian. Elimar Schneider was the reverse of a typical SS man, having been a religious novice before being forcibly conscripted into the Waffen-SS. He was with Wulf's men in a Pak75 tank destroyer which came under machine-gun fire. This is what he saw:

> We could hear the firing growing less intense. From time to time other Pak75s arrived, some returning from the centre of town with *maquisards* tied in front of them as human shields. Fortunately for them the SS respected their FFI armbands, although I knew from the old guys who had served in Russia that they made short shrift of partisans captured there with weapons on them. [I learned later that] my fellow conscript and friend Marcel Most was killed that evening by a partisan in civilian clothes firing a hunting rifle from a window. The bullet entered above the eye and came out through the top of his head, shattering his helmet.[3]

That night, the SS threw a cordon around the town and patrolled the streets in tanks and armoured cars under strict curfew. Setting up his headquarters the next morning at the Hotel Moderne, the senior SS officer Sturmbannführer Aurel Kowatsch – his rank was equivalent to major in the Wehrmacht – threatened to shoot Prefect Trouillé after his men found in the prefecture building a crate of hand grenades left by the FTP the previous day.[4] Trouillé saved his life by begging Kowatsch to visit the hospital, where the German wounded were being cared for. There, one of them explained that they owed their lives in the general massacre to Dr Toty, the chief medic of the FTP, who had prevented Chapou's men from dragging them out to be shot with their comrades.

The story of the mutilated German bodies was commonly believed among the SS, but denied by French sources. Elimar Schneider was one of the men detailed to bury the corpses:

> The chief medic told us that the forty bodies were horribly mutilated. We saw the bodies lying there but did not want to look too closely. The medic tidied them up before letting us carry them away, buttoning a jacket here, doing up a fly there and pulling up some man's trousers, to make them decent.

Being legally a French citizen when telling his story post-war, Schneider was careful to deny seeing any evidence of deliberate mutilation. The official version is that wounds to the bodies were caused by bursts of machine-gun fire from close range and the explosion of grenades in the hands of soldiers killed in the schoolyard. Such wounds would not be unusual for Das Reich men killed in action, so why did Schneider mention that the medic had to do up the fly buttons of some corpses and pull up the trousers of others, which implies sexual mutilation, presumably after death?

Shortly after 0900hrs Major Kowatsch told Prefect Trouillé that the protection afforded to the wounded in the hospital would be 'taken into account' by the German command – he was in radio contact with Lammerding – in deciding on the reprisals to be exacted on the population of Tulle for the previous day's massacre. What else he said is unknown, but at 1000hrs a loudspeaker announcement was made by Trouillé:

> Inhabitants of Tulle, you have followed my instructions and kept an exemplary calm during the days we have lived through. This attitude and especially the way the German wounded were cared for have enabled me to obtain from the German command an assurance that life can go back to normal today.

No sooner had he done this than he was informed by Kowatsch that all men between 16 and 60 were already being rounded up, but that those essential for running the municipal services would be released after their identities had been checked. Charles Buch remembered that, from 0600hrs onwards, SS men had been forcing entry into the houses and dragging out any men found inside who resisted, and arresting any male found on the streets. André Gamblin, a 22-year-old accountant, was out shopping for milk for his baby daughter when they picked him up. *Gazogène* engineer Raymond Lesouëf was having breakfast with his wife and two children when he was led away. Even the priest Father Jean Espinasse was rounded up. In every home, all adult males were arrested and their womenfolk told that this was a simple verification of their ID papers and that there was no need for them to bring along any food. One man who survived what was about to happen said:

> We were escorted by the SS to the Quai de Rigny and joined a larger group. Then another group joined us. Half-tracks and tanks were parked tidily along the pavements. As the tension built up, all our hands were clenched but we walked along with heads held high, trying to conceal our misgivings.

Finally, between 3,000 and 5,000 men – again, estimates vary – were herded inside the walls of the MAT armament factory on Place Souilhac while other SS went around the town, breaking into sheds and barns to collect ladders and rope. They were in no hurry because this was routine work for them. Major Kowatsch admitted as much to Prefect Trouillé: 'We hanged more than 100,000 at Kiev and Kharkov. What we are doing here is nothing for us.'

Trouillé's pleas for mercy ended with the protest that execution by hanging was not customary in France, to which Kowatsch replied that it was standard SS procedure in such cases because it was considered less honourable than death by shooting.[5]

The Mayor of Tulle, Colonel Bouty, appeared soon afterwards at the MAT factory with various heads of municipal departments, the electricity, water and gas companies, the post office, railway station and other town functionaries, attempting to persuade the SS officers to widen the definition of those who were 'essential to the normal running of the town'. Negotiation was mainly by Maurice Roche, secretary general at the prefecture, who spoke fluent German. Doctors, postal clerks, local government employees and even butchers and bakers were now released, until only 1,500 men were left, including – because they had been overlooked – the dentists and teachers of Tulle. The apparent collaboration between the mayor and the SS over who was to be released resulted in later bitterness on the part of those who maintained that he had also identified members of the Maquis to make the Germans' task easier. Had he done so, it was surely to his credit, since it was better for a guilty man to be hanged than one who was completely innocent. Although this is not recounted in most French histories of the hangings, it does seem that the Germans had information on some of the men arrested: a M. Neyrat was set free, while his brother, who was in the Maquis, was placed in the group to be hanged.

Tall, blonde Paula Geissler was well known in the town as the horse-riding, chain-smoking secretary/interpreter of the German manager of the armament factory. She also released twenty or so men she knew because they worked in the MAT factory, as well as the young son of the local pharmacist.

The men who had been released were escorted to the Hotel Moderne[6] to be registered and issued with papers confirming their release. As they returned to their homes, one by one, their families saw the shock on their faces. No one yet knew it was because they had seen nooses hanging from every possible support in the main street.

Towards the end of the morning General Lammerding himself arrived in Tulle, to find everything being done in accordance with his instructions. He later denied that he arrived before the hangings had been carried out. In any event, after the Germans had eaten lunch, leaving their hungry and thirsty victims standing in the sun of the factory yard, at 1330hrs a loudspeaker truck toured the town, announcing that life should go back to normal.

At about 1545hrs Kowatsch brought Trouillé up to date:

> In recognition of your humanitarian gesture in looking after the German wounded, my superiors have cancelled the reprisals which were originally ordered, under which the whole town was to be burned down and 3,000 men shot. But we cannot let what has happened pass unpunished. Therefore only 120 men – exactly three times the number of our comrades assassinated yesterday [sic] – will be hanged and their bodies thrown into the river.[7]

Lieutenant Walter Schmald was a slim, blonde Belgian-born Feldgendarmerie officer who had been stationed in Tulle for five months as interpreter for the Sicherheitsdienst detachment and had narrowly escaped assassination by Chapou's *maquisards* the previous day. Using his local knowledge, he now conducted a further triage, releasing some men and dividing the others into a group of 120 who were to be hanged and the remainder, who would be forced to witness the hangings. Each time someone was liberated from the group of 120 by special request, one of the witnesses was selected to replace him. Schmald's method was simple: any man who had not shaved that morning, or whose hair was untidy, or clothes unbrushed or soiled, was dubbed 'Maquis'. On this 'evidence' he was moved across to the group to be hanged. Final interventions by the borough engineer to the effect that a father aged 30 was innocent elicited from Schmald the reply, 'I know. They are all innocent. But they must pay for the guilty ones who are not here.'

Locked up in the Kommandantur, Adjudant-chef Conchonnet and three other gendarmes were released at 1630hrs, in time to hear another loudspeaker announcement: 'Forty German soldiers were atrociously assassinated by the Maquis yesterday. Therefore, 120 *maquisards* or their accomplices are to be hanged. Their bodies will be thrown into the river.' According to some people present in Tulle that day, a notice to that effect and signed 'The General commanding the German troops' was posted outside the Hotel Moderne.

It now fell to Colonel Bouty to brief the men in the factory not selected in the group of 120 on how to behave when witnessing the executions.

'I ask you to stay completely calm,' he said. 'Do not make any gesture or utter a word.' Escorted out of the factory, these men found ropes with slip knots hanging from every tree, every lamppost and every balcony, all along the street. These preparations had been carried out under the orders of Hauptsturmführer Wulf of the reconnaissance section − equivalent rank, captain − and Oberscharführer Otto Hoff, the company sergeant major of the sappers. When Hoff now asked for volunteers to carry out the hangings, more than sufficient men stepped forward.

From behind curtains and over garden walls the women of Tulle watched one of their sex chatting freely with the SS men who were now killing their husbands, brothers, fathers and sons. From that day, the women of Tulle call Paula Geissler *la chienne* − the bitch − alleging that she laughed at the men being hanged and blew cigarette smoke into their faces. At Bouty's request, Father Jean Espinasse was allowed to accompany each group of condemned men in turn, to give absolution and pray with them as they were hanged. He said afterwards that Geissler was chain-smoking as usual while she chatted with the SS, seated on the terrace of a cafe to watch the executions, laughing and joking with each other while accordion music and popular songs were played on the cafe's gramophone.

The released gendarmes also noted that the SS were in holiday mood, smoking and laughing. Seeing corpses dangling everywhere, the Tulle gendarmes were then escorted to the railway station, where twenty-one colleagues abducted from the Lot *département* as hostages by the SS had already taken off their ties, to speed up their own deaths. Thanks to the mayor's intervention, the gendarmes were not hanged.[8]

A competent amateur sketch exists of the horrific scene. Whether done by an SS officer, as some believe, or not, it shows a recognisable street with soldiers casually walking along the pavement and corpses dangling from each lamppost. In the centre is a group of figures reminiscent of a Renaissance painting of the Crucifixion. An officer watches with hands on hips, a soldier on a ladder against a lamppost is reaching down to help a hostage with his hands tied behind his back awkwardly climbing a second ladder towards the noose above his head. Another soldier steadies the victim's ladder, ready to pull it away as soon as the noose is round his neck. Three or four other victims under armed guard numbly watch what is about to happen to them also.[9]

Father Espinasse described how the SS divided the condemned men into groups of ten, with their hands tied behind their backs:

> When a condemned man's head reached the level of the slip knot, the soldier put it around his neck. The other soldier yanked away the second ladder. So far as I could see, the hanged men showed no sign of life afterwards, which made me think that death was immediate or at least the loss of consciousness was total. In one case, I suppose because the slip knot was carelessly made, the man jerked spasmodically. Then I saw the soldier with the second ladder hit him with it until all movement ceased.[10]

The concern of Father Espinasse and other witnesses was to keep their accounts as painless as possible for the relatives of the hanged men. In several cases a soldier clung to the victim's feet to accelerate strangulation, and some men awaiting their turn were too numbed with horror to step on to the ladder and were beaten with rifle butts to force them forward, being gunned down on the pavement if they could not be forced on to the ladder. And so it went on, ending life after life until it seemed that every balcony, telegraph pole and lamppost along the main street had a body hanging from it, the last ones to be hanged still convulsively twitching.[11]

It is a truism of police work that eyewitness accounts of any event vary. In this case, such was the horror of the scene that no two accounts come even close to each other. Dr Alfred Pouget was present in Tulle that day, attempting to minister to civilians and gendarmes who had been injured and intervening to obtain the release of doctors and other medical workers necessary for this. Even his professional recollection is disjointed:

> The faces of the hanged men were all pale and waxy, with tongues slightly protruding. The knot of the rope was at the back of the neck. Death was due to complete interruption of the brain's oxygen supply inducing an immediate loss of consciousness, followed by convulsions. I noticed the body of Loulou Chieze the barber's apprentice in his check suit. In front of the Tivoli Café there was an SS tank, camouflaged with branches.[12]

One of the many unlikely features of the executions was claimed by Father Espinasse as due to his intervention with Schmald, after he noticed that the penultimate group was comprised of thirteen men. According to the priest, four men were released and Schmald agreed this should be the last group to be executed. The executions thus stopped after ninety-nine men had been hanged. While agreeing that the priest saved the lives of three men in the last group actually hanged – which makes more sense – Colonel Bouty gave the credit for saving the twenty-one men not executed to the literally last-minute intervention of the municipal engineer and company director Henri Vogel, manager of the arms factory.

'Vogel in particular,' he said, 'argued brilliantly with the SS officers present to persuade them to free several of his workmen in what should have been the last group to be executed.' Of several other claims to have ended the executions prematurely, given the severe discipline of the Waffen-SS, the most likely to be true is that which Lammerding made after the war, to the effect that he decided to stop at ninety-nine deaths despite his earlier announcement.

Perhaps to exonerate himself for his minor role in the hangings, Elimar Schneider told it differently:

> I went into the factory yard rather disturbed [sic] and asked the officer in charge of the selections how many men remained to be hanged because we were running out of ropes. Lt Schmald indicated a group of ten kneeling to the left of the entrance gate and another group of about twenty. I went up to the group of ten. In front of them was a sad-looking priest with a dirty *soutane* giving them absolution. This was the next group for execution. I said to the youngest one, 'Don't be afraid. It doesn't last long.' It was a stupid thing to say, but he said, 'Since you can speak French, please tell them that I was not in the Maquis. I work here in the armament factory. Oh, my poor mother. She has nobody else but me.' So I said to Lt Schmald, 'Why are you hanging this one? He worked in the factory here.' Schmald replied, 'Kid, I can't do anything about it. I must have 120 Frenchmen. This is to serve as an example for the whole of France. We're pissed off with the partisans. Haven't you seen what they did to our guys?' That was in German. When I relayed this to the condemned men, the two youngest ones broke down and wept. I wept too. And Schmald said, 'Oh, take the young one then. And you can have the other as well.' So I took Pierre Torquebiau by the arm and he put his arms around me and hugged me so tightly, I couldn't breathe. Then those two were moved across to the group to be deported for the STO, just before Sergeant Piel gave the order for the others to be brought out.

Whatever the truth about the men released from the last group hanged, it was forbidden for relatives or friends to touch the bodies of the hanged men or cut them down. That evening, Maurice Roche wrote a report as follows:

> I went that evening with Col Bouty (and others) to the factory yard. The colonel was near tears describing his sense of impotence and the dignity with which the men died. I was in my civil service uniform and went outside alone to salute the men who had died. It was a terrible sight – all those young men hanging there. They all had their hands tied behind their backs. The expression on their faces was generally calm. Lying on the pavement were some bloody bodies of men whose ropes had been severed by their last struggles, and had been finished off by a burst from a machine pistol.[13]

In fact, other evidence is that only the first men executed had their hands tied. Apparently the cord used for this ran out, so that the others were hanged with their hands free. Roche later went to the site where the SS were burying the first bodies and protested at the lack of respect being shown as corpses were dumped from a truck in the dust. He then negotiated a deal with the SS, under which the young men from the Vichy youth labour camp known as Les Chantiers de Jeunesse were allowed to take the bodies down and dig two mass graves at a municipal rubbish tip outside town, where the bodies were carefully buried. His report continued:

I made the young men from the Chantiers handle the corpses respectfully, four men to each body, and lay them in the grave in ranks of ten separated by a layer of soil about 10–15 centimetres thick. Given the number of men hanged, this was the best we could do. Several times I returned to the scene of the hangings to oversee the work there too. There was nobody about. The streets were full of troops and tanks. Doors and windows were closed and shutters too and I could imagine the terror of the people indoors.[14]

The SS had forbidden Prefect Trouillé to attend the burial as a gesture of respect but, at about 2100hrs, Roche persuaded them to permit this, providing no attempt was made at identification of individuals or to remove objects on their persons. The two senior civil servants were thus present when Father Espinasse pronounced a benediction over the graves, which contained also the bodies of several FTP men shot down along the road in the fighting of the previous day.

On the following day units of Lammerding's force spread out in the countryside, trying to find traces of Chapou's band. Wherever they went, additional reprisals were exacted, both under the Sperrle-Erlass and because local commanders grew increasingly short-tempered after repeatedly having to remove trees deliberately felled across the road to impede their progress. Villages were burned down, farms and barns set on fire. In one incident on the road to Uzerche a half-track rolled into the yard of a farm owned by M. and Mme Bordas, the soldiers loosing precautionary bursts of sub-machine gun fire in all directions. Her testimony was clear:

My husband and my son Pierre were in the yard, bringing the cows into the dairy for milking. The soldiers took aim at them, shouting and saying things we could not understand, except for the word 'terrorist'. Our men were kept under guard in the farmyard while other soldiers searched the house, saying that we had hidden other terrorists there. They didn't find anything and set off in their half-track, making my husband and son march in front of them. My daughter-in-law and I wanted to follow, to see what they did with our men, but they shot in our direction, happily without hitting either of us, but forcing us to turn back. Sheltering in the house, we heard many shots and thought that they were firing into every piece of woodland in case the Maquis were hiding there in ambush. All afternoon we heard them coming and going along the main road, which is only half a kilometre from our house, and we saw the thick smoke going up from houses they had set fire to. We didn't go out to look for our men because we were afraid they would fire at us again. The next day, when the men still had not returned, we went out to look for them, but very cautiously because the Germans were still patrolling along the roads and in the woods. It was about eight o'clock when we found them lying near each other in our meadow, only 150 metres from the house. They had been shot and finished off with a coup de grâce – you could see the hole made by the bullet, the exit wound was much bigger. The Germans had no reason to kill them because they had done nothing, but I think it happened because they had found, on the road leading to our farm, not far from where the bodies lay, a car with German markings that was covered in blood. Near it was a freshly dug grave. So I think they believed that our men had done that. My husband Jean-Baptiste was seventy-two and my son Pierre was forty-four.[15]

It was not always the innocent who were killed. Shortly after the shooting of M. Bordas and his son, three armed FTP men drove a Citroën requisitioned from the Gestapo right into the middle of a German patrol and were taken prisoner. They were driven to Uzerche and hanged there.

On 10 June a further selection was made by Schmald of the men who had been held in the factory overnight, after which the SS transported to Limoges 311 men and 660 young members of the Chantiers de Jeunesse. There, they were subjected to yet another selection carried out by the Milice, at the end of which 162 men and all the youths from the Chantiers were set free while 149 prisoners were despatched to the concentration camp at Compiegne – and from there to Dachau on 2 July. Either in transport or at Dachau, 101 of them died.

Back in the home town they would never see again, after the departure of 2nd Das Reich on 11 and 12 June, the laboratory of the armament factory was used for six weeks as a torture chamber by Schmald and several *miliciens* in attempts to identify the members of Chapou's bands and find where they had gone. On 21 June Prefect Trouillé managed to gain access to the laboratory and found three teenage *miliciens* pouring some kind of acid on the facial scars of a man whom they had severely beaten with coshes. On the same day, a new round-up by the Milice resulted in eighty men being sent to Austria as forced labourers.

Roche's command of German came in useful for his fellow citizens also on 13 June, when he was able to stop the shelling of the town by a German artillery unit installed on the surrounding hills for reasons unknown. On 16 August, nine weeks after Chapou's premature 'liberation' that cost so many lives and ruined so many others, Roche negotiated the surrender of the new German garrison but, his report continues:

> Two days later a German column coming from Clermont-Ferrand and suffering severe losses en route managed to penetrate into the town, despite all the efforts of the FFI present. Both the Prefect and I were compromised because we had been working with the FFI. At 1500hrs on 19 August the Germans took over the Prefecture. In the course of a long interrogation, I explained that the inhabitants had fled the town, not because they were guilty, but from fear of reprisals. The Germans agreed not to blow up the MAT factory and another factory, nor to set fire to the unoccupied houses or houses of people on a list that the Gestapo had with them. The Germans then withdrew peacefully and the FFI re-took control of the town.[16]

Although the rule was for civil servants who had served under Vichy to be automatically dismissed after the liberation, Maurice Roche was allowed to continue in office and received promotion because of the services he rendered to the Resistance and his vigorous negotiations with the Germans.[17]

Today's tourists arriving in Tulle by the *route nationale* from Brive see a neatly kept garden of remembrance beside the road just outside the town limits. It marks the site of the two mass graves. At the war crimes trial that opened in Bordeaux on 4 July 1951, Wulf and Hoff claimed to have 'no recollection' of the executions in Tulle. Sentenced to ten years and life respectively, they were freed the following year. Paula Geissler was sentenced to three years' imprisonment for not having saved the life of an employee of the MAT factory when she could have done so with no risk to herself. Curiously, some years after her release, she appeared briefly in Tulle with a small group of German tourists, but wisely did not stay long. Lammerding was sentenced to death *in absentia*, but was never extradited from the British zone of Germany. He even initiated a suite for defamation against the German magazine *Die Tat* which accused him in 1965 of murdering hostages in France. Lieutenant Schmald was not brought to trial, having been shot by the Maquis in August 1944, muttering, '*Ich hatte Befehl*'. It was the classic alibi, heard so many times in the war crimes courts, meaning: 'I was ordered to do it.'[18]

13

THE WORST ATROCITY OF ALL

On 16 May 1944, in Algiers, General de Gaulle handed to Jacques Soustelle, Secretary General of the Comité d'Action en France, a directive setting out what he saw as the role of the Maquis in the liberation of the country. This document made it clear that armed civilians could only be supportive of the Allied invasion and that for them to rise up independently would be militarily a gross error. When the Allied High Command was given sight of this modest document, its reaction was negative. Basing his reasoning on the professional soldier's traditional mistrust of armed civilians, General Eisenhower considered it badly thought out and far too ambitious.

These reservations failed to reach the men on the ground, who took de Gaulle's directive as a cue for launching their own war. In central France Emile Colaudon, *nom de guerre* 'Colonel Gaspard', had a record of daring sabotage, having severely damaged a steelworks, a German radio transmitter, a liquid oxygen plant and 150 high-tension pylons. With his friend Henry Ingrand – also a member of Frenay's COMBAT movement – he decided on 29 April 1944 to turn three wild areas of the Massif Central area of central France into redoubts where Allied paras could be landed to lead the several thousand *maquisards* of the area in 'an invasion from within'. The most favourable of these was Mount Mouchet, a massif reaching 4,500ft in places.

In this ill-thought-out plan they were fatally encouraged by SOE agent Maurice Southgate, whose cover name was Hector. Many of SOE's records mysteriously and conveniently vanished in a fire after the war, but enough is known of Southgate's activities to piece his story together. He had grown up in Paris, married a Frenchwoman and founded a company designing and making luxury furniture. In 1942, bored with his so far uninspiring career in uniform, he met in London an old pal who had just returned from France. This decided him immediately to volunteer for service with SOE. Since he was an army officer and was to be transferred to the RAF for his SOE work, there was some delay before his training could start. He spent this time living with his mother in London, one day wearing his army uniform and the next, his RAF uniform, causing a neighbour to say to his mother, 'You know, I've never seen both your sons go out together'.

Aged 30 when he was sent into France on 25 January 1943, Southgate set up the STATIONER network, having been warned in London not to have anything to do with the various political movements of the Resistance. He was an energetic agent, who thought big, which is why he got on so well with Coludon when they met. In one ambitious operation that failed, the management of the Peugeot factory in Clermont-Ferrand refused to permit Southgate to carry out a limited sabotage operation, as a result of which 500 aircraft bombed the premises on 17 March, doing great damage but also causing nineteen deaths, injuring twenty-six people and damaging 100 homes.

On the night of 9 April 1944, some pre-war friends of Southgate in Clermont-Ferrand, whose home he used as a safe house, were arrested. That should have been a cue to change all other safe houses, identities and codes. Southgate despatched his wife Josette to London on a Lysander flight, so that she could not be used by the Gestapo to bring pressure on him. By this time his activities were so well known to the Gestapo that there was a price of 1 million francs on his head. At a meeting with Coludon in Montluçon on 15 April 1944 he undertook to arrange airdrops of light weapons and anti-tank bazookas, and to bring in an Allied mission to train the young *maquisards* who had never handled a weapon of war.

On 29 April, Southgate was joined by the Freelance mission, consisting of Captain John Hind Farmer, Captain Denis Rake and another stunningly beautiful female SOE agent called Nancy Wake, whose previous life read like a novel. Her wartime exploits in France are supposed to have inspired the plot of the 2001 film *Charlotte Gray*, in which the lead part was played by Cate Blanchett. Born in New Zealand, Nancy was brought up in Sydney, Australia, as one of six siblings in an unhappy home, which she left at age 16 to work as a trainee nurse until being given £200 by an aunt. Buying a ticket to New York, she worked there for a while until talking herself into a job as London correspondent for the *Chicago Tribune*.

Life in Europe of the 1930s was all she had hoped it would be: all-night parties, love affairs and more travel. At the beginning of the phoney war she fell in love with and married Henri Fiocca, a rich businessman, living with him in style near Marseille until her impulsively anti-German activities resulted in a price on her head. She escaped via Spain, but Fiocca was captured, tortured and killed. Back in Britain, Nancy proved to be the kind of woman SOE was looking for: disciplined, motivated, calm in a crisis and courageous. So successful was she in escaping all the traps set for her that the French *collabos* working with the Gestapo nicknamed her *la souris blanche* – the white mouse.

Southgate was overburdened from his heavy schedule of supervising drops and receiving and despatching agents for SOE, as well as running STATIONER. It is likely that sheer exhaustion lessened his natural caution when he travelled on 1 May to Montluçon, where his radio operator was working in a safe house they had been using for some time in the Rue de Rimard. Someone had sent an anonymous letter to the Gestapo denouncing an STO no-show supposedly hiding in that house. The no-show was Southgate's radio op. About 1500hrs a black Citroën *traction avant*, familiar from so many Resistance films, arrived at the address, where the Gestapo were able not only to arrest the radio operator, but also to lay hands on all the messages sent and received for the previous five days, both in clear and in code. It was the sort of present of which cryptanalysts dream. Despite several people trying to reach Southgate and warn him that the safe house was anything but safe, he walked into the trap at around 1600hrs. At first locked up in Montluçon, Southgate was transferred to the Gestapo HQ in Paris at Avenue Hoche where his captors addressed him by his cover name, 'Hector', blowing any cover story he might have invented.

Southgate was one of the lucky ones, if one may use the word 'lucky' in the context of a concentration camp. Sent to Buchenwald, he survived by using his skills as an upholsterer to work there as a tailor, and was one of four SOE agents still alive when the camp was liberated in April 1945.

Meanwhile, Colaudon continued his plan to raise the local Maquis sympathisers living apparently normal lives at home. These *sédentaires* were ordered on 8 May to present themselves for registration to participate in the coming struggle to liberate France. There was a note of menace in Colaudon's threat that men not reporting would be 'deleted from the ranks of the FFI'. Another arms drop on 10 May convinced him that London and/or Algiers knew what he was up to and was continuing to back him.

A final decision was made on 15 May that Mount Mouchet made the best possible place in the region to create a redoubt. Ten days later an even more explicit summons was issued:

> By order of General De Gaulle, all able-bodied men aged between eighteen and forty-five are summoned to serve as volunteers [sic] in the ranks of the Forces Françaises de l'Intérieur under the orders of General Koenig. They are to report at La Bastide in the commune of Venteuges, there to be inducted into the Lafayette battalion of 91st Infantry Regt and should bring with them provisions for forty-eight hours and be wearing solid boots.

The announcement was, of course, made without the knowledge or consent of de Gaulle, Koenig or 91st Infantry Regiment. The 'Lafayette Battalion' did not exist. Yet several thousand men flocked 'to the colours', some evidently not without misgivings. Historian René Crozet relates the story of one village priest who advised several young men:

> I know you feel that you must join the Maquis. This may be an honourable thing, but you have not thought through what may happen to your families. I beg you to do nothing. I hear things from the [French] Gestapo and [I can tell you that] the German security police know what is going on. Stop before it is too late![1]

Various arms drops provided a total of 3,000 rifles and pistols, 3,500 grenades and 150 Stens, but no heavy weapons. Since many of Colaudon's *maquisards* came from the towns, they had no idea how to behave with the peasants and farmers of Mount Mouchet who were their often unwilling hosts. In one typical crime frequently repeated, hungry young men from towns and cities would requisition for slaughter at gunpoint one of a peasant's pair of oxen, unaware that the owner needed both to pull his plough.

In response to the call of 25 May, Colaudon had an army of 2,700 men, organised in fifteen companies. Each man was issued a rifle, carbine or Sten and wore a uniform of khaki shorts, a brown or black windcheater with a red armband on which was a blue Cross of Lorraine on a white background. They were shod in good-quality British footwear, specially parachuted in, the Vichy shoes and boots available by then being of such poor quality that a few weeks' rough usage would make them fall to bits. Five companies also had light machine guns and 100 hand grenades each. Another 1,200 men joined Colaudon's army and were organised into companies numbered 31 to 36. Even Colaudon was embarrassed when a further 400 men arrived, for whom he had no weapons. They were told to go home again as there was no way of arming them or feeding them. Some of them were arrested by the Milice on the way back and shot.

The pessimistic priest was proven right on Sunday 28 May when seventy *maquisards*, about to set off on an ambush were themselves ambushed by a mixed force of GMR and German troops, who killed thirty-two of them outright and took twenty-seven prisoners. On the Monday eight others, mostly wounded, surrendered and were shot out of hand. The twenty-seven prisoners were tortured for information and then shot. In all, three men survived the tragedy of 28 May.

This was only a foretaste of what was to come. Newly arrived in Clermont-Ferrand to suppress all Maquis and Resistance activity in central France, General Fritz Brodowski gave Major General Kurt von Jesser a mixed force of 2,800 Waffen-SS and Wehrmacht troops, supported by GMR and *miliciens* who knew the territory, to eliminate the Maquis on Mount Mouchet. At dawn on 10 June they attacked the south flank of the massif with automatic weapons and mortars.

Von Jesser's private army was variously designated in different accounts as a division, a column, a brigade and a *Kampfgruppe*. The *Kampfgruppen* were battle groups constituted in emergency from men from many different permanent units, adapting themselves to orders from officers they did not know. Their creation in the brutal chaos of northern France after the Allied breakout from the beachheads, and their effectiveness, came as a surprise to many British and American commanders, who had thought the German soldier a hidebound creature who would simply surrender when his command chain was broken with no chance of being restored.

Von Jesser's brigade comprised six *Kampfgruppen* designated A to F, each including Wehrmacht, Waffen-SS, Sipo-SD security troops, sappers, an armoured company, two battalions of infantry and anti-aircraft units. Significantly, in view of the reputation they earned in central France, they also included battalions of Volga Tatars, Ukrainians and Azerbaijani troops conscripted in the Caucasus, making a total of 2,550 men travelling in 500 vehicles. By this stage of the war, the faces and skin colour of the men in Waffen-SS uniforms bore little resemblance to Himmler's Aryan ideal.

Of course, von Jesser did not deploy all his troops at the same time and same place. They were usually, as in this case, divided up and allocated to the needs of each of the multiple anti-partisan conflicts in central France during the summer of 1944, sometimes being the aggressor, but sometimes being ambushed several times in a day as they moved about the country. Again, one could write a book about the little-known war von Jesser led against differently armed and trained FFI groups in the three months from June–August 1944. After being talked out of destroying Tulle by Maurice Roche on 18 or 19 August, the column was ambushed five times on the 75-mile journey to Clermont-Ferrand.

Fighting on Mount Mouchet continued all day. In the evening, von Jesser's men retired after suffering casualties. The *maquisards* congratulated themselves that they had won a battle, but all they had done was to allow the enemy to measure their strength and assess their arms and equipment. Now considerably less confident than he had been, Colaudon organised an evacuation of arms and ammunition in expectation of a renewed attack in the morning. It began at 0900hrs with artillery support. Casualties among the defenders were high: some companies lost a third of their men. Ordered to hold until 0000hrs, they then filtered away towards the neighbouring La Truyère massif, so that when von Jesser's men reached the remote forestry camp that had been Colaudon's HQ they found nothing – except ten badly wounded men who had not been able to accompany the others. Their death by shooting almost certainly came as a relief. To punish the neighbourhood, at the village of Ruynes von Jesser's men shot twenty-seven male inhabitants in front of their wives and children. Other villages were pillaged and burned down. By the evening of 14 June, the day's total of civilians executed had mounted to fifty-four. Captured *maquisards* were also shot, regardless of their uniforms and FFI armbands.

By 20 June the forces that had driven Colaudon's little army from Mount Mouchet had also encircled the Massif de la Truyère, burning homes and whole villages as they came. By the time he was ordered by his FFI superiors to disperse his forces, his initiative had cost the lives of 280 men killed and 180 wounded in action, with a further 100 civilians executed in reprisals. Colaudon seems not to have understood that the airdrops of heavy weapons and paratroops he expected could never have materialised while the holding of the Normandy bridgeheads was the overriding Allied preoccupation. In the legends of the liberation, the Battle of Mount Mouchet was credited with delaying the arrival of a whole division in Normandy. The locals, on the other hand, had suffered greatly, for no advantage that any of them could see.

By this stage, the Allies had landed 325,000 men in Normandy, which was a formidable achievement logistically, but territorial gains had fallen far short of their objectives. In the west, VII Corps of the US First Army had failed to occupy the line it was meant to have reached on D-Day. In the east, British I Corps under General John Crocker was still nowhere near occupying the town of Caen, which had been its target for D-Day – this despite massive air raids and naval bombardments of the town that killed hundreds of civilians and very few Germans.

In addition to the severe delays in breaking out of the Allied bridgeheads, on 13 June the first V1 cruise missile landed on London, making the launch sites in northern France the top priority targets for the overstretched Allied air forces based in Britain. There was thus less chance than ever of bombers being spared to drop arms to the Maquis or fighters being despatched to support a rising in central France that should never have taken place.

Meanwhile, a company of Lammerding's 2nd Das Reich Division had been writing its name in blood. If the hanging of ninety-nine men at Tulle was arguably no more than predictable reprisals for the illegal killing of the German garrison by Chapou's FTP, 3rd Company of 2nd SS Regiment Der Führer immortalised the division's name at a village that had done nothing to merit its complete eradication from the map after the massacre of virtually the whole population.

At 1400hrs on the balmy summer afternoon of Saturday 10 June, 120 men under Major Adolf Diekmann cordoned off the village and ordered the mayor to assemble the inhabitants for an identity check by beating the traditional drum. In such a quiet village, unlikely to be the target of Allied air raids, there was no warning siren. Obediently, the adult population emerged from homes and shops and workshops and gathered in front of the *Mairie* to hear whatever announcement was to be made – as did the teachers and pupils of the village school and the school for refugee children from Lorraine who were living there. By a cruel irony, few children were absent that afternoon because the local doctor had just arrived to give them all a medical check-up. His car still stands where he parked it, in front of the main school with the tyres burned off, the window glass cracked by heat and the bodywork rusted by seven decades of wind and rain.

The single child not present at the mock roll call was a boy from Lorraine, 8-year-old Roger Godfrin. Many of the Waffen-SS men were *malgré nous* conscripts from Lorraine. Overhearing what they were saying to each other in dialect, he hid himself in a garden. By the end of the afternoon Roger Godfrin was to be the sole child alive in Oradour.

A party of cyclists – five thirsty young men and a girl seeking refreshments in the village – were allowed through the cordon to share the fate of the villagers, as were a number of mothers living in outlying hamlets who came looking for their sons and daughters after the time they should have returned home from school. Eventually, 240 women and 205 children – some accounts say 247 children – were herded into the church at gunpoint. That sounds an orderly, if menacing, procedure, yet evidence was given at the post-war trial that groups of men, women and children were also shot in the streets, perhaps to terrify the rest into obedience. Some of them were left there wounded and finished off later. That could account for the discrepancy in the body count of children killed. Several of these bodies were stuffed down a well only 60cm in diameter.

The 202 adult males rounded up were locked inside several barns. Of these, only five survived to testify that the SS shot at the mass of bodies jammed into their barn, aiming low to hit the legs and throwing straw and other combustible material on top of the bodies, most of them still alive and writhing in pain from their wounds, before setting fire to everything by throwing in several phosphorous grenades and barring the doors. While 197 of their friends and relatives died of wounds or were burned alive, the five survivors threw themselves flat when the first shots were fired and crawled into a corner of the barn that the flames did not reach, subsequently finding a way out and making their way with extreme caution into the countryside.

The SS next turned their attention to the church. The one woman who survived the massacre later testified that at about 1700hrs two soldiers carried in a large chest with fuses coming out of it, which they lit and retired. At the eventual trial, witnesses said that the chest contained what they described as 'asphyxiating grenades'. Whatever that may mean, the church swiftly filled with choking smoke that panicked the 240 desperate women into breaking down the door into the sacristy, where they found SS men standing at the windows with sub-machine guns, like farmers waiting for rabbits to break from the last stand of corn to be harvested. Bullet scars and holes still visible in the masonry show how they shot without discrimination in all directions at the trapped women and children.

In desperation, 47-year-old Marguerite Rouffanche used the stepladder kept for lighting the altar candles to climb up to a stained-glass window behind the altar. She smashed a hole in the bottom panel and fell through it, landing on the ground outside. Another woman climbed up the ladder and threw her baby to Madame Rouffanche. It fell to the ground, both mother and child being immediately shot. Madame Rouffanche, although bleeding from several bullet wounds, managed to drag herself behind a stone wall in the presbytery garden, where she was found by civilians the following morning.

At 1900hrs the evening commuter tram from Limoges was halted at the SS cordon, instead of proceeding as usual to the tram station at the other end of town. The tram lines are still there and the terminus station still awaits the last passengers of the day, who never arrived. Those passengers who could show identity papers with a domicile other than in Oradour had come to buy black-market food. They were ordered back on board and allowed to return to Limoges. The twenty-two passengers whose papers showed Oradour as their place of residence were lined up against a wall with a heavy-calibre machine gun pointing at them.

One can imagine their feelings as they were kept there, with the smoke from the burning village darkening the evening sky and their nostrils filled with the stench of burning human flesh. Many of the SS were drunk on looted wine and spirits, but after three hours the twenty-two terrified people were simply told to get lost. Entrance into the village being forbidden to them, they hurriedly sought refuge on nearby farms or hid in the woods until dawn.

By the time a late summer dusk hid some of the horror, out of all the people in Oradour when the SS cordoned the village off from the rest of the world that morning, only the boy from Lorraine, one woman and five men were still alive. Of the 642 people definitely killed only fifty-two corpses were positively identifiable; the others were so badly carbonised that many were not even recognisable by their nearest and dearest as human remains. Some time after dawn on 11 June, when the church bell should have been tolling for Mass, the last SS departed and the handful of surviving inhabitants of Oradour walked into the stinking, smouldering ruins that had been their homes. Every house was gutted. Nearly seven decades later, rusting motor vehicles and children's prams and bicycles have almost completely disintegrated. The melted bronze bell still lies on the church floor for tourists to photograph.

14

'UNDERSTAND? OFFICER, BANG BANG!'

As to the reasons why it all happened, on the French side it is claimed that there was no Resistance activity in Oradour-sur-Glane. This version maintains that Major Diekmann misread his maps and that his company should have been at nearby Oradour-sur-Vayres, a village where the Maquis had been active. The German version does not differ greatly as far as the massacre of the men is concerned, but claims that the village was the right one, to be destroyed in reprisal for three local Resistance operations, in which an ambulance convoy had been ambushed and two German officers had been kidnapped by the Maquis, and one of them killed.

In the first of these operations, Lieutenant Gerlach – unit unknown – was about to be shot by *maquisards* who stopped his vehicle at gunpoint in some woodland. After being forced to strip to his underclothes, Gerlach managed to escape while his captors were busy machine-gunning his driver. Finding his way back to his unit by following a railway line through the woods, he indicated that the incident had occurred near Oradour-sur-Glane. After his traumatic experience, and since he had fallen into the hands of the Maquis after misreading his map and getting lost, he may well have confused one village called Oradour with the other. Two unidentified *miliciens* also directed the SS to Oradour-sur-Glane on the morning of 10 June.

In the second incident, a German ambulance unit was attacked by *maquisards*, who set fire to the vehicles and burned alive the medical personnel and the wounded soldiers they were transporting.

In the third event, while prospecting ahead of his unit Major Helmut Kämpfe, a personal friend of Diekmann, was taken prisoner by a band of FTP *maquisards*. The major's personal papers were found by a Wehrmacht despatch rider the next day, on a road where he had presumably thrown them to leave a clue to his whereabouts while being transferred from one vehicle to another. An offer to return him unharmed against the release of *maquisard* prisoners was agreed to. There was also an unverifiable rumour that gold bullion, looted from a dynamited bank by the SS, was handed over as a ransom. Whatever the truth of that, the Maquis killed him anyway. His remains were found by a German war graves team after the war, with 10 June 1944 given as the date of death. It was afterwards claimed by the Maquis that he was killed in retaliation for what happened at Oradour.

With the *maquisards* involved neither wearing uniform nor carrying their arms openly, the Sperrle-Erlass required reprisals, including the executions of hostages. Major Diekmann, commanding the troops at Oradour, alleged that he found bodies of murdered Germans on arrival there, as well as caches of weapons and ammunition. According to his account, there was no intention of killing the women and children, but when their homes were set on fire the flames spread to the roof of the church, where the Maquis had a store of explosives, which blew up and brought the flaming roof down on to the victims below, producing sufficient heat from their body fat to melt the bronze bell.

Diekmann's immediate superior SS Colonel Sylvester Stadler was sufficiently disturbed by the number of civilians killed to refer the matter to General Lammerding, who on 5 June had issued divisional orders to arrest 5,000 hostages as 'punishment for attacks on German personnel by mobile bands of terrorists'.[1] Hearing what had happened at Oradour-sur-Glane, Lammerding ordered an investigation 'as soon as the situation permitted'. Given the urgency of getting his tanks and men to the Normandy front as swiftly as possible with insufficient wheeled transporters and a lack of many spare parts for the tanks,[2] this was unlikely to happen in the near future. Whatever his intention, when on 29 June Diekmann was killed in action together with many of his men who had taken part in the 'operation' at Oradour, the idea of an official inquiry, followed by a possible court martial, was abandoned.

At the post-war trial – there could hardly not be a trial for what had happened at Oradour – an unrepresentative few of the killers of Oradour were arraigned by the Haut Tribunal Permanent des Forces Armées sitting in Bordeaux from 13 January to 12 March 1953. Strangely, General Lammerding was not extradited to give evidence, nor ever brought to trial, although known to be practising as a civil engineer at Düsseldorf in the British zone of Germany. He subsequently claimed to have offered to attend the trial in Bordeaux and also to provide the war diary of 2nd Division Das Reich to be used in evidence. Whether he did or not, neither he nor the war diary was called in evidence. Lammerding died of natural causes on 13 January 1971 at Bad Tölz in Bavaria.

Forty-three members of Diekmann's company were condemned to death *in absentia*, most of them having been killed during the subsequent fighting in Normandy after the tragic event at Oradour. Present in court were seven Germans and fourteen men from Alsace and Lorraine – one volunteer and thirteen conscripts. Whether for political reasons – Alsace and Lorraine were technically German in 1944 but belonged to France again in 1953 – or for diplomatic reasons with the Cold War at its height, or because of a need to cover up the alleged Maquis atrocities, the sentences were not exemplary.

The senior accused was sentenced to death, as was one Alsatian volunteer. Nine of the conscripts were given forced labour ranging from five to twelve years; one was acquitted.

In the Limousin, the sentences were considered outrageously inadequate, yet in Alsace-Loraine there was public indignation that the *malgré nous* conscripts should be sentenced at all for obeying German orders, no matter what they had done. Since the accused had already spent eight years in custody, the Alsatian and Lorrainer conscripts were released immediately, as the judges had known would be the case when passing sentence. All the Germans, except the one sentenced to death, were liberated a few months later. The two death sentences were commuted, with both men released in 1959.

Oradour-sur-Glane has become France's national shrine to the tens of thousands of victims who died during the German retreat. It lies some 65 miles north-east of Tulle and 15 miles from the major city of Limoges. Frozen in time, the roofless homes and shattered shops, barns and workshops could be the result of an earthquake or area bombing. As the roofs collapsed they brought the walls down with them in many cases. Yet, 1940-model cars, prams and bicycles stand or lie rusting but otherwise undamaged. It is hard to think that all this ruination was accomplished by men, many of whom had grown up as French, using a few bullets and some phosphorous grenades.

When the author first visited Oradour, the ruined village was open to all comers. Parking a car and walking into it was like stepping back into a Ground Zero of horror. The site is now walled and fenced off from the modern world and the only access is through a visitor centre, where one goes underground to emerge into a nightmare scene, frozen in time. Many visitor centres ruin the effect of the sites to which they guard access. The one at Oradour is respectful and informative, with facsimiles of contemporary documents and also personal mementoes: the intact porcelain inkwells from the school desks, of which the woodwork was burned to a cinder, some children's shoes, a faded junior school photograph – the last ever taken in Oradour. This is all that remains of the little children in their best clothes, gazing solemnly at the camera with no idea of the terrible fate awaiting them.

Oradour is far from the only town or village in France to suffer like this. Most tourists and international truckers hastening along the A10 motorway 25 miles south of Tours on their way to south-west France, Spain or Portugal have no idea that, in passing the picturesque little village of Maillé, on the western side of the motorway, they are at the scene of another massacre in summer 1944. On 25 August – the very day that Paris was liberated and the tricolour flag was flying on the Eiffel Tower – a detachment of German troops commanded by Second Lieutenant Gustav Schleuter, a Nazi Party member since 1931, who was stationed in St-Maure-de-Touraine, killed 124 people in Maillé, allegedly in reprisal for Resistance activity in the region. Most of the victims were women and children.

Only 241 people lived in the village, including eighty-eight refugees. Many of them were personally known to German officers and troops who had been billeted in the village for several weeks. The Resistance had been active in the region, actually blowing up the railway lines in Maillé station three times since the Normandy landings. On 11 August an RAF pilot had parachuted from his stricken aircraft and been spirited away from the troops searching for him.

The reprisal 'operation' was methodical and thorough. During the night, Schlueter brought up the supporting artillery and concealed the trucks of his reinforcements among some trees. At 0800hrs his men blocked all access to, and exits from, the village. A squadron of RAF aircraft chose this moment to overfly Maillé and attack a train passing through, destroying one of Schlueter's 88mm cannons. Unfortunately, the noise of the attack distracted the villagers, some of whom might otherwise have realised what was going to happen in time to flee. Waffen-SS men started shooting dead any person – adult or child – they came across. People in hiding were dragged out and shot. Those who tried to escape were hunted down like animals. In early afternoon, with 124 people killed, the troops set fire to many houses before withdrawing to leave a clean field of fire for German artillery, including several 88s to shell the village. The shelling continued until late evening.

In the village post office that morning was postmistress Jacqueline Roy and her neighbour Christiane Benoist, who worked as housemaid for Maillé's two schoolteachers. Long afterwards, Madame Roy, who was a girl of 18, pregnant with her second child at the time, talked about the experience to a grandchild:[3]

That morning, I was on duty alone. My daughter Liliane was 15 months old and asleep in her bedroom. My husband, who was the postman, had left on his bicycle with the outgoing mail that had to be taken to the main post office in Celle St Avent, the next village. We heard the train being machine-gunned by the English planes. My husband was about to use the level crossing and had to throw himself into a ditch to avoid all the bullets. He rode back to the post office and told me that something strange was going on. He had seen smoke rising from [some outlying farms that had been torched] but we thought it was coming from German vehicles that had been attacked by the RAF.

Our neighbour André Metais came in at the same time and said that there were German soldiers in camouflage uniforms firing at people near the cemetery. I was worried and went to get my little daughter from her bedroom. When I came back, my husband and Monsieur Metais had decided to go down into the cellar, where we could take shelter. From some instinct – I don't exactly know why – I refused to follow them, so they agreed we should all go next door to Monsieur and Madame Gandar, the schoolteachers. We tried to slip quietly through the gardens, but the communicating door was locked, so the men had to break it down.

Madame Gandar saw us in the schoolyard and made signs for us to follow her down to the cellar beneath the school, where we found her husband and children aged 2 years and 10 years old and seven other people. The cellar door was closed and we sat among the wine casks. Through the ventilation holes in the walls we could see booted feet in the garden we had just run through. There were some bursts of fire very close and bullets pierced the door of the cellar, but no one was hurt. The children were terrified and crying, but we had our hands over their mouths to silence them. We smelled smoke. The teachers' apartment over our heads was burning. We heard the noise of china and glass shattering.

Then everything seemed to calm down. Madame Gandar opened a jar of conserved fruit for the children, who were hungry and thirsty. About two p.m. the shelling started, with some firing closer. It went on until around five o'clock. The men went out of the cellar and peered over the garden wall, to see bodies on fire lying in the street. My husband hurried to our house to get the baby's pram and some milk for her, but found himself facing three young Germans pointing rifles at him. They shouted, 'Terrorist!' He replied, 'No, not a terrorist,' and they let him go.

Abbé Payon, the parish priest, now came along with some Germans. Madame Gandar asked them to help us leave the village, which they did. The priest came with us as far as the level crossing and told us to walk slowly, stay together and not look back. We spent the night at a farm, how I don't know. In the morning, Madame Gandar and my husband went into the village. Most of the houses were burned down, but the post office was still standing, although a shell had blown away the gable end. A grenade had been thrown into its cellar, where we should have died, but for my sudden panic. My sister-in-law Georgette was killed in her cellar with her little 4-year-old boy. His father was a prisoner of war in Germany, so he never saw his child. Fifty-six years later, I still wonder by what miracle we were spared.

Christiane Benoist, the other young woman in the post office that morning, wrote down her account:

I had left school at fourteen and went to work in the home of Monsieur and Madame Gandar. This all happened on the day after my seventeenth birthday. That morning, the sky was blue and the sun already hot. We had been occupied for four years and we knew that the war must end soon. I heard a train being machine-gunned by English planes and, not realising the danger, went up into the attic to see what was going on. I'm not sure what the time was. There was smoke going up outside the village and I thought the planes must have attacked a German convoy. It was time to prepare the vegetables for lunch, but Monsieur Gandar told me to go down to the cellar. I hadn't realised there were bullets flying around outside, and I took the potatoes with me to continue peeling them down there. With us were Monsieur and Madame Roy and their little girl, and a neighbour called Metais. We shared our fears but soon fell silent.

Her account continues similarly to that of Madame Roy, except after they left the cellar, when:

… the soldiers lined us up against a wall, pointing their sub-machine guns at us. I was standing next to Madame Gandar. It seemed to last a long time. When she changed her little girl Annette from one arm to the other, she put her free arm around my shoulders and said, 'Be brave, girl. We're all going together.' That was when Abbé Payon came up, talking in German with the soldiers. It seemed to go on for a long time until he said to us in French, 'I'm going to come with you to the level crossing. Keep calm.' When we got there, he went back into the village. We had no idea then how terrible it had been. Next morning I had to let my parents know that I was all right. Madame Gandar tried to stop me by saying it was too dangerous. but I went anyway, keeping off the roads, walking through the fields and crawling at times until I got down to the river. At the slightest sound, I hid in the long grass. I was frightened when a man approached, until I recognised my father, who took me across the river in his little boat, back to our home. I didn't sleep properly for more than a month. On the Sunday we all attended the mass funerals, feeling completely numb. Now, fifty-six years later it still gives me pain to write these lines.

Although Schlueter was condemned to death in his absence at a trial in 1952, he was never tracked down. Unlike Oradour, which was preserved as the symbolic 'martyred village', Maillé was completely rebuilt by 1950.

There were, sadly, many Oradours and Maillés during that awful summer of 1944. As late as 29 August an unidentified Waffen-SS unit shot eighty-six men, women and children in and around the village of Couvonges in Lorraine, and thus technically German under the armistice agreement of June 1940. It was a small village of not more than 120 inhabitants, most of whom earned a living on the land. On 27 August a retreating column of 3rd Division of Panzer Grenadiers arrived and requisitioned accommodation. The locals, mistrusting the intention of all soldiers by this stage of the German retreat, although never guessing what was in store for them, set about hiding everything stealable, from household linen to wine, food and clothing. In the evening of 28 August the news went round that trains from Germany could get no further into France than nearby Revigny-sur-Ornain. After that, the lines had been blown up. Artillery fire could be heard to the west and the sky in that direction was lit by explosions at night.

On the morning of 29 August the artillery fire was much nearer, making windows rattle. At 0500hrs a motorised Wehrmacht column halted at the entrance to the village. Some of the German troops got out, seemingly to stretch their legs before concealing their vehicles in a barn. An NCO asked the mayor three times whether there were any partisans operating locally. Each time he was told there were none. At 0700hrs a Waffen-SS convoy rolled up with men dressed in khaki shorts and shirts. They set up two machine guns at the entrance to the village and two more by the church. The officer in command ordered the mayor to stay in his house with his family while soldiers searched the place, stealing everything that took their fancy. He then announced that no one might leave the village without written permission, but the villagers were not unduly worried as yet because this seemed reasonable in expectation of the arrival of American spearheads.

On the contrary, they set about making themselves as comfortable and as safe as possible from both German and American fire once the battle started. Eight men were arrested. Two were released. An accusation was made that arms were hidden in the village and that someone had fired on the Germans, which was patently untrue and made the villagers uneasy. It sounded like an alibi. One soldier with a conscience advised an elderly couple to hide in the woods. In broken French, he said, 'Understand? Officer, bang, bang.'

An Italian living in the village who could speak German asked several soldiers what was happening. Looking pale with shock, he translated for the villagers' benefit: 'They are going to kill all the men and set fire to the village. But they will spare the women and children.'

Accused again of harbouring partisans who had attacked German troops, the mayor denied the charge and asked what had become of his two sons, arrested shortly before. A lieutenant took him to where all the men had been lined up and freed the two sons, ordering them to stay indoors with their father all day. Two FFI men travelling through Couvonges, but without weapons, were arrested. Three Waffen-SS men headed for the post office, where they tore out the cable of the only phone in the village, helped themselves to money from the cash drawer and took the jewellery of the postmistress at gunpoint.

Around midday, after pillaging and looting every house, soldiers with flame-throwers and phosphorous grenades set fire to buildings at both ends of the village. Other soldiers were breaking down doors and arresting all the men found in the houses, herding them into a barn. Two young girls were raped in front of their mother's eyes. By 1300hrs the fires had taken hold and the whole village seemed to be burning. The prisoners in the barn were marched into a field and lined up in front of the machine guns, to be mown down like grass before the scythe. People running out of their burning homes were gunned down and the bodies robbed of anything of value. So terrified were the villagers who had escaped the massacre that it was three days before they dared to return and bury the bodies, which by then were decomposing in the heat.

One could go on, listing the villages and towns of France that were pillaged and burned down in autumn 1944, with all or most of their inhabitants killed for no military purpose, since Germany had obviously lost the war long since and liberation by the Allied spearheads was in many cases only a matter of hours away.

15

THE TOWN WHERE NOTHING EVER HAPPENED

During the occupation, the town of Bourges in central France stood just 4 miles north of the Demarcation Line, firmly in the Occupied Zone. In the Gestapo wing of the Bordiot prison torture was routinely used to extract information from the *résistants* and others arrested for helping people cross the line. One of them, Marc Toledano described his first agonising session as follows:

> Scharführer Schultz looked like a rat. Everything about him was grey: his uniform, his hair, his skin. He was like something that had never seen daylight. As a torturer the Gestapo could not have made a better choice. His henchman was Ernst Basedow. I thought Schultz was going to kill me [in the interrogation cell]. He grabbed a pistol, cocked it, took aim at me and changed his mind. Then he got a dog whip and swished it through the air so that the lash caught me on the eye. The pain was so acute that I lost my balance and fell. Later, Schultz forced my head right down the dirty toilet, blocking the outflow while Basedow repeatedly activated the flush so that I was drowning.

Between two sessions of torture, Toledano was lying in a dark cell, his hands cuffed in front of him. The handcuffs had sharp teeth on the inner faces that cut into the flesh and nerves of the wrists, like the jaws of a man-trap:

> I was in a semi-coma, when a man appeared, placed his hand on my face and whispered in heavily accented French, 'Don't move. Don't say anything. I am a German nurse, Brother Alfred of the Order of St Francis. I've come to look after you, to comfort you and take care of you.'

Toledano was not hallucinating. This was his first meeting with Wehrmacht corporal Alfred Stanke. He was born at Danzig in 1904 into a Polish Catholic family, whose original name was Stanicewski until his father changed it to sound more German. A religious child from very young, Alfred entered the Franciscan order of nursing monks dedicated to the Holy Cross. The community must have appreciated his talents in the staff kitchen, because four years later he was officially appointed cook to Pope Pious XI in the Vatican.

Returning to Germany, he became a nurse in a hospital in Cologne run by the nursing nuns of the Order of Poor Clares. There, for the first time, he was in daily contact with extremely poor people in ill health, who could not afford to pay for treatment. Imprisoned by the Nazis when another convent in which he was working at Coblenz was closed down by them in 1936, with all its property confiscated, Brother Alfred experienced the inside of a cell at first hand. Released and compulsorily mobilised for military service in 1940, he found himself a Wehrmacht corporal in the very different world of the occupation forces in France. By 1942 he was working as a warder/medic in the Bordiot prison at Bourges. There he became known to hundreds of grateful detainees as 'the Franciscan of Bourges'.

The worst tortures, the effects of which he tried to alleviate, were carried out not by the German Gestapo but a Frenchman from the area named Pierre-Marie Paoli, whose many specialisations included the pulling out of fingernails, use of electric shocks and slicing prisoners' skin in fine strips with a razor – known to Chinese torturers as 'the death of a thousand cuts'. A fluent German-speaker, this former tax clerk had first been employed as an interpreter until his sadistic inclinations led to him being enlisted in the Gestapo, where his workload rose to 'treatment' of as many as 300 victims in one year, almost all of whom either died in the prison or were transferred to concentration camps.

On arriving in Bourges, Brother Alfred could hardly speak French. Georges Ruetsch, the interpreter at the prefecture, spoke fluent German and agreed to teach him French. The teacher-pupil relationship soon exceeded language lessons by far. On one occasion, Ruetsch confided that the Resistance was planning to attack the prison and liberate the prisoners. Brother Alfred saved many lives by warning him to abort the plan because the prison guards were too numerous and too well armed.

In the same building as Paoli, Schultz and Basedow, Brother Alfred was ignoring all the regulations and doing his best to alleviate the sufferings of the prisoners by comforting them in any way possible and moving them into cells with their comrades so that they could prepare uncontradictory watertight defences and possibly avoid an appointment with a firing squad. He also carried messages to and from their families outside. By offering to do other warders' night duties, he not only had more freedom to help the prisoners during the hours of darkness when the prison was less well staffed but also got paid for the favour. The money was used to buy food for the starving prisoners. In this way men and women suffering from the tortures of Paoli and the other interrogators were given back some strength in the hope that this might enable them to survive the rigours of deportation under atrocious conditions. Brother Alfred was, in short, a saint, albeit never canonised.

It was a black day for prisoners in the Bordiot when he was discovered by an officer praying at the grave of a recent victim of the prison firing squad – something strictly forbidden by the Vichy government and totally *verboten* for a German soldier. Aghast, the officer screamed at him, 'This is a serious affair. I am compelled to take severe measures against you.' As a result, Brother Alfred was posted to another prison at Dijon in April 1944.[1]

On the other side of the Demarcation Line – about 20 miles south of it at the nearest point – the twin town of St-Amand-Montrond boasts that it is the plumb centre of France. Geography teachers and students may like to know that the precise coordinates are longitude 2° 52" E and latitude 46° 72" N. A stele in the neighbouring commune of Bruère Allichamps supposedly marks the exact spot. It was originally a Roman milestone erected in the reign of Emperor Alexander Severus to mark, uniquely, the junction of three imperial roads, and was later hollowed out for use as a sarcophagus. Unearthed in the eighteenth century, it was placed in its present position in 1758.

In terms of tourist attractions, the casual visitor to St-Amand can go fishing in the Canal du Berry – Berry was the pre-Revolutionary name for the region – or take river trips on the canal in gently puttering motorboats. The twelfth-century parish church is an interesting mixture of Romanesque and Gothic styles. The Cité de l'Or is a permanent jewellery exhibition celebrating St-Amand's position as the third most important jewellery producer in France. There is a medieval castle in Montrond, unfortunately largely dismantled for building materials by an impoverished owner in the nineteenth century. The twelfth-century Cistercian abbey at Noirlac still stands and is worth a visit. The Musée St Vic purports to trace local history over the past 100,000 years. Local history there certainly is, for Berry was the heartland of witchcraft in medieval France.

In the Place de la République is a handsome bronze bust of General de Gaulle. There is also a memorial to the commander of the locally recruited 1st Infantry Regiment, who died in a German camp. The *mur des fusillés* is a wall of remembrance commemorating 'our brothers who died so that we might be free' and were shot there on 8 June 1944, two days after the Normandy landings. In many places in France, when war memorials have to be refurbished, the current European political correctness apparently demands that the wording is changed, so that *fusillés par les Allemands* – shot by the Germans – becomes '*tués par l'occupant*', meaning 'killed by the occupiers'. It is politely vague and may mean nothing to most people in a couple of generations. Here, on this wall, the visitor is left to guess who committed the deed, since the perpetrators are not identified.

Near the wall is a plaque noting that the Croix de Guerre was awarded to St-Amand-Montrond in 1958. The inscription reads:

> First town in France to be liberated by the Resistance on the very day of the Allied landings, 6 June 1944, St-Amand-Montrond suffered enemy reprisals on 8 June 1944. Situated in the Free Zone at the beginning of the war, it became the refuge for many Jewish families who did not escape the persecutions of 24 July 1944.

Still, no mention of who the enemy was. Asking at the tourist office for information about the Resistance who liberated the town on 6 June, when the nearest Allies were more than 200 miles distant and having too many problems of their own to worry about St-Amand, the visitor is greeted with a blank look and a shrug that seems to say, 'Nothing ever happens here'.

On 5 May 2010 a ceremony was held to honour the many Gentile families in the area who were awarded the title 'Just Among The Nations' for saving the lives of Jewish children and adults during the Second World War. Next to the commemoration wall for the men shot on 8 June is a plaque reading:

On the night of 21–22 July 1944 the Gestapo, guided by the Vichy Milice, arrested seventy-one French Jews and imprisoned them at Bourges. In two groups, on 24 July and 8 August thirty-six of these men, women and children aged between sixteen and eighty-five were driven to the military zone at Guerry in Savigny en Septaine. There, they found horror and death, being thrown, mostly still alive, into the well shafts. Because they were Jews, they were the victims of Nazi barbarism. St-Amand-Montrond remembers them.

This plaque is dated 24 July 1994, which makes one wonder why it took half a century for the town to erect it. And why are there two misleading untruths in the 102 words of the French inscription? Firstly, the vast majority of the Jewish victims, if not all of them, were not legally French at the time of their deaths. Retroactive nationality was awarded post mortem as a gesture of guilt from the post-war government. Secondly, many of the men who killed them in a particularly barbaric manner were French.

Go to almost every place in France where the Resistance or Maquis was active, and you will find a Musée de la Résistance or a memorial to the fallen featured as one of the places of interest in tourist brochures and on the municipal website. Yet, the website of St-Amand-Montrond, while boasting of its goldworking and jewellery industries, remains mute about its experience of the Second World War. One does not need to be Hercule Poirot to surmise that this is a town hiding a great shame.

16

A RECIPE FOR DISASTER

The texts of Churchill's and Eisenhower's early morning broadcasts on D-Day were printed as leaflets airdropped all over northern France. Ever the realist, Eisenhower also had in a uniform pocket a personal apology he had drafted, to be transmitted if the invasion turned into a ghastly mistake with the troops involved wiped out or taken prisoner on the beaches, as had happened at Dieppe. In the broadcast messages both Allied leaders exhorted the civilian population to do everything possible to assist the invasion.

Two days before, Churchill learned that 200 Free French liaison officers, who had been attached to Allied units to go in with the first waves, were being unilaterally withdrawn by de Gaulle because no agreement had been reached with the Allied command on their duties and functions once ashore. In the event only seventy-seven French marines, who were embedded in other units, did land on D-Day – a fact commemorated in 1984 when President François Mitterrand unveiled a monument at Ouistreham in their honour.[1]

Relations between the Anglo-American leaders and de Gaulle were so fraught that, at one point that morning, Churchill dictated a deportation order and gave orders for the leader of the Free French to be arrested and flown back to North Africa, in chains if necessary, so that he might never set foot in France again. Mid-morning on 6 June brought cautious confirmation of the first landings. To enlist the support of the French population, the British War Cabinet considered it imperative that de Gaulle should add his voice to those addressing the people of his country at this critical moment. De Gaulle agreed, but the Foreign Office insisted on vetting what it feared might be a denunciation of the Allies in general and Britain's prime minister in particular. In the face of de Gaulle's intransigence, a compromise was reached, with the BBC authorised to record the general's speech, which could afterwards be suppressed if too inflammatory. By noon it was being recorded. De Gaulle opened with:

> The supreme battle has begun. It is, of course, the battle of France and the battle
> for France. The sons of France, whoever and wherever they may be, have the simple
> and sacred duty to fight the enemy by whatever means they can … The instructions
> of the French government, and the French leaders which it has appointed, must be

followed exactly. Behind the heavy cloud of our tears and blood, the sun of France's true might is dawning ...

When a transcript of the speech was read at the Foreign Office shortly afterwards, it was noted that de Gaulle had called the body of which he was leader 'the French government' and not the 'provisional French government'. After brief reflection, the speech was reluctantly approved for transmission while, just around the corner, the War Cabinet was still discussing whether de Gaulle should be punished in some way for failing to dance to the American tune. President Roosevelt planned not to liberate France, but to occupy it and replace the Vichy regional prefects by 'sixty-day wonders' – US officers and civilians who had been given a two-month course in Virginia before shipping overseas that supposedly qualified them to take over the civilian administration of France as the occupation forces were driven out of each *département*.

Had they been installed, it is more than probable that a second military occupation following immediately on the heels of the German occupation would have fuelled a nationwide resentment, giving the PCF exactly the leverage it needed to stage a coup d'état that wanted only a propitious moment. To short circuit this, de Gaulle intended to replace the Vichy prefects with his own regional commissioners in each area liberated.

Although furious at the way he had been sidelined throughout the planning of Operation Overlord and because neither Churchill's speech nor Eisenhower's acknowledged his role as military leader of Free France and political head of the provisional government constituted in Algiers to replace the totally discredited collaborationist government in Vichy, de Gaulle was not a man to let his personal feelings interfere with the main priority, which was to drive the German armies out of France.

Much oil was poured on the troubled water between Downing Street and his headquarters in Carlton Gardens so that the hastily composed message could be transmitted by the BBC at 1730hrs on 6 June. It included the instruction that the civilian population should take orders only from Gaullist officers. This was his attempt to cut the ground from beneath the feet of other Resistance factions with their own agendas, especially the Moscow-line communists.

Unfortunately, the haste with which the message had been drafted left a great ambiguity. The phrase 'The sons of France ... have the ... duty to fight the enemy by whatever means they can' was about to be taken as authorisation for the hideous game played out in many places, including Tulle and the little-known market town in the plumb centre of France. St-Amand-Montrond lay some 250 miles from the landing beaches, but only 30 miles by road from the major city of Bourges, where large Wehrmacht, Gestapo and Milice units were stationed. Before dawn on 6 June, while the alarm sirens were still wailing on the Atlantic Wall at the first sight of the enormous invasion armada off-shore and the first wave of landing ships was heading shoreward, four local FFI commanders met at the home of 37-year-old René van Gaver in Coust, a village 5 miles south-east of St-Amand. Two of the other men present at van Gaver's house were 25-year-old Parisian Daniel Blanchard from the right-wing COMBAT network and Hubert Lalonnier, the 37-year-old commander of the local FTP. He was a hard-line Marxist who had served in the International Brigades during the Spanish Civil War.

Before undertaking any military action, all Resistance and Maquis commanders were supposed to clear their plans with COMAC, the Comité d'Action Militaire of Jean Moulin's Mouvements Unis de la Résistance (which became in December 1943 the Mouvement de Libération Nationale (MLN)). COMAC for the area in which lay St-Amand was controlled by PCF members Pierre Vrillon, Maurice Kriegel-Valrimont and Alfred Malleret-Joinville. The confusion of initials and code names they used was deliberate, to obscure the long arm of the Comintern in Moscow, which had ordered the PCF to conceal its preparations for a coup d'état to take place in the power vacuum after the liberation by operating under the cover of ostensibly popular front organisations. If their actions succeeded, the party could emerge from the shadows and claim the credit; if they failed, the other political parties in the umbrella organisations could be blamed.

COMAC had already called upon all member groups to support plans agreed with London in the run-up to D-Day. Plan Green was the sabotage of railways, which was already very effective, slowing down by days or even weeks the arrival of much-needed German reinforcements and deliveries of materiel, like the spare parts for Lammerding's tanks. Plan Slowcoach was the blockage of roads, more difficult to make permanent because a road usually has alternative routes and can be more easily repaired. COMAC's Directive No. 10 dated 29 May 1944 included the words:

> In the coming weeks, each of us must prove that he is worthy of the post he occupies by loyally obeying the orders of COMAC … [and] by the way in which, during the operations against the enemy in connection with the landings and the Allied offensive, he demonstrated his initiative, daring, spirit of sacrifice and devotion to the nation.[2]

As the independently minded FFI boss of the Limousin region Georges Guingouin later wrote:

> The Gestapo had decapitated the military leadership of LIBERATION-SUD in the spring of 1944, after which its current leadership on 6 June was really the clandestine secretariat of the PCF, giving orders without taking any account of the military realities. To declare an insurrection is one thing. To 'liberate' towns and hold them against reprisal (by regular forces) is quite another.[3]

On 6 June even de Gaulle's BCRA in London was unaware of the extent to which local commanders were about to take unauthorised initiatives that would expose uninvolved civilians to the terror of German reprisals.

Two days previously, on 4 June, there had been a village fête in nearby Châteaumeillant, where Blanchard and his fellow *résistant* and brother-in-law André Sagnelonge got stinking drunk. When Blanchard's disgusted wife told the men it was time to stop drinking, he told her to get lost because 'It's the last piss-up we're ever going to have'.[4]

The senior military officer in the FFI of the Cher *département* was Colonel Bertrand, a career soldier who had been underground with the OAS since the Armée de l'Armistice was disbanded. He had not been invited to the early morning meeting on 6 June, and had been deliberately excluded from a preparatory meeting held on 29 May – this on the instructions of the fourth man present at van Gaver's house while the first wave was fighting its way ashore in Normandy. Fernand Sochet was a militant PCF member posing as the politically neutral regional organiser of the multi-party Front National, and had cut Bertrand out of the chain of command to prevent the colonel's professional appreciation of the military situation from acting as a brake on what Sochet was planning. That was nothing less than exploiting the local *maquisards'* pent-up frustrations after four years of humiliation during the occupation. In a metaphor used by one communist *résistant* involved: 'We were driving the latest model Citroën *traction avant* car, while [Bertrand] was riding a bicycle.'[5]

In those first hours of the invasion, when even Eisenhower was uncertain that the Allied bridgeheads could be held, they should all have been on metaphorical bicycles and keeping well off the main roads. However, between the two meetings in St-Amand, van Gaver and Blanchard did contact Colonel Bertrand and gave him a vague outline of their idea for a 'spontaneous' liberation of the town. Bertrand was horrified: a single glance at the map was enough to show that any local uprising in St-Amand would call down immediate reprisals long before any Allied troops could fight their way through from the beaches of Normandy to support it. After the savage reprisals on the Maquis and uninvolved civilians in the Glières and Vercors and many other regions of France, there was no doubt that this would result in considerable bloodshed.

In addition, Bertrand had received from Free French HQ in London an order dated 16 May to the effect that no confrontation was to be sought by the FFI in the early stages of the invasion because 'an unplanned uprising by diverse factions of the Forces Françaises de l'Intérieur risks breaking the impetus [sic] of the French Resistance and causing considerable harm to the general population, without any compensating gain'.[6]

This was particularly likely to be the case at St-Amand. After the disbanding of the Armée de l'Armistice on 27 November 1942, Pétain's Secretary of State for War, General Eugène Bridoux, started lobbying for a military force of some kind by arguing that it could be usefully deployed against the Maquis and Resistance groups. Six months later, in a meeting with Hitler at Berchtesgaden on 30 April 1943, Laval obtained the Führer's agreement for a new and smaller Vichy army to be created for this purpose and placed directly under his control.

On 23 July 1943 Bridoux authorised the formation of the Premier Régiment de France (1RF), a force of three battalions, maximum total strength fixed at 2,760 officers and men. General Antoine Berlon, an officer whose pro-German sympathies were punished with five years' deprivation of civil rights after the liberation, was given overall command. The 1st Battalion of 1RF was stationed at Le Blanc, 70 miles south-west of Bourges, but 3rd Battalion was stationed at Dun-sur-Auron, only 15 miles southeast of Bourges and therefore within a short drive of St-Amand. Even more to the point, 2nd Battalion was actually stationed in St-Amand-Montrond, which meant that the best part of 1,000 officers and men owing allegiance to the government in Vichy were within a few minutes' march of Sochet's planned uprising. Knowing that, in this confusing time, many 1RF officers were anti-German despite the task they were supposedly fulfilling, Colonel Bertrand did the only thing possible in the circumstances.

He unofficially sent a message through mutual friends to Major Ardisson, the officer commanding the 1RF troops in St-Amand, to do everything possible to prevent or at least retard any intervention by the battalion, no matter what happened in the town on D-Day.

The stage was nevertheless set for a tragedy, of which the unlikely heroine was a powerful woman named Simone Bout de l'An, whose husband Francis[7] had taken over as national head of the Milice after its founder Joseph Darnand was promoted to the post of Secretary of the Interior at the beginning of 1944. Like many Vichy politicians, Bout de l'An had flirted with the left during the 1930s and even visited the USSR. It was that visit which persuaded him to abandon communism and head right. Spells of teaching history and geography in Teheran and Damascus were followed by a return to France in 1941, just in time to be in at the beginning of Service d'Ordre Légionnaire that became the Milice.

In April 1944 Bout de l'An had come to St-Amand for a political meeting. Looking for a safe place to leave his wife, their two sons and his ageing mother – partly because he enjoyed the pleasures of a bachelor life away from them – he had chosen St-Amand because it lay as far as possible from any French coast that might be invaded and because it enjoyed the reputation of being 'the sort of town where nothing ever happens'. With its own Milice headquarters and the presence of 2nd Battalion of 1RF, what could be safer?

In an endeavour to minimise civilian casualties after the first landings in Normandy, German-controlled Radio Paris broadcast repeated warnings that the occupying forces would have to take 'exceptional measures' in the combat zones and that the population should 'not allow itself to become involved in the fighting'.

Blanchard and Sagnelonge, pumping adrenalin and with a sense of mission, took de Gaulle's broadcast on the evening of 6 June as a blessing on the local initiative they were planning. Thirty minutes later, some seventy men gathered at the lock-keeper's cottage on the Canal du Berry at Clairins, just outside St-Amand. The Renseignements Généraux (equivalent of British MI5) attempted to justify the lack of action by local forces of law and order by alleging there were 'between 700 and 800 individuals armed with sub-machine guns and automatic rifles'. Communist historians also exaggerated the numbers threefold in an effort to prove the popular support for the uprising. However, survivors of those at Clairins on that evening are definite that they numbered no more than seventy.

They were a mixture of young *maquisards* from various bands in the region and older *sédentaires* living at home, apparently normally, while they awaited the call to arms. Most of the younger ones were simply out to seize what they thought would be a good opportunity to prove their courage and manhood after four years of submitting to German occupation. Others went along with the rest because they were afraid of being called cowards if they did not. Because there had been little open contact in the past between the different Maquis bands, introductions at Clairins were made at the same time as Sten guns and automatic pistols parachuted by the RAF to COMBAT were handed out to men with no military training. Most of them had never previously handled anything more lethal than a shotgun. The immediate result was that one man was shot dead accidentally before they learned how easy it was to loose a burst of fire from a Sten.

Even at this stage the ultimate tragedy could have been averted, save for the instruction received by the minority of PCF members present, who had been secretly briefed to 'exterminate all the German garrisons and … kill without mercy all the murderous rabble of the Milice'.[8] The second part of the order was effectively a declaration of civil war. There was a fail-safe plan decided on at the meeting of 31 May: should it prove impossible to hold St-Amand after its 'liberation', the various elements would flee into the nearby Massif Central, where it would be difficult for German anti-terrorist troops to track them down. Since many French towns and villages had been punished for Resistance and Maquis operations with which they had nothing to do, what did van Gaver, Blanchard, Sochet and the others think would happen to the civilian population of St-Amand after their withdrawal? Nobody knows.

The unfamiliar, but obviously lethal, British weapons in their hands made all the men at Clairins very gung-ho. In trucks, private cars and on motorbikes they drove back into town. The time was now 1830hrs. Hubert Lalonnier took command, splitting his forces into three groups. The first, under van Gaver and Sochet, occupied the sub-prefecture without meeting any resistance. Van Gaver installed himself in the sub-prefect's office.

The second group headed for the town hall. There also, there was no resistance. At the Gendarmerie, it was the same story because the senior officer there was a clandestine member of OAS. Two German civilian administrators of the STO – some reports say three – were arrested, but not maltreated. At the post office a *milicien* in the wrong place at the wrong time was so badly beaten up that he was left for dead. Barrages were set up on the principal roads into the town. At the barrage on the road to Bourges a car was stopped in which two *miliciens* were travelling, their automatic weapons out of reach on the rear seat. Arrested and led to the war memorial, the two prisoners were shot and their bodies left lying there all night.

The third group of insurgents, led by Lalonnier and Blanchard, surrounded the Milice headquarters in St-Amand at 1900hrs and opened fire at will. An impressive hail of bullets struck the building without hitting anyone inside. Nor did the return fire or the few hand grenades thrown by the *miliciens* score a hit until a stray shot – no one knew whose – killed an incautious passer-by. Having no overall command, each *maquisard* kept in touch only with comrades from his own group. In the resultant confusion a *milicien* with more guts than the others decided to act.

Clément Marchad was a Parisian waiter who had joined the Milice to save himself from the STO. He now took off his uniform jacket and slipped on a civilian coat, jumped out of a window at the rear of the building and was surprised to find no one there. Grabbing a motorbike, he rode off to a public telephone, where he called the Milice HQ in Bourges with a vivid account of Allied parachutists dropping on St-Amand and attacking the town. Whether he made this story up to justify any accusations that he had deserted his post or simply because the general confusion made it hard to know exactly what was going on, no one is sure. In either event, his news was swiftly relayed from Bourges to Vichy.

Inside the building still under attack, Simone's younger son was suffering from bronchitis and needed to be taken to hospital. Furious at the incompetence of the men supposedly protecting her and her children, and who were plainly unable to drive off what she called 'the rabble outside', she gave them all a good tongue-lashing, on the lines of, 'Call yourselves men?' She then ordered the senior *milicien* to inform the FFI by telephone that they were prepared to surrender for the sake of the women and children in the building, provided they were guaranteed their lives. On the other end of the line, Lalonnier agreed to this, without any intention of keeping his word to men, some of whom had arrested and beaten up his comrades in the past. After Simone thrust a white sheet out of a window about 2300hrs the firing stopped. Eight *miliciens* walked out, hands on their heads, followed by several women and the two children. Lalonnier wanted to kill the men there and then in compliance with the PCF directive, but gave way to Blanchard and van Gaver, who insisted they be treated as POWs and locked up in the sub-prefecture because the *miliciens* were, after all, in uniform.

Since one of the Bout de l'An boys was visibly ill, it was decided to send the two of them and their grandmother to the hospital. The male prisoners were locked up in the cellar of the town hall and the women, including Simone, who protested that she should be with her children, were put into the office where the mayor normally offici-ated at marriages.

Because no one in the Milice had the presence of mind to destroy their files of informers and sympathisers before surrendering, the *maquisards* now used these to launch a witch hunt in which many people were dragged out of their houses and marched off at gunpoint to be locked up in the town hall, where the German STO administrators were also interned.

Lalonnier, meanwhile, had driven off in a truck to inform all the local villages of St-Amand's 'liberation'. As dawn approached, villagers eager to join the celebrations mingled with those who would anyway have come into town for the market. Most of the shops stayed closed. At the sub-prefecture a cask of wine was broached with free drinks for everyone who looked in. Tobacco being normally scarce, a chest of it was also made available to anyone who smoked. Rumours flew from mouth to mouth: the Allies had landed in the south of France too; Bourges was besieged by the FFI. Hastily printed posters suddenly appeared on walls announcing a general mobilisation for males of military age to join the FFI.

The Rex cinema, owned by van Gaver, was turned into a recruiting depot, where the general euphoria produced a sudden flood of volunteers wanting to enlist. Their enthusiasm was somewhat dampened when they could only be issued with three car-tridges per man and a hunting gun from the store of those confiscated after the defeat. Slowly the numbers of men in St-Amand armed with some kind of firearm mounted until they approached 300 maximum. One of them is worthy of note. Jewish, but iden-tified only as 'the traitor', he had been arrested by the Gestapo and released shortly before members of the LIBERATION-SUD movement had been betrayed. Suspected of being responsible for the betrayal, 'the traitor' was shunned by everyone. Coming out of the cinema with the gun he had just been issued, he announced grandly: 'They didn't want me in the Resistance, but now I am.'

The police tried to keep some kind of order and prevent pillaging of property belonging to known supporters of Vichy. In the general confusion, the chief *milicien*, who had not been in the headquarters building at the time of the attack, put on civil-ian clothes and caught the early train to Bourges. In the sub-prefecture, van Gaver was working the phones and finding that none of the neighbouring towns had risen up against the occupation. There was some fighting in Guéret between local FFI and mixed Milice/German forces, but that was 80km distant and no help could be expected from that quarter. From a patrol of 1RF, who did not otherwise intervene, he also learned the disquieting news that the Allies were still bottled up in a few square miles of Normandy beachhead and fighting desperately not to be pushed back into the sea. When he expressed his concerns, Sochet brushed them aside, stating with the blitheness of ignorance that it must be possible to hold St-Amand for the few days it would take the Allied spearheads to reach them.

17

A COUNTRY IN CHAOS

Francis Bout de l'An was awoken in his Paris hotel on the morning of 7 June with the news that his wife and children were held hostage by the FFI. Darnand, also in Paris, authorised him to use all necessary German and French forces to re-take the town and liberate his family. Telephoning the sub-prefecture in St-Amand in the hope of getting an update from a Vichy official, Bout de l'An found himself talking instead to van Gaver, sitting in the sub-prefect's chair. The conversation rapidly degenerated into an exchange of insults that became threats. After collecting thirty *miliciens* in Vichy, Bout de l'An stopped at Moulins, where the local Wehrmacht commander promised to attack St-Amand in force the following morning. Meantime, throughout the afternoon of 7 June, he was receiving intelligence on enemy strength from the pilot of a light observation aircraft, who reported that the town was in a holiday mood, with people thronging the streets and only a few makeshift barricades here and there.

The FFI, having neither camouflaged their transport nor even parked it under cover, panicked at the sight of the small aircraft with Maltese cross markings flying low overhead, believing that it meant German troops would arrive imminently. A few prudent people in the crowds took it as an evil omen and hurriedly packed a suitcase, to leave town as soon as possible. Towards 1500hrs Simone was allowed briefly to visit her children in the hospital and then forced to clamber aboard one of the FFI trucks with the *miliciens'* girlfriends. Although her captors knew exactly who she was, and rightly considered her more valuable than all the other prisoners put together, she alone among the hostages showed no sign of fear, openly despising the anguished girlfriends of the *miliciens* – or 'little sluts' as she called them – with characteristic lack of tact. With the male prisoners in another truck, the FFI then left town after posting warning notices in prominent places:

> We have taken thirty-six men and women of the Milice prisoner. This is to warn you that, if *miliciens* from elsewhere take reprisals in St-Amand, the hostages will be shot.

The notices were signed 'The Committee of the Resistance'.[1]

An hour later the trucks returned, Lalonnier having failed to find a safe house in which to detain his prisoners. They were again locked up in the town hall, while their captors took stock of the situation, which was not all as they had hoped. A sympathetic gendarme at Charenton, only 8 miles to the east of the town, telephoned to say that a large German force was on its way. The news compelled a move out of St-Amand, but not during daylight, when they could be tracked by the spotter plane. Those who had not slept for forty-eight hours were sent home to grab a few hours' shut-eye. The signal to report back and leave town was to be the traditional roll on the town crier's drum.

For the most part roused in time – three were left behind, sleeping – they returned to the Rex cinema, where various groups were allocated to different trucks. A number of the prisoners were released for reasons about which no one seemed clear: friendship, probably. Finally, Simone and the six girlfriends were placed in one truck with eighteen *miliciens* in another. As to how they were selected to be taken, while ten others were left in the town hall, to be liberated by the Germans, most survivors claimed that those taken along for the ride were the ones guilty of excesses, not that there was anything like a trial; everything was done on hearsay. Apart from Simone, the tearful girlfriends in the first truck were thought to be a useful bargaining counter, if and when one was needed. There was also a masculine desire to punish them for 'sleeping with the enemy' – a 'crime' for which so many thousands of Frenchwomen would be punished by public humiliation in the months to come.

The trucks departed at various times between 2200hrs and 0100hrs. In the confusion and darkness one man was shot dead after being mistaken for a German. At Châteaumeillant, only 4 miles away, the convoy assembled, to hear that the warning of the Germans' proximity was apparently a false alarm. Unbelievably, they turned round again and headed back to St-Amand. Just outside the town limits two civilians warned them that a battalion of the von Jesser brigade had already cordoned off the other side of the town and was making its way through the south-eastern suburbs.

Soon after the convoy had finally left, at about 0500hrs von Jesser's troops headed into the town centre, wearing camouflage smocks and with blackened faces. Guided by two *miliciens* – one was the man who had been badly beaten up at the post office – they arrested anyone incautious enough to be in the streets and all those identified by their two guides as having been involved in the uprising until they had 200 people to lock up in the sub-prefecture. There, they also released some of their own men left in the cells by the Maquis.

On Thursday 8 June, André Sagnelonge woke up at 0700hrs. Whoever was supposed to have awoken him for the departure with the other *maquisards* had forgotten to do so. Hearing the sound of firing in the streets, he hurriedly dressed and, with a young neighbour, went outside, his jacket sleeve still bearing the FFI armband. Surrounded by German troops after only a few paces, he threw down his rifle and put his hands up. Ordered to stand facing a wall with several other men, he awaited the command, '*Feuer!*'

Instead, he heard an argument behind his back, after which the local Gendarmerie captain Cholet told the men to put down their hands and attempted to release those whose guilt was in any doubt. Thanks to his armband, Sagnelonge knew he could not be one of them. A man of unusual initiative, who had escaped from German POW camps five times and been re-captured each time before making his successful run home in 1942, he waited until the nearest soldier was looking the other way and then leapt over the wall, followed by his young neighbour. Cholet attempted to place himself between the soldiers and the running men. Two shots rang out. Both men fell. A third shot, missing its target, hit Cholet instead, and killed him.

The next victims of the day were seven FFI men who had not departed with the others because they were still looking for fuel for their *gazogène* truck. Recognised by the *miliciens* accompanying the German soldiers, they were arrested and shot, with one other man, their names recorded to this day on the *mur des fusillés*.

Alarmed by a burst of fire released accidentally by a *milicien*, the Germans set fire to six buildings in the town centre, using flame-throwers and phosphorous grenades. They then prevented the fire service from doing its job. It was a day of terror for everyone in the town, a total of nineteen men being shot and six homes burned to the ground. As one of the survivors bitterly remarked: 'On 7 June, the Maquis bought drinks all round and left us to pay the bill next day.'[2]

The only German casualty was the pilot of the spotter plane, who misjudged clearance over a treetop and crashed in flames. Finding their three civilian compatriots unharmed, the Wehrmacht withdrew in good order, handing the town over to the Milice, who plundered and burned the homes of the departed FFI men, arresting people at random and locking them up temporarily in the 1RF barracks. And there the sorry episode would have ended, but for the hostages.

Arriving about noon, Bout de l'An visited his sons and mother at the hospital and had them driven to safety in Vichy. He then interrogated Major Ardisson as to why 2nd Battalion of 1RF had not intervened the previous day. Ardisson replied that he was not there to fight the Maquis – a reply that saw him arrested and sent to the prison in Bourges. Bout de l'An then took a posse of *miliciens* and scoured the nearby countryside for traces of the men holding his wife. Apart from beating up a few people who could tell them nothing useful, it was a waste of time.

Bout de l'An now returned to Vichy, showing no concern for the *milicien* hostages because, in his view, they should have died fighting. The thought of a bunch of *maquisards* having the temerity to keep his wife hostage, however, sent him into a fit of rage. After St-Amand's mayor René Sadrin negotiated the release of some of the townspeople locked up in the barracks, Bout de l'An was furious and decided that the local Milice was too soft or too involved with local people to be entrusted with reprisals in the town.

One Milice officer who would go all the way was Joseph Lécussan, a tall, heavily built ex-naval officer whose hair-trigger temper matched his red hair. A chronic alcoholic, Lécussan was rarely sober, and had indulged his hatred of Jews and communists while director of Jewish Questions in Toulouse by brutal interrogations that killed at least one detainee and by extorting money and valuables from many others in return for promises of leniency that were never kept. After joining the Milice in 1943, this record was enough to see him swiftly appointed its regional head in Lyon.[3]

An uncertain progress saw the FFI convoy still only 50 miles away, arriving in Guéret, capital of the neighbouring *département* of Creuse, to find the town in a state of civil war with roads barricaded and many buildings on fire. After the regional FFI under its tyrannical 34-year-old commander Albert Fossey, using the *nom de guerre* 'Major François', had besieged the Milice and the German garrison, both groups had surrendered and been locked up without ill treatment. Some *miliciens* were still at liberty, however, and three of the prisoners were shot in reprisal for their continued resistance.

The hostages from St-Amand were herded into the town's prison, their captors grabbing the chance to sleep wherever they could find a bed. The early risers among them were taking breakfast on a cafe terrace when a German aircraft flew in at rooftop height and machine-gunned the centre of town. 'François' – as commander of all FFI forces in zone R5 – ordered an immediate evacuation, conveniently forgetting to advise the local FTP fighters as a way of settling an old score with them. The straggling convoy of trucks – all the *gazogène* wood-burners had run out of fuel by now and had to be towed – made off towards the south and were strafed several times by German planes, but miraculously without casualties.

In the early afternoon the trucks were hidden beneath trees while a council of war was held. Lalonnier took the view that the convoy was too big and far too visible from the air, and therefore had to be broken up. Preparing to spend the night there and travel on in the morning, the FFI had an unforeseen problem. One of the 'little sluts' was having a miscarriage, brought on by all the bumping on the hard wooden seats of the trucks. Simone took charge, despatched two men to fetch clean water and looked after the terrified girl.

Posters printed in Vichy were displayed all over St-Amand, warning that the 200-odd hostages would be executed and the whole town burned down if Simone Bout de l'An was not liberated within forty-eight hours. To avoid the destruction of his town and the massacre of its inhabitants, Mayor Sadrin undertook a seemingly impossible task: to catch up with the Maquis convoy and negotiate an exchange of hostages.

So, on that awful Saturday morning when Oradour was about to be destroyed and almost all its inhabitants massacred, 150km to the north-east he and two other mediators from St-Amand were stacking up the miles hunting for the FFI and their hostages taken from St-Armand. Their deadline had already been extended several times. On one occasion they missed a rendezvous with the *maquisards* by less than a kilometre due to a misunderstanding.

Drinking heavily from the moment he arrived in St-Amand, Lécussan ordered a number of houses to be blown up and a curfew to be imposed, starting at 1800hrs. Returning exhausted from his fruitless hunt for the Maquis, Sadrin met Lécussan for the first time. Armed with a pistol and several hand grenades and rapidly emptying looted bottles of fine wine, he was holding twenty terrified additional hostages in the sub-prefecture. Arguing that they had nothing to with the events of 7 June, Sadrin offered to be shot in their place. Lécussan refused.

People with hidden radios, on which they had listened to the BBC against a background of explosions from the *miliciens*' demolitions, passed on in whispers the warning broadcast by General Koenig, C-in-C of the FFI, in an attempt to defuse the several premature uprisings in France, that it was impossible for the Allies to supply the food, arms, ammunition and military support for any guerrilla activity. His advice was, in short, to cease guerrilla activity, to stay in small groups and not to band together. If only, the terrified inhabitants of St-Amand must have thought.

The Maquis convoy was still only at Boismoreau-les-Mines, 15 miles south-east of Guéret, taking stock of their situation and deciding what to do next – something they should have thought about before starting their insurrection. When told that the convoy was splitting up and given the choice of going with the communist FTP or the right-wing COMBAT fighters, most of the men had no political preference. The question had to be simplified: 'Do you want to go with Lalonnier or Blanchard?' Blanchard made certain to keep control of most of the weapons, since they had been dropped to the COMBAT network, to which he belonged.

On Sunday 11 June the fatal split took place – fatal for the hostages, that is. Lalonnier wanted nothing more to do with them, so they had to depart with Blanchard's group. But they were cheerful enough, little guessing what the future held. Coming from the same town, it was not surprising that, in the five days since being taken prisoner on 6 June, cautious moves had been made between captors and captives to renew old friendships, for these were men who had been to school together, played football in the same teams, got drunk together and, in some cases, courted the same girls.

On the same day, back in St-Amand Lécussan embarked sixty-five hostages in motor-coaches, escorted by carloads of armed *miliciens*, destination Vichy. There the men were beaten – some to insensibility – in front of their wives. Bout de l'An arranged mock executions and shouted that everyone in St-Amand would die if Simone was not returned within the time limit. It was pure terrorism, since the hostages could do nothing to assist or accelerate the return of his wife. One of the female prisoners was 16-year-old Thérèse Lamoureux, whose father and brother were in the Maquis. Shown coshes and whips to be used on her if she did not talk, she was told that she would be forcibly undressed for her beating, and she replied defiantly, 'You won't see anything new. My body's just the same as other girls.' In reluctant admiration, a *milicien* whispered, 'We need chicks like that in the Milice'.[4]

The original limit expired and was extended by twenty-four hours. But everything possible went wrong for Sadrin and his companions: their car broke down and had to be pushed through a rainstorm to re-start it; Sadrin, in his mid-sixties, sprained an ankle while pushing it; the windscreen wipers would not work; they repeatedly lost their way.

Just before the two groups went their separate ways from Boismoreau-les-Mines, a messenger from Sadrin who had come all the way from St-Amand by bicycle caught up with them, giving the latest news. This was the first time Sochet, Lalonnier and Blanchard learned that the hostage ploy meant to protect their families and friends had misfired and put those very people and many more at risk in St-Amand. But they were not free to make their own decision, being subordinate to 'Francois' so long as they were in Region R5 – the Creuse and the southern half of the Cher. He refused even to contemplate giving up the *miliciens* or the women, no matter what happened. However, to gain time, Sochet persuaded Simone Bout de l'An to write a letter to her husband. It read as follows:

> My dear Francis,
>   I am in the hands of the liberation army. I am being well treated. Spare the hostages to avoid the worst happening. I put my trust in God. I am worried about what's become of the children. Give them a hug for me.
>   Fondest kisses, Simone

18

NO TIME TO WASTE

It sounds unbelievable, but Sochet took the letter himself by bicycle all the 80 miles back into the Cher *département*, intending to confide it to the mayor of a neighbouring commune to forward to Bout de l'An since he could not risk entering St-Amand with it in his possession. From commune to commune he cycled, without finding any mayor willing to risk delivering the letter and be suspected of having links with the Maquis. Late at night, Sochet at last found a mayor's secretary not far from St-Amand who had the courage to telephone the Milice in St-Amand with the news of the letter.

By that time, a German detachment had tracked down the *maquisards* hiding in Boismoreau-les-Mines, who succeeded in breaking off contact and slipped away towards the village of Sardent, where a column of SS Division Das Reich had just shot sixteen local men in passing through. Even before that, the local Maquis had experienced a hard time, living under hidden tents or semi-dugouts deep in the woods. A guarded truce between them and the newcomers was made more uneasy by Lalonnier's men stealing a considerable number of weapons. With no intention of living rough any longer than necessary, Blanchard, van Gaver, Georges Chaillaud and half a dozen other bosses installed themselves comfortably in the Château de Mérignat with one of the hostages and a German prisoner preparing their meals for them. Their men were left to bed down in nearby barns. The prisoners, too, were confined in a guarded barn with a rough partition between the *miliciens* and the women, where Simone took to lecturing her guards that they were wrong to regard the Milice as enemies because they too were working for the liberation of their country.

Surprisingly, at this time of undelineated battle lines many Maquis groups were living similarly, with the bosses enjoying privileges and comfort denied to the rank and file. One such man, who is now a neighbour of the author, openly criticised the leadership of his FTP group over the hypocrisy of communists behaving in this way. They offered him the bribe of coming to live in the château with them, if he would shut up. Disgusted and disillusioned, he chose instead to walk 200 miles home and took no further part in the Maquis.

Life at the Château de Mérignat was comfortable, if not luxurious. Opinions are divided as to where all the funds came from, but money there was, sufficient to pay a butcher to come and slaughter a requisitioned calf every day. There was little coffee, which was in short supply everywhere, but always hot chocolate and plenty of milk. One of the survivors recalls never eating so much meat each day in the rest of his life, although the menu was boring: veal stew twice a day. A semblance of discipline was enforced by Blanchard. He obliged one of his men, who had taken tobacco from a local shop against a promise of payment after the war, to return the tobacco and apologise to the shopkeeper. Similarly, when a silver plate disappeared from the château, Blanchard assembled everyone who had access and threatened to refer the theft to 'François', who had already had a man shot for cowardice during an attack. The threat was enough to see the plate returned the next day.

The big problem was boredom. Even though ammunition was in plentiful supply, each man now having 150 rounds for his weapon, it was impossible to train with live ammunition in case the noise alerted any Germans passing nearby.

With the extended deadline expiring in the evening of 12 June, it had become more urgent than ever for Mayor Sadrin to arrange the exchange of prisoners. As the go-between in a climate of extreme mutual mistrust, his own position was far from enviable: some in the FFI regarded him as a Milice stooge and Lécussan made no bones about letting him know that he considered the Mayor of St-Amand a closet *résistant*, to be liquidated after he had served his purpose. Six days after the departure of the Maquis and their prisoners, Sadrin was still without any real news of their whereabouts.

Simone's letter having at last reached St-Amand, its contents were relayed by telephone to her husband in Vichy. Although use of the term 'liberation army' and the mention of being well treated implied that part of the message had been dictated, the letter proved to Simone's husband that she was still alive … unless she had been executed by her captors after writing it. He opted for the sane course, despite Lécussan's impatience to kill someone – anyone – and agreed to a further prolongation of forty-eight hours in the deadline.

It was ironic that Simone had now become the one person who could save the lives of the hostages in the hands of the Milice, considering that they had been arrested in order to force her return safe and sound. Nobody had time to appreciate the irony of that, nor to reflect that the Maquis decision to take the hostages when they left St-Amand as a way of preventing reprisals by the Germans was itself the cause of the reprisals by the Milice.

Sadrin now being immobilised by his damaged ankle, the office manager of the sub-prefecture, Bernard Delalande, was lent a car by the Milice and set off with the two remaining negotiators to a rendezvous with some local *maquisards*, including one man who had been with the men from St-Amand. Although initially only offering to drive the others, Delalande was to play an increasingly important part in the negotiations. Driving into the Creuse *département*, contact was made with a local *maquisard* whose *nom de guerre* was 'Roger' and who took their message to 'François'. He refused to consider any exchange of hostages, saying, 'Tell those middlemen from St-Amand to piss off, unless they want trouble with me. Madame Bout de l'An is staying where she is. We're keeping her, come what may.'[1]

At a loss of what to do next, the negotiators returned to St-Amand, where Sadrin was trying to secure the release of the arrested families by persuading five other local notables to join him as substitute hostages. Equally as stubborn as 'François', Bout de l'An would hear none of this, adding, 'Even if they call me Bout de l'An the Butcher, the hostages will be shot and the town burned down, if my wife is not released'.[2]

Desperate, Sadrin even wrote an appeal to Prime Minister Pierre Laval, begging him to intervene, but received no reply. Archbishop Lefebvre of Bourges was also brought into the act, to plead for the hostages, even offering himself in their place, but Bout de l'An was unmoved – until the prelate simplified the issue: if the hostages were killed, Simone would never be seen again and her children would grow up motherless. Bout de l'An at last gave way and agreed to stop ill treating the hostages and to send back three of them who had not even been in St-Amand during the premature 'liberation'. However, running out of patience at 1700hrs on 17 June, he again threatened Sadrin that, if the negotiations did not swiftly end in success, he would cut off the gas, electricity and water supplies to St-Amand and, when the town was burned down, only the hospital would be spared because it had cared for his children.

A bizarre convoy then set off for Vichy to see him in person, consisting of Delalande and the other negotiators with a Milice escort, which saw them through one German roadblock after another. Meeting Bout de l'An in the Milice HQ, they were able to obtain the terms of a possible settlement: so long as Madame Bout de l'An and the women were released, all the hostages would be freed, with the exception of those arrested while carrying weapons. As to the *miliciens* involved, he said, 'They are soldiers. Their job was to fight. They should have died defending the woman they were supposed to protect.'[3] To the end of this convoluted tale, he never showed the remotest interest in their fate. The negotiators also got the clear impression that he would rather know his wife had been killed than submit to any blackmail using her as a pawn.

He also spelled out the consequences of any refusal of the other side to negotiate Simone's release: the hostages at Vichy would be shot, the families of the leading 'terrorists' would be arrested and their property declared forfeit. In other words, whatever the Maquis did, he would reply by escalating the violence to another level. As a favour, the team from St-Amand was allowed a brief visit to the female hostages. After a few hours' sleep, they drove back to St-Amand to try again to pick up the trail of the elusive *maquisards* holding Madame Bout de l'An. Passed from one contact to another, the negotiators finally met 'François' in pouring rain in the morning of 17 June at a rendezvous on a country road near Sardent.

A tall man in uniform, with a large black Basque beret tilted over one ear, he was at pains to impress on them that he held the reins of power in Resistance zone R5. Recently promoted to the rank of lieutenant colonel, he was on his way to arrest a female spy and had just had five of his own men shot 'for unworthy conduct' during the fighting. He appeared unable to understand why the negotiators had been chasing round the country on their quest, since they had no personal motive to do so. The idea of a humanitarian gesture seemed as foreign to him as to Lécussan. So far as he was concerned, doing a deal with the traitors of the Milice was out of the question and, if a town of 10,000 people was destroyed as a result, that was not his fault.

He did, however, propose a counter-deal. Claiming that Simone was the mistress of Secretary of the Interior Darnand, he ordered them to persuade Darnand to effect the release of a man arrested by the Gestapo on 2 June, in return for which he would send Simone back to her husband. The dismayed negotiators could not believe that he wished to introduce the Gestapo into the already problematical power struggle in which the hostages on both sides were enmeshed. 'François' dismissed the soaked negotiators with the threat that they were Milice stooges who would be hanged if he set eyes on them again. He then dictated a letter to Darnand in which he declared that any harm to the hostages would result in Simone being killed, cut up in small pieces and posted back to him in several parcels.

On 18 June, the only good news was that Bout de l'An had heeded Archbishop Lefebvre's appeal from the pulpit and given permission for the hostages to be overseen by the Red Cross. The bad news was that he had also appointed Lécussan sub-prefect in St-Amand, with instructions to bring order back to the rebellious town.[4]

It was in the morning of 19 June that the weary negotiating team set off yet again for another fruitless meeting with 'Roger', the current whereabouts of 'François' being unknown. The following day, they again drove into the Creuse, talking their way through roadblocks, some manned by the Maquis and others by the Milice, where Delalande's function in the sub-prefecture established their bona fides. The whole country was now effectively in a state of civil war. On 21 June at 1100hrs they missed a rendezvous near Sardent due to the roads being blocked by flocks of sheep and herds of cattle. Desperate pleas to 'Roger' finally bore fruit: at 1700hrs, they met the elusive Maquis overlord himself at Pontarion. To their surprise, 'François' agreed to Bout de l'An's latest offer: to exchange the hostages in Vichy and the *maquisards'* wives in return for the women held hostage in the Creuse.

The return of the haggard negotiating team to St-Amand was a nightmare journey. Delalande dared not switch on his headlights for fear of ambush by one side or the other and drove at a snail's pace along unfamiliar roads in the gloom, at one point missing by minutes an ambush set by Lalonnier's men, who had heard that the car was carrying Milice spies. Reporting back to the sub-prefecture in St-Amand on the morning of 22 June, they found all the personnel terrified by Lécussan's speech of the previous day, during which he threatened them with a loaded revolver and said, 'I have been sent here as a *Gauleiter*. I shall certainly burn down the whole town, if the order is given. I can shoot whom I want, when I want. I demand your complete submission to my authority.'[5]

In comparison with that, Bout de l'An sounded sane when they relayed to him by phone the terms of the offer by 'François'. However, he said that he could not return the wives because the rail connections between Vichy and St-Amand had been cut by sabotage. It would thus be necessary to backtrack to the previous deal. Delalande and the others were dumbstruck and horrified to hear Lécussan add that if Simone was not released that very night, he would begin reprisals at dawn. Exhausted and demoralised, they set off yet again into the Creuse and tracked down 'Roger'. He, however, had no idea where 'François' now was.

While hunting for him, 'Roger' bumped into van Gaver and Blanchard entirely by chance. They were on their way to find 'François', who had never bothered to inform them of the negotiations with Delalande. 'Roger' thus brought back to Pontarion not 'François' but the two St-Amandais, who were horrified to hear of the prolonged negotiations over the hostages, for which the final deadline was to run out so soon.

They all agreed that there was no time to waste. If their families were not to suffer, the exchange was a matter of urgency. All five were about to leave for the Château de Mérignat when 'Roger' showed up again and told them that 'François' now refused to let the exchange of hostages go ahead.

Another hour was wasted while van Gaver and Blanchard were driven by 'Roger' to argue their case with 'François', who heard them out, still unmoved by the thought of St-Amand being razed to the ground, but eventually told them disdainfully to do whatever they liked with their female hostages. It was by then too late for the exchange to take place that evening, so a handover was agreed for the following morning.

Delalande had no way of knowing that German military units had moved into St-Amand, ready to effect the reprisals the following morning. This was to prove the decisive moment in the drama because there was no room in his vehicle for the male hostages, even though van Gaver wanted to release them with the women, despite Bout de l'An not including them in the deal.

After an uneasy night, Delalande's team was up at 0530hrs, with two and a half hours to go before Lécussan's deadline. At 0730hrs Delalande managed to wake up a sleepy village postmaster whose telephone was still working and got through to Lécussan. For once – perhaps he had not yet started drinking – the self-styled *Gauleiter* of St-Amand sounded quite rational. On being told that the women had been handed over to Delalande and would be back in St-Amand by early afternoon, he stood down the German troops, who returned to base, and agreed to have the hostages brought back from Vichy.

At 1000hrs Delalande was waiting at a crossroads when one of Blanchard's men drove up with Simone and four of the 'little sluts', all blindfolded so that they could not lead anyone back to the château where they had been held. The two other girls had opted to stay with the Maquis. In one case, this was because the girl was afraid to return and face the wrath of her father for sleeping with a *milicien*. The other girl's motive remains unknown, but since she was just referred to as *la Juive* – the Jewish girl – she was a strange person to find consorting with the anti-Semitic Milice. Simone promised to confirm the two other girls had stayed behind of their own accord, so that there could be no going back on the deal when they arrived in St-Amand.

Delalande made her and the four girls promise on their honour not to divulge anything about their captivity. Simone installed herself beside him on the front bench seat, with the four girls in the rear, and off they set. A stop en route had to be made for one of the girls who was ill. Another girl wanted to be put down at her family home, but Delalande refused to permit this, although she was allowed to greet her family as they passed by. It was thus 1345hrs when the unshaven team drove into St-Amand with their relieved passengers, and halted outside the sub-prefecture. The relief for Sadrin and everyone present can be imagined. Lécussan, who was probably drunk by then, unpredictably burst into tears of joy. Asked for the record what she thought of her erstwhile captors, Simone said they were patriots, and that it should be possible for a dialogue between them and the Milice. Unable to believe his ears, Sadrin murmured tiredly, 'Perhaps you could work on that, Madame'.

Refusing a celebration meal that had been prepared for the occasion, Simone departed for Vichy to rejoin her children, leaving Sadrin, Delalande and the other wondering whether they had been duped, for there was no sign of the hostages from Vichy. Seven prisoners were released in St-Amand, which went some way to assuage their fears. But Bout de l'An kept his word, possibly under the influence of Simone, who assured him that she had not been physically ill treated during her captivity.

At last, about 1500hrs on 25 June, the convoy of hostages from Vichy, escorted by the Gardes Mobiles, arrived in St-Amand amid great rejoicing. The indefatigable Delalande then headed for Vichy to try to make a second deal for an exchange of the *milicien* hostages who were considered not guilty of any particular crime or act of violence against a number of relations of *maquisards* who had been taken prisoner. Bout de l'An did not say yes or no, but Lécussan made it plain that he would do everything possible to frustrate this new initiative. Before that could be sorted out, news came that all communication with the Resistance and Maquis units in the Creuse had been cut, due to a major anti-terrorist drive launched by the von Jesser Brigade to eliminate all FFI units in the Creuse, Haute Vienne and Corrèze *départements*.

The *milicien* hostages still held at the Château de Mérignat were an assorted bunch of twenty men and women. There were the eight men who had been defending the Milice HQ when it was besieged, several of whom came from the disbanded 1RI regiment – not to be confused with the new 1RF regiment. Some of these were on the black list of those known to have denounced *résistants* and Jews and therefore had a number of deaths to answer for. There were also ten other men arrested in the night of 6 June. They had joined up for different reasons – to escape the STO, because their parents told them to earn some money, etc. – but had nothing bad known about them. Then there were the two remaining female hostages.

After the departure of Simone and the other girls, one of the male prisoners attempted to escape. A cobbler by trade, physically feeble and obliged to walk with a crutch, he never washed and stank so badly that he was shunned even by his fellow prisoners. When caught before getting very far, he was given an impromptu trial and shot. Blanchard also presided over a hearing of evidence against 'the traitor', accused of responsibility for the near-fatal return to St-Amand on 8 June by falsely alleging that it was safe to do so when the German reprisal force was already in the town. Suspicions about him were voiced by several men, but there was no firm evidence. Blanchard therefore gave him the benefit of the doubt and freed him. In view of what was shortly to happen, it is noteworthy that Lalonnier and Chaillaud disagreed vehemently with this decision. They wanted him shot, for the safety of the group.

For the national holiday on 14 July, the nearby towns of Bourganeuf and Sardent were *en fête*, with garlands strung across the streets, a celebration dance organised and a victory parade of the Maquis held on the field where airdrops had taken place, after which 'François' – in a better mood than usual – awarded some medals and promoted several men, including Blanchard, now designated 'Captain Blanchard'. The celebrations were cut short by news of the approach of one of von Jesser's columns. Down came the garlands as the Maquis drove out to ambush the enemy. Once again, the plan went wrong. Alarmed by Allied aircraft flying overhead, the German vehicles left the road and disgorged the soldiers just before the ambush, where they found themselves face to face with the *maquisards*. In the fighting, two of Blanchard's men were killed, as was 'Colonel Kléber', who had caused all the deaths in Tulle.

The survivors retreated into what 'François' called the Iron Triangle of Bourganeuf, Guéret and Aubusson, which he declared a no-go area for von Jesser's men. Days slipped by. Then, on the night of 16 July German forces surrounded the hideout of 'François'. He managed to escape and sent couriers to all the Maquis bands in zone R5 to split up and vanish into the countryside. Blanchard's men decided to head back into the Cher *département* and rendezvous there, where they could count on the support of the population. They split into four parties: one headed north in a small van; the biggest group, totalling ninety men, including van Gaver and Blanchard, set out to march back into the Cher; a smaller section commanded by Chaillaud kept all the heavy weapons; and thirty men planned to slip back using tracks and little roads.

The prisoners were also split up. The two girls and a man who should never have been taken prisoner were left with a local Maquis band, instructed to release them as soon as this was safe. Three hostages who wanted to change sides were taken with Blanchard. The thirteen others were handed over to Chaillaud's section, a decision that sealed their fate.

Again, nothing went as planned. The largest group marched off to the north until van Gaver, a townsman unused to physical exercise, began to limp. A halt was called in some woods and men despatched to secure meat and other food for the night. At 0600hrs men were again sent out to find food. Before they returned, shots were heard and some other *maquisards*, who had been hiding nearby, ran past, screaming, 'Get the hell out of here. The Krauts are on our tail!' The firing was getting nearer. A man fell, shot through the head. A fusillade rang out, proving that the Germans had taken position along one side of the woods and were beating in from the other side, to drive the Maquis on to the guns. Mortar shells began bursting among them and then stopped as the attackers were among them: men in camouflage jackets with machine pistols, who spoke not German but Ukrainian. *Maquisards* who continued fighting were shot down like rabbits. The rest threw away their weapons and waited, hands on their heads in the building heat of a scorching summer day, for the German officers to arrive.

Fifteen men only had escaped through the woods. The wounded men were finished off where they lay. Hours later, sixty-two others were marched off under guard, leaving nine bodies on the ground. Transported in trucks to the town hall of Bourganeuf, they were handed over to the SS, who proceeded to interrogate them with threats and violence about identities, weapons caches and so on. One of the *maquisards* bravely stepped out of line to point out the three *miliciens*, so that they would not be beaten up. They were released. Lined up in the courtyard, all the other men expected to be shot at any minute, until an officer informed them that their execution was to take place at 0500hrs the following day. Locked up in a medieval prison nearby, the prisoners were hungry and terribly thirsty. Some men urinated on their hands, to moisten their lips with the only liquid available.

They were let out of their cells at 0900hrs, whereupon men knelt in the filthy urinals and licked the walls. The SS took pity on them and brought some water. Early in the afternoon, they were herded into trucks. Some men were handed bread by their captors; others received nothing. At Aubusson, they got down to be locked up in the technical college, guarded by Czechoslovakian conscripts who made no secret of their delight that Germany was done for and told them of the assassination attempt on

Hitler's life and reassured them that they were not going to be shot. Nor could they be deported to concentration camps because of all the railway sabotage. A visit from representatives of the Red Cross was also comforting.

On 23 July, they re-embarked in the trucks, to be driven along the winding little roads of the Massif Central, expecting at every turn to be saved by 'François' and his men ambushing the column. It was not to be. He had retreated into a fantasy world, issuing communiqués claiming victory in massive battles with high body counts that had never taken place.[6] Arriving in the major city of Clermont-Ferrand, the prisoners were again interrogated, this time violently by the Gestapo and the Milice, but without premeditated torture as such. Two days later, they were put on a train to Dijon, where they were handed over to soldiers of the Wehrmacht. Greeted by the Milice escort with cries of 'We bring you the criminals!', the commanding officer did not return their Hitler salutes. He replied dryly, 'There are criminals everywhere, including among those who bring others here.' It seemed a good augury, the prisoners thought.

On 29 July they were herded into cattle wagons that rumbled over the tracks, heading east. Four days later they were hauled out of the wagons and found themselves in the Reich after all. And not only in the Reich, but in that state-within-a-state ruled by the Allgemeine-SS. Split into small groups, the survivors of Blanchard's group were despatched to Buchenwald, Neuengamme, Dora and Mauthausen – concentration camps from which they had little chance of emerging alive and where there was every chance of dying an unheroic death from disease, malnutrition and ill treatment.

'Live free or die!' had sounded fine to Tom Morel's men on the plateau de Glières all those months before. Now, for Blanchard's men the most appropriate slogan was Dante's '*Lasciate ogni speranza, voi ch'entrate*' – 'Abandon all hope, ye who enter here …'

19

BODIES IN THE TREES, BODIES DOWN THE WELLS

Lalonnier's group meanwhile had managed to escape direct contact with von Jesser's Ukrainians, thanks largely to two local women, known only as Alix and Jeannine, who guided them by little known routes out of immediate danger and into the neighbouring Indre *département*.

The section of thirty-five men under 28-year-old Chaillaud and their thirteen Milice prisoners managed to get completely lost after changing direction and back-tracking repeatedly to escape their pursuers. It was hardly surprising: during the weeks they had spent at Château de Mérignat nobody had thought about getting a compass and the only map they possessed was a very small-scale one on a post office calendar.

The men were depressed by news of what had happened to Blanchard's group. They were also continually hungry and missing their regular food supply at the château. Finding food for so many men was becoming more and more difficult as supplies ran low even in the towns. Each time they narrowly escaped encirclement by von Jesser's troops some muttered that it was time 'to get rid of' the *milicien* hostages who, they alleged, were deliberately slowing them down. Since so many old friendships had been renewed during their six-week odyssey, it was hard to decide what to do. The only certain thing was that the *miliciens* could not be released because they would then identify all their captors, which would lead to reprisals on their families at home.

On the morning of 20 July the only food being cooked for the midday meal was a pot of beans. Men in German uniform were seen jumping out of their trucks across the fields. Chaillaud gave the order to move immediately. Once again, they stole away, leaving their food behind. Luck was with them. Before the circle around the farm where they had been hiding was complete, they managed to get away. However, it was becoming more and more obvious that they were the target of a massive sweep by von Jesser's anti-partisan units and their luck was likely to run out at any moment.

After several hours' march, the enemy was still so close that, if one of the hostages had shouted, he would probably have been heard. Chaillaud made up his mind that the only way of moving faster was by executing the hostages, which would also reduce the problem of securing enough food. The problem was that each one was known personally to one or more of his captors, who argued that chance alone had led one man to the Maquis and another to the Milice. Chaillaud himself owed his freedom, if not his life, to the senior *milicien* Louis Bastide, who had knowingly allowed him to get rid of compromising papers some months previously by tearing them up and flushing them down a toilet just before he was to undergo an interrogation.

To justify his decision, Chaillaud said, thirteen years later in 1957:

> There was no question of shooting the prisoners because the nearest Germans would have heard the shots. So we hanged them. We made slip knots with parachute cord attached to high branches. We didn't have a step-ladder or a chair, so we put the cord around their necks, lifted them as high as we could – and let them fall. When I told [Bastide] that they were going to be killed, he said simply, 'You chose England and we chose Germany. You've won and we've lost.' The *miliciens* died bravely.

Accounts of the hangings by other men present differ. It seems that Louis Bastide vainly begged the man whose life he had saved to spare his in return.[1] In any case, the same parachute cords could have been used to tie up and gag the *miliciens*, leaving von Jesser's men to find them alive, instead of thirteen strangulated corpses hanging from the trees. But then, they could have given away their captors' names, so the gruesome hangings can be attributed to Chaillaud's fear of reprisals. In the event, several of his men were so disturbed by seeing old friends hanged in this way that they threw away their weapons and took a chance on being able to walk home. Within hours, Lécussan received a phone call from one of them, later identified as 'the traitor', saying that eight of the *milicien* hostages had been hanged, which suggests that he had downed arms in protest after the first batch of executions before walking out in disgust. At any rate, the exact number of men hanged was not important to Lécussan, whose rage was about to be directed at his favourite target.

There had been few Jews living permanently in St-Amand before the invasion of 1940 brought a number of refugees from the north-east and Paris to the area, using the same rationale as Bout de l'An: that it was a safe place, where 'nothing ever happened'. St-Amand being in the Free Zone after the armistice, nothing much did happen to them until June 1944. Although thousands of Jews were deported by the Vichy regime to concentration and death camps in the Reich, exemptions could theoretically be made for those who had French nationality, a French spouse or children, also for pregnant women, ex-servicemen and the disabled and those over 60. In the latter cases, this was to preserve the fiction that the deportees were going to work camps in the east.

In St-Amand during 1943 officials of the sub-prefecture had tried to make Jews leave on the pretext that their accommodation was required as billets for the officers of the newly created 1RF regiment, but the drive had not been very successful, largely because the civil servant responsible was a clandestine *résistant*, who frequently warned those at risk.

Lécussan intended to change all that. Had he needed an excuse, it came in the early morning of 28 June when a team of *résistants* wearing Milice uniforms and bearing false papers managed to penetrate inside the Ministry of Information in Paris, where the virulently anti-Semitic and pro-German politician Philippe Henriot was sleeping. They shot him dead in front of his wife, who had pleaded with him not to open the door to their quarters. Lécussan's hatred of Jews making him believe that they had been behind the assassination, he ordered several to be arrested in St-Amand, torturing some before killing them all, their bodies left floating in the canal.

On learning of the hanging of Chaillaud's hostages in the afternoon of 20 June, Lécussan went berserk. The perpetrators were out of reach, so he decided that the Jews of St-Amand must be considered guilty in their stead. Determined to make St-Amand *judenrein* – or cleansed of Jews, to use the Nazi terminology – Lécussan now ordered a total round-up for the following day.

His most enthusiastic collaborator was the sadistic 23-year-old Gestapo interpreter Pierre-Marie Paoli, already notorious as a torturer and so hated in the region that the FTP had mounted an attack on him in April 1943, which left him with a bullet in his belly that required surgical removal and three months' convalescence. Fully recovered and delighted to be working with Lécussan, whose reputation was well known, Paoli obtained the go-ahead from the Bourges Gestapo boss, Erich Hasse, and gathered a task force which included forty-five German soldiers, fifteen *miliciens* and several French and German Gestapo officers.

Paoli, Hasse and their men arrived at St-Amand at about 1600hrs. The men were accommodated in the cinema, the bosses repairing to a hotel for a generous meal with plenty of alcohol. It was not difficult to know where the Jews were living because Vichy legislation made it compulsory for the heads of families to declare their place of residence to the local authorities. That night, starting at 2300hrs, doors were smashed in by rifle butts and seventy-one victims were dragged out in night attire or underclothes. Some elderly men and women were even forbidden to collect their false teeth or spectacles, or to get dressed. Under Paoli's direction, nationality was ignored as they were all – French-born and foreigners alike – herded into the Rex cinema.

No one bothered to use the customary pretence that they would be deported to a labour camp. One bewildered old lady, arrested with her 3-year-old grandson, asked permission to bring her sewing things, only to be told, 'You won't need them. You're going to paradise.' Already dressed and waiting for Paoli's men to arrive, 76-year-old veteran Colonel Fernand Bernheim told the *miliciens*, 'You must have sunk really low to come and arrest the likes of me'.[2]

In the cinema an ex-serviceman prisoner named Léon Weill asked politely for his confiscated identity papers to be returned. The reply was a sneering, 'You won't need them any more'. Interpreting this correctly and without being noticed, Weill managed to open a pass door that led to the next-door cafe also owned by van Gaver. He crossed its courtyard, climbed a wall and leapt down into another courtyard, where he threw himself on the mercy of the household, who hid him for thirty-six hours at the risk of their own lives, until he could be taken to a Resistance safe house. Many others thought of escape before it was too late, but could not leave behind their spouses or children. Fortunately for him, Weill was single and had no one to think of except himself.

Back in the Rex cinema were twenty-eight men, thirty-eight women and ten children, including a baby of ten months old. Of these, one man, three women and the baby were released on the ground that they were not legally Jewish, although related to Jews. At 0700hrs the other prisoners were herded at gunpoint into trucks. As they drove off, the Milice HQ in St-Amand resounded with gunshots as the *miliciens*, drunk off looted liquor, celebrated their 'victory'. After spending the day without food or drink in the stifling courtyard of Bordiot prison, the prisoners from St-Amand were locked into overcrowded, stiflingly hot cells, where eighteen people had to share one stinking toilet bucket, emptied every twenty-four hours. The only food was a ration of dried beans twice a day and there was no longer any Brother Albert to soften the treatment or bring extra rations. Any valuables had been stolen. In the afternoon of 24 July Lécussan arrived to oversee what he considered proper revenge for the killing of the *miliciens* taken hostage at St-Amand. In this he was enthusiastically assisted by Paoli, wearing his German uniform.[3]

The full details are too obscene to recount, but in short twenty-six male Jewish prisoners were crammed into a closed van with barely space for half that number by Paoli and his men, and then driven to a deserted farm in a military training ground a few kilometres from the town at a place called Guerry. In groups of six they were made to carry heavy rocks and solidified sacks of cement weighing 50kg each to a deep well, where *miliciens* armed with automatic pistols and sub-machine guns were waiting.

Instead of shooting the prisoners so that the bodies fell into the well shafts, their killers made them kneel by the parapets and pushed them over alive head-first, with the rocks and sacks of cement thrown in afterwards. The lucky ones died from a crushed skull or broken neck, others more slowly by drowning, already injured, under the weight of subsequent victims as more bodies and rocks crashed down on them, making a tangle of bodies that later took local firemen several days to extricate.

Once the prisoners waiting their turn realised what was happening, they were frozen in terror with the exception of one young man named Charles Krameisen, who decided that he preferred to die with a bullet in the back while attempting to escape rather than submit like a beast to the slaughter. Told to get out of the van in the last group, he was careful to be the last man to emerge, having already taken off his heavy boots to make it easier to run faster. Marched outside the courtyard of the farm where the van was parked, he overheard one Gestapo man say to another, '*Hier werden wir die Hasen töten*'. Understanding German, he realised that the talk of killing hares was a jokey way of saying that they were going to kill their prisoners.

His run for freedom took the two guards at the rear of the group by surprise. By the time they started firing, he was sheltered by a corner of the farmhouse, off which the bullets ricocheted as he ran through scrub and low bushes, tearing clothes and flesh on brambles and thorns. Afraid that others might try the same trick, the guards designated one man to pursue the fugitive while they stayed with the group. One other man did try to escape, but was immediately shot down. Hiding in brambles, Krameisen heard several shots fired in his direction by the man detailed to kill him, who eventually went back to the others and saved face by reporting that he had killed the runaway and thrown his body down another well. Waiting until after darkness, Krameisen emerged from hiding shocked and dishevelled, to knock on the door of a peasant family with eight children living on a farm near the execution site, by whom he was taken in and given food and clothes.

The sorry story did not end on this note of courage and humanity. The female hostages were still locked up in Bourges prison, with a gruesome fate awaiting them too.

The *miliciens* and Gestapo officials were by now mostly preoccupied with saving their skins before the Allied spearheads drove into the town. So the women might have survived until the liberation of Bourges, had not the commander of the local Milice been assassinated on 7 August. With no chance of catching the assassin, his men used the same 'logic' as Lécussan and decided to execute their Jewish hostages in reprisal.

Since all the male Jews taken from St-Amand were dead, it was the turn of the women. For 'humanitarian' reasons, those with children were exempted, but two women who had claimed to be childless, so that their children would not be rounded up, were included in the ten who were now told they were to be deported to a concentration camp in Germany. In the prison courtyard, as they were being herded into the Milice van, a German officer saw one of them weeping. Fortunately for her, she could speak enough German to explain that she was not Jewish, and was returned to the cells with another woman. The other eight and a male Jewish *résistant* who had been held in the prison for two months were then driven off to the killing ground at Guerry.

As evidenced by bloodstains and bullet scuffs on the parapet of a different well that was used for this round of killings, the man and five of the women were probably first shot before being dumped in the well. The body of the youngest, aged 18, was naked and mutilated, with indications that she had been raped. The last woman to be pushed in before rocks were dumped on the bodies was Marthe Krameisen, who should not have been there because she had two children, but had denied this to save their lives, as she thought.

Between 9 and 11 August the Gestapo and their French hangers-on evacuated Bourges in style by motor transport, ignoring the plight of many Wehrmacht soldiers who had to commandeer bicycles after all their transport had been destroyed in combat or when strafed by Allied aircraft.

When the town was finally liberated on 17 August by a mixed force of FFI men, Free French troops and some SAS paras, the gates of Bordiot prison opened to release twenty-five women and nine children who survived the tragedy of St-Amand. Not for them the dancing in the streets of Bourges that went on until dawn. All they wanted was to get home and try to put their lives together again.

Administration in the areas that had been liberated by the Allied advance was complicated by de Gaulle insisting on replacing any functionary who had served under Vichy with a man untainted by his activities during the occupation. In Bourges the unanimous choice for the new mayor was a 77-year-old retired schoolteacher. Charles Cochet had been active in the region's political life for many years until declared unsuitable for public office by Vichy because of his frequent criticisms of the regime.[4] In a climate of vengeance that saw a number of *collabos* beaten up and some killed, Cochet and the local liberation committee made an announcement that this impromptu *épuration* – or purging – was to stop: anyone who had an accusation to make should contact the forces of law and order, whose job it was to make arrests for punishment after due legal process.

The new incumbents all over liberated France had their hands full simply arranging food and shelter for the local inhabitants and the thousands of refugees unable to return to their homes on the wrong side of the battling armies. In this context, it is understandable that no one in Bourges had the time to listen to Charles Krameisen's account of what had happened to him and others at Guerry, partly because he spoke French poorly and also because it sounded like the ravings of a madman. The missing Jews from St-Amand having been temporarily listed as missing or deported to camps in Germany, Krameisen was written off for several weeks as a man demented by suffering. Finally, on 18 October 1944, he was able to guide an ad hoc commission of inquiry to the killing ground at Guerry, where the presence of a US army photographer and cameraman permitted irrefutable coverage of the atrocity. The decomposing corpses of twenty-six men and eight women in the two wells used for the executions bore out Krameisen's gruesome story. The first body to be brought out of the second well was that of his wife Marthe, recognisable only by the torn and soiled dress she had been wearing.

In October 1945, Paoli was condemned to death *in absentia* for the crime. He and the other guilty men had fled Bourges with their Gestapo protectors, but not headed straight for the illusion of safety in the Reich, as did so many of their ilk. Paoli and nine others, including François Rutz, heavyweight boxing champion of France in 1938, posed as a travelling band of *maquisards* in the Ardennes and elsewhere en route, repeatedly dodging the advancing US troops of General Courtney Hodge while tricking many genuine FFI groups into accepting them as comrades. Because they moved about frequently and covered their tracks well, there is no count of the number of their victims duped and killed in this way, but it is considerable. At some point, they retreated into Germany, where Paoli asked Gestapo HQ in Berlin to arrange German nationality for him. After this was refused, he and his band finally gravitated with some 2,000 French fascists and other Vichy riffraff to Sigmaringen in southern Germany, where Pétain was being held under house arrest.

In the final days before the German surrender, Paoli's gruesome odyssey ended at Flensburg in Schleswig-Holstein, a few kilometres from the Danish border, where the last German troops were still holding out. It was there that he was arrested by British military police on 16 May 1945. In January 1946, he was handed over to French justice after many delays by the British occupation authorities. Others of the band were later also handed over. At his retrial in Bourges, Paoli lied consistently. Defying the incontrovertible evidence of the autopsies, he pretended that all the hostages from St-Amand had been humanely executed by the traditional bullet in the back of the neck before being dropped into the wells. On 15 June 1946 he was executed in Bourges prison, scene of his many depredations. The previous week, four other *miliciens* were also condemned to death and executed. Defiant to the end, one of them cried out to the firing squad, not '*Vive la France!*' but '*Vive Bucard!*' Marcel Bucard was the founder of the pre-war French fascist party known as 'Francisme', whose followers had been the most enthusiastic members of Darnand's Milice.[5]

Accorded French citizenship in recognition of his suffering, Charles Krameisen died in a mental hospital. Lécussan was tried for his crimes and executed in Lyon in September 1946. Simone Bout de l'An and her children remained in France, but her husband fled to Italy and lived there to die a natural death in 1977. Chaillaud returned to St-Amand, always ready to justify the hanging of the Milice and became an increasingly bitter man, angry that more people were not punished for collaboration.

Thus ended the sad story of St-Amand – the town 'where nothing ever happened'.

20

KILL THE HERO!

In the days, weeks and months after D-Day, General Eisenhower and the Joint Chiefs of Staff were concentrating on the drive out of Normandy and eastwards into Hitler's industrial heartland in the Ruhr as the quickest way to end the war in Europe. They had no wish to expend non-French lives in liberating areas of France outside this grand design. Since de Gaulle was the man who had given them so much trouble in the past with his insistence that he knew what was best for his country, the task of liberating areas of France irrelevant to the drive into the Reich was largely left to his Free French forces, in collaboration with the local units of the FFI under the command of General Koenig.

While most PCF members blindly obeyed the party's instructions during the months of France's slow liberation with no thought for the lives of those who would be killed in German reprisals after spurious 'liberations' that lasted hours or a few days, 31-year-old schoolteacher Georges Guingouin was one party member who refused to do this. Brought up by his schoolteacher mother after his father died in the First World War before Georges' second birthday, he had a strong sense of right and wrong, which often conflicted with the PCF party line. As one example, in September 1940 he refused to distribute issue No. 9 of *La Vie du Parti*, in which the editorial urged party members to be 'without hatred for the German soldiers [because] we are against de Gaulle and the capitalist clan whose interests Vichy shares'. That may not seem much of a rebellion, but it meant that he was a marked man in the eyes of the PCF leadership.

Guingouin fought his own war, going underground in February 1941 to escape arrest and setting up a clandestine printing press in a remote area, where he lived in abandoned houses, huntsmen's cabins and even caves that had not been inhabited since the Wars of Religion in the Middle Ages. To the party, he was known dismissively as 'that crazy man who lives in the woods'. His tracts, never tame reprints of the party line, were distributed by the thousand wherever people gathered at traditional fairs and agricultural meetings. He also augmented rations by stealing the entire stock of ration cards in St-Gilles-des-Forêts, a crime for which he was sentenced in his absence by a Vichy court to hard labour for life. In May 1943 the PCF ordered his execution for defying party discipline and raising a band of partisans that blew up essential equipment in a rubber processing factory in Limoges, but Guingouin was not an easy man to kill, although one of the party's later attempts very nearly succeeded. Two months later, another of Guingouin's coups was the sabotage of the underground cable connecting the U-boat base in Bordeaux with the HQ of the Kriegsmarine in Berlin. So successful was his personal brand of communism that the German occupation forces branded the eastern part of Haute Vienne *département* where he held sway 'little Russia'.

When the Vichy administration crumbled away after the invasion, rather than allow a power vacuum in which gun law predominated, Guingouin effectively became the one-man government of a large slice of the Limousin in central France. His printed communiqués, signed in his own name as 'Prefect of the Maquis', fixed agricultural prices and banned black marketeering. The penalty for transgression was not a fine, but a bullet. Guingouin also used traditional trade unionist methods to slow down industrial and agricultural production in the area and thus delay fulfilment of the last spate of German requisitions, rather than inciting obvious sabotage which invited reprisals. Even the millers – traditional enemies of the peasants who grew the grain – were forced to pay reasonable rates and produce a flour of better quality than the Vichy standard, which by this time included various additives, including sawdust. In the Limousin dialect of Occitan, they said, '*Que lo Maquis qui nos baillen lou po blanc!*' – 'It took the Maquis to deliver us white bread!'

Guingouin was one of only twelve PCF members later honoured with the title Compagnon de la Libération – in his case for disobeying party orders to attack the German garrison in Limoges in July 1944 because he judged it pointless to 'liberate' the city for a few hours and then retreat, calling down severe reprisals on the population, as happened in Tulle. Events nearly overtook him nevertheless after American Flying Fortresses made a major airdrop of arms on 14 July in the wild scrubland and forests of Mount Gargan, a chunk of the Massif Central near Limoges that rises to 2,000ft.

As in the Vercors, the drop was clearly visible to German forces in the area – in this case a 2,500-man mobile armoured anti-partisan column commanded by monocled Lieutenant General Otto-Ernst Ottenbacher, plus 2,300 assorted other German and Milice units. On 18 July a battle commenced in which Guingouin commanded his private army of 3,500 men, including Vichy units that had changed sides to fight with the Maquis. By the end of the afternoon the Germans had succeeded in breaching the FTP lines and followed up this advantage in the following days.

In six days of fighting, Guingouin lost thirty-eight dead, fifty-four wounded and five men missing in action against an alleged casualty total of 342 killed and wounded on the German side. Although the FTP were forced to withdraw, they did so successfully, and melted away into the countryside, taking with them the arms dropped on 14 July.

On 4 August, after learning that the Gestapo were intending to execute all their partisan prisoners before withdrawing, Guingouin disposed his considerable forces around the town and attempted to negotiate the surrender with the officer commanding the garrison, Major General Walter Gleiniger. It comprised 1,400 men including 19th SS Police Regiment, eleven squadrons of the GMR and 300 Milice. On 17 August 1944 the Milice drove away from Limoges, fleeing the Allied advance. On Saturday 19 August Limoges was paralysed by a general strike. Knowing that the town was surrounded by several thousand FFI, Gleiniger indicated that he was ready to negotiate – but not with 'terrorists'.

A solution was found when M. Jean d'Albis of the Swiss Legation offered his services as intermediary. On the night of 20 August the GMR decided that the war was over and came over to the Maquis en masse. On hearing this news, General Gleiniger was overwhelmed. In the afternoon of Monday 21 August he, his deputy Lieutenant Colonel von Liebich and Captain Noll met at d'Albis' home with representatives of the FFI and an inter-Allied mission. Present were Major G.M.Staunton[1] of SOE, American Captain Charles E. Brown and representatives of the FFI and Free French forces. Their presence enabled Guingouin to tell the German commandant that failure to surrender meant that the town centre would be bombed flat by the Allied air forces.

The meeting broke up after two and a quarter hours of discussions with an agreement to reconvene for the signature of the capitulation document at the German HQ in the Hôtel de la Paix at 2030hrs. On the German side, that was just a device to gain time. In the Hôtel de la Paix Captain Noll gave the Allied team the dramatic news that Gleiniger and von Liebich had been abducted by the SS, who had succeeded, despite numerous FFI ambushes and roadblocks, in breaking out of Limoges with the majority of the garrison some time after 1815hrs. That their escape went unnoticed was due to many FFI men deserting their posts in order to join a parade celebrating the liberation of the town. Noll was then informed that the act of capitulation was without effect and that the FFI would force a surrender of those remaining. At 2210hrs Noll, twelve other officers and 350 men were taken prisoner.

Wild rumours circulated – and continue to be believed – to the effect that Gleiniger had committed suicide or that he had been assassinated by the SS before their withdrawal. In either case, where was the body? The truth was that Gleiniger was present in the convoy that left town with the SS, but not as their prisoner. On the road to Clermont-Ferrand the convoy had been ambushed and the civilian car near the head of the column in which Gleiniger and von Liebich were riding was machine-gunned with both men killed. There is some doubt of what happened to the general's body, which was recorded as being buried in the town cemetery of Guéret and later removed to the German military cemetery at Berneuil, near Saintes in south-west France, together with the remains of three other German soldiers killed in the ambush.

In Limoges, de Gaulle's wish that France should be seen to be liberated by Frenchmen came true. It is for this reason that Guingouin is remembered every 16 August when wreaths and bunches of flowers are placed at the war memorial in the Orsay gardens, from where a procession of local notables, ex-servicemen and people of all ages walk to the prison and the prefecture before ending at the Hotel de la Paix on the Boulevard du Fleurus, where the surrender of the German garrison was not signed nearly seven decades before.

PART 3

THE SAVAGE REVENGE

21

ROUGH JUSTICE

Nobody talks now of *l'épuration* – the purge that followed the liberation. During research for this book, the author asked a woman whose mother was sent to a concentration camp and whose father and his friends never returned from death camps in Germany why no one had ever attacked the neighbour who betrayed them to the Gestapo. She replied simply, 'We had had enough of all the killing. We wanted to get on with our lives.'

But some wanted vengeance and could not wait for the due process of law to be reestablished. This is an eyewitness account by Claude François, a printer's apprentice in Limoges who later became a journalist:

> The prison gates opened and the prisoners were replaced by alleged *collabos*. One shopkeeper was a Pétainist who had been in the habit of giving the Hitler salute every time he met a German. He was dragged out of his house and taken to the prison. That is a distance of about half a kilometre. All the way, a furious crowd of people spat on him and kept pushing and shoving to try and get a blow in. It was a horrible sight.

Jacques Valéry was a 15-year-old runner for the Resistance. He recalls the same day:

> All the buildings that had been used by the Milice, the Gestapo and the Service d'Ordre Légionnaire were invaded and pillaged, and all the papers thrown out of the windows. It wasn't done by the Maquis because they wanted to keep these documents and use them to identify the *collabos*. The FFI had warned when it entered town that it wanted no excesses, but you have to remember the brutality of the Milice, the Gestapo and the GMR. There were 250 GMR men in Limoges. Okay, so the FFI persuaded them to change sides, but just a few months earlier they were tracking down *résistants* and some of them kicked their prisoners' head in. It's not easy to forget that sort of thing.

Résistant Nestor Spel had this to say:

In the prefecture, we found more than 10,000 denunciations of *résistants* and Communists, but husbands also betrayed the lovers of their wives and wives betrayed their husbands. And there were hundreds of applications to become 'guardians' of confiscated Jewish property. When you think of all those documents, you can't say that the revenge was terrible. In the mood of that time, if no one had stopped us, there would have been many more executions.[1]

Lawyers, priests, shopkeepers and politicians were dragged out of their homes or shot in them without trial. One 18-year-old boy, who was suspected of betraying a Maquis band wiped out by the SS, was tied behind a car and dragged along for miles until multiple injuries caused his death. In some cases, men accused and killed by one Resistance group were given an honour guard from another group at their funeral. In an attempt to stop this sort of impromptu vengeance, many of whose victims were later exonerated, Guingouin arranged with the officer commanding the FFI to install throughout the five *départements* of the region temporary tribunals to judge accused collaborators. Jacques Valéry said, 'It was an *attempt* to restore order.'

In legal terms, even the tribunals had the air of revolutionary committees. They consisted of three FFI men or officers – the oldest was often no more than 21 years old – advised by other FFI officers, a lawyer and a representative of the Comité Départementale de Libération (CDL). Since lawyers had continued exercising their profession under Vichy, few of them were accepted as suitable defence counsel. Of forty-one practising in Limoges, the tribunal accepted only four at first. Later fourteen were 'approved' and allowed to practise again. Three verdicts only were handed down: acquittal, death and execution within twenty-four hours or imprisonment 'until a judgement can be made after the complete liberation of France'.

The tribunal in Limoges was afterwards alleged not to have been free of personal vengeance. One shopkeeper, spoken for by members of the CDL, was found innocent, but shot all the same. A prostitute accused of having slept with 100 Germans retorted that she had also French clients and even one Chinese man. She was also shot. Another prostitute, known to her clients as 'Big Marcelle', showed a certain *sangfroid*. Claude François recalls her asking the firing squad for five minutes to do her make-up so she could leave this life looking her best. A number of *maquisards* were also judged and shot after being found guilty of rape and/or obtaining money at gunpoint.

Not until the end of October were the military tribunals stood down after the restoration of a civil judiciary. It seems from the latest researches that approximately 250 people were executed in the Limoges area in addition to all those simply shot out of hand in the first days of the liberation of the area.

Guingouin was elected Mayor of Limoges by its grateful population in 1945, despite the PCF leadership and his old comrades in the region doing everything possible to undermine his election campaign. Labelled a Titoist deviant, he was expelled from the party in 1952 and thus deprived of its political protection. In the aftermath of the 1953 amnesty for collaboration crimes, many counter-accusations were levelled at former *résistants*. Guingouin was named by the Marxist periodical *Le Populaire du Centre* in the context of its denunciation of 'the killers of the Resistance' as 'Colonel Masakrov', who allegedly had killed personal enemies during the liberation.

While in prison, on Christmas Eve 1953 Guingouin survived a murder attempt by former party comrades, as a result of which he was released in June 1954, when his physical condition gave cause to consider him in danger of dying. Not until 1998 did PCF General Secretary Robert Hué publicly apologise for the harassment of this renegade communist. Asked for his reaction, Guingouin replied, 'I've reached the age of serenity. It's a problem for the party and no longer concerns me.'[2]

Charles Guingouin died of natural causes in 2005 and was buried in St-Gilles-les-Forêts, the scene of his 'liberation' of the ration cards sixty years earlier.

As each *département* of France was painfully released from the German yoke, the Gaullist enforcers of law and order who replaced Vichy's judges repeated that any idea of vengeance on *miliciens*, police, gendarmes and other functionaries tainted by their activities under the occupation must be left to the courts to decide. By then, it was often too late because so many people had been tortured and imprisoned, or seen their loved ones thus treated or killed during the German occupation. There were countless executions after kangaroo courts by groups of *maquisards* or no trial at all. In addition, many individuals settled private accounts during this period, knowing they were unlikely to be exposed. It was not difficult in a country in turmoil, with a total war still being waged on its soil, to find a weapon and shoot a personal enemy dead in the night.

In Cahors, a picturesque tourist town in south-west France, the last Germans drove away on 17 August 1944. Hard on their heels, the FFI took over the town and the whole Lot *département*. As reported on the front page of *Le Partisan* of January 1945:

Two days after the liberation of Cahors, the Resistance disinfected [sic] the town. Fifteen traitors, guilty of the most serious and monstrous accusations, atoned for their crimes in the cemetery.

Behind that bald statement the truth is both simpler and more complicated. The simple reason for the executions is that a communist teacher named Maurice Faurant and fellow members of the PCF posing as the Front National had grabbed the reins of power in the FFI of the Lot. Being a stranger to the region, Faurant wished rapidly to acquire authority, and the best way to do that was to execute, with a semblance of justice, a number of people suspected of collaboration. The complicated side of the bloody equation is that sixty-nine men and thirty women accused of various crimes were arrested by the FFI and vilified by the euphoric crowds celebrating their liberation in the town as they were marched off to the prison known as Le Château du Roy.

The unluckiest fifteen were hauled before a court where 'evidence' against them was heard in a commotion recalling the crowds howling for the blood of the nobility during the French Revolution. Most were not allowed to utter a word in their defence, nor to question their accusers before they were judged guilty. So blatant was the fake trial that the prison staff refused to hand over the illegally condemned prisoners to the FFI until obliged to do so at gunpoint. The fifteen were then driven to the cemetery and shot between the graves.

Among the fifteen, only one had served in the Cahors Milice. Two others had been members of the Service de l'Ordre Légionnaire. Two more had been members of a right-wing organisation called Collaboration and two had been members of another pro-German party led by Jacques Doriot, formerly a prominent communist. But if those six were guilty enough to be shot, why were not all the former members of all the collaborationist parties been rounded up and shot? At least one of the fifteen was afterwards proven to have been accused by a father and son who were themselves guilty of denunciations to the Gestapo and were making sure that he was killed before he could tell what he knew about them. Most of the condemned had never even figured in the lists of 'those to be punished after the liberation' which had been published in the clandestine Resistance publication *Le Lot Résistant*.[3]

So it was all over France: thousands of hasty executions of people, some guilty and others patently not deserving their fate. This extra-judicial purge, as it is officially called, was said by Minister of the Interior Adrien Tixier in November 1944, when Alsace and Lorraine were still occupied, to have caused 100,000 deaths. That statistic is now thought to be a wild exaggeration. A Parliamentary inquiry in 1952 differentiated between 8,867 people killed for collaboration and 1,955 killed during this period for reasons that were never clearly established, making a total of 10,822 executions not sanctioned by law. Historian Robert Aron believes this is a severe underestimate and stands by a figure of 30,000–40,000.[4] The currently accepted statistic is that at least 8,775 Vichy *collabos* were killed without trial.

The judicial purge which followed involved more than 300,000 accusations heard in duly constituted courts, which handed down 97,000 convictions ranging from five years' deprivation of civil rights to banishment, usually for a year, from the *département* in which the convicted person had lived to the death penalty. To be judged *interdit de séjour* in one's home *département* was not only a punishment, but also a way of removing the guilty from contact with those they had wronged and thus avoiding illicit retribution.

Official figures list between 767 and 791 death penalties handed down by the courts and 769 imposed by courts martial. This brings the total to somewhere between 10,000 and 11,000.[5] The two most famous cases involved Marshal Philippe Pétain and his prime minister, Pierre Laval. Pétain was condemned to death, but the sentence was commuted to life imprisonment by de Gaulle in view of his advanced age and senility and because of his undeniable services to France in the First World War, for which he won the honorific 'The Hero of Verdun'. Laval escaped to Spain, but was such a hot potato that Franco sent him back to the US zone of Germany, where he was arrested and handed over to the French authorities. His trial in October 1945 was a travesty, in which he was frequently prevented from putting his case forward because of his brilliant record practising law before becoming a politician. Condemned for treason on 9 October, he was shot a week later.

During the occupation, the head of the vast Renault motor empire Louis Renault had used his factory to repair and produce vehicles for the German forces under the control of Daimler-Benz. He could hardly have refused, since the factory in western Paris was equipped and staffed to make tanks and trucks for the French army. Arrested in 1944 as a collaborator, he was so savagely attacked in jail by PCF prisoners that he died before being brought to trial. His commercial empire was nationalised as additional punishment for the Renault family.

It is impossible to estimate how many thousands of *collabos* were beaten up, threatened or robbed during this unhappy time of purges, legal and otherwise. De Gaulle's

post-war government and its successors, however, understandably thought it imperative to weld into a composite nation a population deeply fragmented by the political
schisms of the 1930s and the years of the occupation. They thus gave amnesties in
1947, 1951 and 1953 to many people convicted and imprisoned for crimes committed
during the Vichy years. Meanwhile, they had been locked away, not just in prisons but
also in the same concentration camps used by the Vichy government for its victims,
under the same conditions of malnutrition, inadequate sanitation and medical care,
and discomfort.

22

PUNISHING THE WOMEN

One 'crime' not listed as such in the French legal code, but for which a particularly savage punishment was reserved all over France during the period of the purges, was *la collaboration horizontale* – in other words sexual relations between a French girl or woman and a German serviceman or civilian. Particularly savage treatment was reserved for wives of POWs absent in Germany who had found a German boyfriend, perhaps to guarantee extra food for themselves or their children. Prostitutes who had had a few German clients were usually left alone as that was 'business as usual'. Other women who had worked for the Germans as cooks, waitresses, washerwomen or housekeepers were presumed by jealous neighbours to have given their bodies to their employers in return for favours, and fell victim to vigilante squads of men who rounded them up for ritual humiliation.

There were also many thousands of women who had genuinely fallen in love with a German during the four long and grim years of the occupation, and many of these liaisons had produced babies. These women were subjected to the humiliation of having their heads shaven in public, with swastikas painted on their scalps or breasts before they were driven on trucks or dragged on foot through the streets of their home towns, sometimes naked but always surrounded by a jeering crowd. Many were forced to hold their babies and young children in their arms during the ordeal.

Because none of them were actually reported killed and because often local police or gendarmes did not want to admit they had been present at these scenes – either to ensure things did not go too far or for personal reasons – no official statistics are available. Another reason is that the French nation regards the love affairs that produced *les fils de Boches* – the Krauts' kids – as a 'national shame' or pollution of the race. It took more than fifty years before researcher Frédéric Vergili broke the taboo in 2000 by publishing a book about it.[1]

The liberation of France lasted eleven months, from 6 June 1944 to the signature of the unconditional surrender by General Alfred Jodl on 7 May 1945 in Rheims, after which the last German pockets of resistance at Dunkirk and elsewhere in France also surrendered. Vergili concluded that the most conservative estimate from documented cases was that more than 20,000 women were publicly shamed in this period, with the head-shearing and humiliation reaching a peak in August and September 1944. Months later, some Frenchwomen who had been volunteer workers in Germany had their heads shorn on return to their home towns.

Who were these women? The majority were aged between 17 and 34, but cases were recorded as young as 15 and as old as 68.[2] Many of their lives were irrevocably shattered in a few minutes by the razors, scissors or clippers wielded by their tormentors in these public humiliations. They came from all walks of life, although the rich were usually able to buy their way out of trouble.

Mademoiselle Z[3] was sentenced by a purge court to ten years' deprivation of civil rights for 'passing intelligence to the enemy'. Today, her daughter speaks out at the monstrosity of the sentence:

> My mother was seventeen years old! What political motive could she have had? She was condemned for bearing a German's child. After five years in Troyes prison and at the camp of Jargeau where they put all the unlicensed prostitutes, when she came out, she was completely unstable. Her life was ruined.[4]

As another of the 'children of national shame' said:

> If it had been a one-night stand, there was always the traditional way out of the problem. In those days, single mothers left the baby on the doorstep of an orphanage, a convent or the local presbytery. But our mothers chose to keep us, so we must have been conceived in love.[5]

Certainly Anne S. showed devotion for Günther, her German MP lover, throughout the four years of their relationship. As the daughter of a railway worker she repeatedly travelled free by train to wherever he was posted in France. During the liberation he was taken prisoner and imprisoned in a POW camp near Lyon. To help the father of her child, she persuaded her brother-in-law, who had made false ID papers for *résistants* during the occupation, to make papers for Günther, but he broke a leg while escaping. This accident led to Anne being sentenced to six months in prison, during which time her only joy was to see through the bars of her cell once a week the sight of her small son being carried in his grandmother's arms along the street outside the prison. Anne's mother paid the owner of the local paper not to report the affair and shame the family, but he printed it all the same.[6]

Anita A. brought up her German lover's child in an abusive household. Married after the war to an alcoholic ex-*résistant* who knew of her 'shame' and used it as his excuse to beat and humiliate her regularly, Anita accepted the abuse as atonement and spent hours on her knees in the bedroom praying for forgiveness. Only after the husband committed suicide in 1999 did her daughter find on going through family papers that her own birth certificate bore the stigmatic 'Father unknown'. Among her mother's papers were dozens of exercise books filled with the repeated phrase 'I must atone, I must atone'.[7]

After the capitulation of the La Rochelle pocket on 7 May 1945 the little seaside resort of Fouras on the Atlantic coast saw thirty or so local women dragged by neighbours to the picturesque Victorian bandstand where concerts had been given for summer visitors before the war. Renée X. was cleaning the tables in her aunt's restaurant, which had been requisitioned by the Germans to serve as an officers' mess, when four male neighbours with guns forced her to accompany them to the bandstand. There, she was prodded up the steps to where the women were kept waiting. They were, in her words, 'like sows in a market pen' except that sows do not get spat on or have fists shaken in their faces.

With clippers and scissors, the self-appointed justiciars started cutting hair – blonde hair, dark hair, red hair, Renée remembers it clearly – until the women were standing on a carpet of their own hair, symbolising their deprivation of the femininity they were accused of soiling. Long afterwards Renée recalled:

> I walked back to the hotel through the crowd. It was not far, but it seemed a long way. My little daughter Mylène was there with my parents. There was no need for her to see that.

Renée had been 16 when she fell in love with Mylène's father. Posted elsewhere, he left his signet ring as a token and departed, unaware that she was pregnant. His daughter Mylène, now a middle-aged woman herself, wonders:

> Will people ever understand that that not all Germans were swine who raped women, and that not all French women who slept with them were sluts? My mother has felt guilty all her life.[8]

The standard punishment for sleeping with the enemy in twentieth-century Europe seems to have begun in Belgium after the German withdrawal of 1918, and was widely used during the occupation of the Rhineland after the First World War, when German women suffered the same fate for relationships with French soldiers. It also occurred during the Spanish and Greek civil wars.[9] The victims were being humiliated for having enjoyed preferential treatment in terms of food, clothes, make-up, but there is more to it than that.

Young girls naturally fall in love with young men, especially those in uniform, which is seen to endow them with all the masculine virtues. If tens of thousands of young Frenchwomen flirted with, or had affairs with, young German soldiers during the occupation when most Frenchmen of their own age were locked away in POW camps, on the run with the Maquis or in Germany with the STO, was that treason? Estimates are that between 49 per cent and 57 per cent of the women punished were accused of no other crime,[10] so for what exactly were they being punished?

The only theory that rationalises the shearing of women's hair in liberated Denmark, Belgium, Holland, the British Channel Islands, Italy, France and elsewhere is that the child-bearing potential of women's bodies is regarded as national property, so that the woman who uses hers against the common will must be shown the error of her ways – as continues to happen in peacetime to girls of strict religious or racial communities who dare to 'marry out' or have a relationship with a man unacceptable to their ethnic or religious group.

Perhaps also, the collective need to punish anybody vulnerable after the humiliation of the defeat and occupation seized upon women during the liberation as victims because the act of shearing is a physical and psychological act of violence with a strong element of fetishist pleasure and yet is generally sanctioned – few people of either sex spoke out against it at the time – because it seems less permanent than retributive violence directed against guilty men, who have to be beaten, injured or killed. The catharsis felt by the crowds watching after women had been shorn – there were catcalls and spitting on the victims, but little overt physical violence – seems to indicate that all of these explanations are partially true.

Since the act of punishment was always decided and usually executed by men – although with women approvingly present, some with small children in their arms – it can be seen as their way of reclaiming the masculinity lost in military defeat. By disciplining the vulnerable 'guilty' women, the males of the herd consider themselves back in control and no longer subjugated to a more potent, male, enemy.[11] That the act of shearing the head hair was inflicted for many other offences on women,[12] but very rarely on men, is taken to mean that shearing was a sexual punishment for a crime rather than a punishment for a necessarily sexual crime. One victim was popular singer Vera Valmont, who was accused of only one known 'crime', which was that she had accepted professional engagements on Radio Paris during the occupation.[13] The humiliation and the assumption that her broadcasting contracts concealed something more shameful destroyed her professional life, while Maurice Chevalier, Yves Montand and many other male singers who had performed for German audiences went on to have successful post-war careers.

Illicit affairs with German personnel during the occupation resulted in only 30,000 declared births according to French records although, in the northern zone, by mid-1943 80,000 French women had applied for child benefit from the German authorities, asking that their offspring be given German nationality because they were fathered by a German soldier.[14] Taking the lower figure of 30,000, to this must be added all the children who were 'fathered' on paper by a subsequent unwitting or consenting French partner of the mother.

Conservative estimates currently put the total above 70,000, which compares with 5,500 known births to German fathers in Denmark, with a population one-tenth the size of France.[15] The true figure may well be higher: on 14 September 1942 the Propaganda Abteilung reported to Obergruppenführer Karl Oberg, Hoherer SS- und Polizeiführer Frankreichs, that some 3,000 children had already been fathered by German personnel in Normandy alone.[16] Whichever figure one takes, if pregnancy resulted in only 5 per cent of cases, there must have been several hundred thousand emotional liaisons between Frenchwomen and German men. Viewed by the French as the ultimate national shame, this is only now being discussed and written about openly, two generations later.

What strikes one on looking at photographs of the shorn women, whether clothed, semi-naked or, in some cases, completely so, swastika-branded on scalp or breasts or with a 'confession' pinned to their blouses, is the range of facial expression. Old and young, pretty and ugly, some show lip-biting anguish; others, submission or bewilderment; a few glare angrily at the camera or defiantly brush the hair clippings off their shoulders. Very few weep, and some have eyes downcast as if praying for the nightmare to end, blessedly unaware at the time that their hour of shame was frozen forever by an unforgiving camera lens. Photographs of the women shorn in Bergerac were even printed as a souvenir set of postcards for public sale.[17]

But what was in people's minds at the time? A personal acquaintance of the author was an 18-year-old girl at the time of the liberation of the town of Auch in south-west France, staying with her mother in the last of the borrowed homes in which they had hidden since November 1942. After several days of watching open Wehrmacht trucks heading north carrying wounded German soldiers, they heard on 19 August that the German garrison in the town had received orders to regroup further north. One imagines the civilians at moments like this huddled in cellars, to keep out of the way. Reality on that day was very different. Madeleine Martin's[18] mother had packed her children off that day to the local swimming pool with a picnic, to keep them out of harm's way. Learning just after midday that the last Germans had left Auch, Madeleine ran back into the town. Speaking perfect English – the formerly affluent Martin family had always employed British nannies before the war – she jumped aboard the first Allied jeep to enter the town and kissed a wounded British liaison officer sitting in the rear seat, Captain T.A. Mellows. Colonel Hilaire of the OAS and an American officer also got a kiss, as did the Polish driver, before Madeleine was told to get down and behave herself because they were there to kill Germans, not to be kissed by pretty girls.

Throughout her wanderings under false names, because the family was partly Jewish and her husband was an officer in l'Armée Secrète sought by the Milice and the Gestapo, Madeleine's mother had kept intact her last packet of tea in the assumption that her liberators would be English and in need of a good cuppa. When she now proudly presented the officers in the jeep with her precious gift, the result was laughter all round: tea was one thing they had a-plenty.

Despite the public relief in Auch that the enemy had gone, Mellows warned the family that the war was not yet over. Retreating German forces had been halted at a barricade on the bridge at Isle-Jourdain manned by local Maquis units, from where the sound of gunfire was audible. Dusk came with a stalemate, the Germans unable to cross and the Maquis unable to prevail. After dark, the FFI Armagnac Battalion arrived and completely surrounded the German positions. At dawn, sporadic firing intensified until the arrival of an FFI formation known as Corps Franc Pommiès. Now outnumbered, the scattered groups of Germans on the wrong side of the river surrendered, one by one.

Since that left no armed enemy forces in the *département* of Gers, everyone congratulated themselves on having liberated their part of France without Allied intervention. Groups of musicians were playing in the streets of Auch, with people of all ages dancing from sheer joy. For Madeleine and her family the morning was tinged with sadness at the news that Captain Mellows had been killed in a nocturnal skirmish only a few kilometres away.

Elation after years of fear combined with a sleepless night to trigger one of those shameful scenes of the liberation in which people who had never lifted a hand in anger during the occupation exorcised their guilt by humiliating the most vulnerable members of their community. In Auch that morning, a number of *miliciens* and other male *collabos* were rounded up and forced to parade around the town with some forty women, most of whom had been shorn. Joining the crowd screaming at and spitting on its victims, Madeleine was so carried away by the general excitement that when someone accused a woman of having denounced her husband, who had been deported to Germany, Madeleine took the scissors from her and continued hacking off her victim's hair until she was completely bald.

Now she says, 'It was such a terrible thing to do, but at the time, I just wanted to hurt someone to make up for those awful four years of fear and unhappiness.'[19]

23

PAYING THE PRICE OF LOVE

Statistics, and even the photographs taken over half a century ago, convey nothing of what the experience was like for the 'guilty women'. Perhaps their feelings were as different as their facial expressions. To research even just one personal story was not easy, for even those who had survived their humiliation without trauma were not prepared to talk about it so long after the event. Who can blame them? Through a trusted mutual female friend, the author was able to interview one of what the French call *les tondues* – the women with shaven heads.

The family photographs in the sitting room of Marie-Rose Dupont[1] date back to the late 1940s, with no earlier images in sight. They show her as a stunningly beautiful young woman who matured into a fashionably dressed and extremely attractive middle-aged lady with a very handsome husband, now deceased. In her mid-eighties she is still a very attractive and elegant widow with a face strangely unwrinkled that gives away nothing of the trauma she lived through.

Her parents were poor peasants scraping a living off a small property near Valence in the Tarn-et-Garonne *département* of south-west France. When Marie-Rose was only 14 her mother, desperate to be rid of a mouth to feed, tried to engage her to a well-off older man. For the first time in her life, the daughter refused to obey her parents. Since the alternative to marriage was to earn her own living, she left school to start work as a hairdressing apprentice. Hard work and a talent for the job saw her opening her own salon in Valence two years later in 1936. Marriage to a work-shy alcoholic husband who sold off all her possessions prompted her to divorce him in 1939, leaving her the single parent of their 12-month-old son.

After the defeat in June 1940, she was relieved to find that the regular customers still came to have their hair done regularly and some apparently penniless refugee women seemed able to find money for this small vanity. Apart from the difficulty of procuring shampoos and hair dyes, which could only be found on the black market, life had never been better for Marie-Rose. The problems of being a single working parent were alleviated by her parents' help looking after her son in the daytime and she was able to spend all her Sundays with him. Her parents were pro-Pétain Catholics, so when the marshal came to Valence and addressed a full house in the local cinema Marie-Rose was present to hear him repeat the phrase: '*J'ai fait à la France le don de ma personne*' – 'I have given myself to France'.

She felt like weeping. Around her, many people did shed tears. This was the Messianic side of Pétain.

Although the salon was prospering, the country was in mourning – for the defeat, for the 1.6 million POWs languishing in Germany, for its own self-esteem – and public displays of gaiety were frowned upon, especially dances. Since they could not be organised publicly, *les bals clandestins* took their place – private dances organised by word of mouth. Friends whispered of a rendezvous in a house with a room large enough for a dozen or so couples to dance to the music of a portable wind-up gramophone and, for an hour or two, the occupation was forgotten in the arms of one's partner.

Marie-Rose was not only beautiful, but also professionally made-up and coiffed. As owner of her own salon, she could always swap a free permanent wave or hair-do for an article of clothing, so she was also well dressed. But she turned down all propositions for more than just a few dances. Given the total non-availability of contraceptive devices for civilians, casual sex was out of the question and she was certain that she never again wanted to be tied to a husband.

For a single mother coming from a peasant home, she had good reason to feel pleased with her life – and no thought of what the future might hold. Why should she, when the only interference from Vichy was the visit of a gendarme on 27 March 1942, bringing her an extract from the *Journal Officiel* obliging her and all other salon proprietors to collect hair clippings for mixture with rayon fibres in a specialised factory in Calvados that produced up to 40,000 pairs of bedroom slippers a month?

Valence was well inside the Free Zone and even after November 1942, when the Germans occupied the zone in response to the Allied invasion of North Africa, few soldiers in field grey were seen on its streets. Having been brought up by her father, who had been a POW in Germany in 1914–18, to think of *les Boches* as the enemy, Marie-Rose was shocked on visits to big towns like Montauban and Toulouse to see uniformed German soldiers walking arm in arm with French girls.

One busy morning a Frenchman in civilian clothes entered Marie-Rose's salon, flashed a Gestapo ID card and asked her to step into the apartment behind the salon, so they could talk in private. She explained that the apartment was let, without saying that her tenants were a Jewish refugee couple. The *gestapiste* refused to talk in the street, because it was 'too public', and said he would return when she closed at noon. She could not imagine what he wanted, unless it was in connection with her black-market purchase of essentials for running the salon. When he returned at midday there was still one elderly lady under the dryer.

'Get rid of her,' he ordered.

'I can't,' Marie-Rose explained. 'Her hair's still wet, but she can't hear anything with the blower on. What can I do for you?'

He showed her a list with four names on it. Realising what was going on, the woman in the chair pushed the dryer hood back and shouted at the top of her powerful peasant voice, 'Why are you bothering my daughter? Go away and leave her alone!'

To Marie-Rose's astonishment, the *gestapiste* blushed and fled in confusion, leaving the list of names on the cash desk.

'That's the way to treat those swine,' observed her client, calmly pulling the dryer back over her head.

One of the names on the list was of a man working in an office opposite the salon, so Marie-Rose hurried across the road to warn him. He disappeared that afternoon, and presumably so did the other three, but she never knew what that was all about.

One of her more affluent clients named Madame Delmas, whose husband was a POW in Germany, owned a smart hotel and restaurant in the centre of town. When 2,000 Waffen-SS troops straight from the Russian front were posted to south-west France to regroup and refit, she organised *diners dansants* for the SS officers on Friday evenings. Each Friday afternoon she came to have her hair done in Marie-Rose's salon, so as to look her best that evening. Food and alcohol could always be found on the black market; her problem was finding sufficient attractive girls to amuse the clients. Several times, she invited her beautiful young hairdresser to come along and have a good time, promising that the food was excellent and the officers' behaviour always very correct.

'Nobody's going to make you do anything you don't want to,' she promised. 'So where's the harm?'

In the salon, Marie-Rose frequently heard women discussing girls who went with Germans; it was hinted darkly that they would 'have to pay for it' after the liberation. It was not that which held her back, but rather that she did not want to get involved with the very manipulative Madame Delmas. One Friday evening in April 1944, her demanding client telephoned just before closing time to say that she had been unable to get away that afternoon for her hair appointment. The plea ended, 'Couldn't you, just this once, come to the hotel and comb my hair out? I'd be so grateful.'

Reluctantly, Marie-Rose agreed to help a regular customer in a fix and packed a few essentials in a bag. After arriving at the hotel, she was kept waiting by Madame Delmas until it was almost time for the guests to arrive. To escape after doing her hair, Marie-Rose used the excuse that she had to get home and look after her son, but Madame Delmas brushed this aside: 'Let your parents take care of the boy. Stay just for a while and enjoy a good dinner. You deserve it.'

The food was well cooked and of such a quality and quantity that it had obviously been purchased on the black market. The atmosphere was very relaxed, with all the officers in their immaculate SS uniforms being very charming and attentive to the ladies. One of these, acting as interpreter for the officers who could not speak French, was a vivacious multilingual Jewish refugee from Latvia called Masha, whose 'racial impurity' did not appear to worry any of the SS officers. Several times Marie-Rose danced with a blonde, blue-eyed Austrian officer named Willi, who told her he was an engineer in civilian life. She was 23 years old, he three years older.

Good food, a glass or two of wine, the elegant atmosphere and the polite manners of the men smilingly chatting up the girls with champagne glasses in their hands in the moonlit garden behind the hotel, all put Marie-Rose off her guard. The only things she knew about Willi were that he was unmarried and came from Vienna. Yet when he asked whether they could meet again the following Friday, she blushed to hear herself say that she would like that.

It seemed a very long week. Two weeks after their second meeting they became lovers. Sometimes they met, not entirely by chance, on the street by the salon or on the beach where local families and the German soldiers went to swim in the River Tarn with an unspoken demarcation line separating the two groups of swimmers. Then they could only share a few glances, for romantic attachments were forbidden to an SS officer, even had Marie-Rose been prepared to 'come out' and let the neighbours know. Only among the regulars in Madame Delmas' hotel could she and Willi openly be together.

At the beginning of June, he was due for fifteen days' leave and tried to persuade Marie-Rose to travel with him to Vienna in order to meet his parents who, he was sure, would raise no objections to their marriage after the war. Whether it would actually have been possible for her to go there, Marie-Rose never found out because she told Willi that she could not leave her son. He therefore spent his leave in Valence, meeting her discreetly dressed in sports shirt and shorts after the salon closed in the balmy early summer evenings.

Masha earned her living by giving German lessons in Montauban and Toulouse. It was a boom market, with the number of German-language students at Berlitz schools in France rising from a pre-war 939 adults to 7,920 in 1941 and continuing to increase until D-Day.[2] On the morning of that day, she and Marie-Rose were driven by an Italian SS auxiliary to Montauban, where Masha was to give some lessons and Marie-Rose hoped to buy supplies for the salon. They arrived before midday, took an early lunch in the Sans Souci restaurant and then split up, having agreed to rendezvous back there at four o'clock.

Returning to the restaurant, Marie-Rose found Masha agog with bush-telegraph reports of the landings in Normandy. The Italian driver was nowhere to be found and all the German troops in Montauban were hastily departing, so the two women had to take a train back to Valence. The streets of the town were deserted, except for the last SS-men loading equipment on to trucks to head north. Willi was gone. Marie-Rose had no idea where until she received a letter from him explaining that he had been wounded fighting with his unit on the Normandy front and then been invalided back to the Reich. Thus began a correspondence that lasted two years.

A few days after the liberation of Valence by local FFI units on 20 August 1944, Marie-Rose was playing with her son in the garden of her parents' home when four men carrying rifles and wearing FFI armbands drove up and ordered her to get into the back of their black Citroën. Neither then nor at any time later was she accused of anything, nor did anyone mention Willi. One of the men in the car was Albert Dumas, whose family were clients of the salon and all the others were known to her by sight. They drove her to the *collège* or middle school, which the FFI had made their temporary headquarters. There, she was locked in a classroom with twenty or thirty other men and women. Unable to look at the others, she huddled in a corner with eyes closed, praying to the Virgin Mary to let her be released so she could return to her son.

Two days later all the detainees were driven by the FFI to the Gendarmerie in Lauzerte, 25km to the north-west. Since there were far too many prisoners for the cells to hold, they were locked in an office where they had to sleep on the floor, suffering frequent verbal abuse for collaboration from anyone who felt like dropping in, but not otherwise maltreated.

Back in Valence after nearly two weeks' confinement, Marie-Rose was interrogated by FFI men hunting a *collabo* who had gone to ground. Unable to tell them anything, she emerged with cuts to her body and severe bruising on her legs caused by blows with the butts of their rifles. On the following Sunday – exactly two weeks after the liberation of the town – she and three other female detainees were taken out of the *collège* and herded at gunpoint through the streets to the square in front of the main church, where a wooden dais had been erected. Praying that none of her family was there, Marie-Rose stared straight ahead as she was led through the large crowd waiting to see the fun.

A colleague of hers who ran a barbershop in the town was supposed to shave the women's heads, but could not bring himself to do this to Marie-Rose, with whom he had been at school. Unable to look her in the face, he handed the clippers to one of the FFI men, who did not know how to handle them. Her public humiliation was thus both clumsy and painful as she tried to block out the ugly noise of the crowd's insults by praying to the Virgin Mary. By keeping her eyes raised to the sky, she avoided looking at the people below or the other women on the dais, but she does recall that one of them was an 18-year-old prostitute from a local *maison close*. Presumably this girl's crime was to have fallen in love with a German client. It is interesting that well-connected Madame Delmas, at whose *diners dansants* Marie-Rose had met Willi, was denounced neither then nor later.[3]

Armed FFI men roughly bundled their shaven victims off the platform and on to the back of a flatbed truck. With two armed guards jeering at them, their shame was then paraded around the town for two hours, the klaxon blaring to attract attention. For the same reason, the driver made a long halt outside the hairdressing salon, where a number of Marie-Rose's clients were watching. None of them showed what they were thinking, except for a mild-mannered little music teacher who had taught her in the *collège*. He came up to the truck and took both her hands in his. Ignoring the FFI men and the crowd staring at them, he said, '*Courage! Ça va bientôt se terminer*' – 'Bear up, it'll soon be over.'

It was his sympathy that broke the dam of her self-control. Tears streaming down her face, Marie-Rose was driven away with the other shorn women and again locked up in the *collège*. A guard whom she knew told them their ordeal was over and they would soon be released. Neither of her parents came to visit Marie-Rose, but her brother brought food several times during the next four days' confinement. One day at 0600hrs the women were released, the time being chosen because few people would be in the streets to see them. Setting out to walk the few miles back to her parents' home, Marie-Rose was given a lift by a Spanish refugee who had lived in Valence since the civil war. On the way, he tried to comfort her with the reflection that most people soon forget everything, both the good and the bad.

For a week she dared not set foot outside, but then courageously decided that the first step in re-starting her life was to make herself a wig, so she could get back to work. As she says, 'I was lucky. At least I knew how to do that for myself.'

Re-opening the salon, she found that, far from losing customers, all the regulars came back as though nothing had happened. In addition, a whole crop of new customers booked appointments as a tacit gesture of sympathy from the women of the town. Marie-Rose Dupont corresponded with Willi for a year without ever mentioning her public humiliation. Twelve months after her day of shame, with her natural hair fully re-grown, she left Valence and its memories and found work in a hairdressing salon at Nice. When a male colleague fell in love with her, she told him about Willi. He said, 'We'll pull the curtain on the past. It's all over and done with.'

His price for marrying her and accepting her son was that she destroy all her carefully hoarded letters and photographs. After they set up home in Valence – she to re-open her salon and he working as travelling rep for a hair products company – it seemed that everyone had forgotten the shearing. Then, to her horror, she came into the salon one day and found her 8-year-old son sitting in one of the chairs, totally bald with a pair of clippers in his hand. Of her humiliation in September 1944, she never spoke again to him or anyone else until interviewed by the author in January 2006.

EPILOGUE

What did they achieve at such disproportionately high cost in lives, suffering and grief, the Resistance and the Maquis? There is no question that the widespread sabotage of railway communications in the run-up to, and after, the Normandy invasion was instrumental in its success by denying urgently needed reinforcements and materiel to the German forces on the Western Front. The spare parts for Lammerding's tanks thus delayed are one example of many. Some of the intelligence culled by SOE agents and Resistance networks throughout the occupation was also of critical importance in selecting important targets for Allied strategic bombing raids – none more so than the courageously stolen details of the V1 launching sites that were brought into operation one week after D-Day to bombard London into submission, but were then swiftly bombed out of existence, thanks to this intelligence.

Yet the decision to form underground armies composed of heroic amateurs – and there were many lesser-known such groups in addition to those in the Glières, the Vercors, at Mount Mouchet and Mount Gargan – flouted all the canons of guerrilla warfare and proved those 2,500-year-old canons valid: never concentrate your forces and never be drawn into a pitched battle. Much French blood was shed in this way during late 1943 and 1944 to no apparent military gain. The premature liberation of individual towns before and after D-Day – but long before the invasion forces could possibly reach them – were, as Georges Guingouin fortunately realised, at best just bravado that invited reprisals against the civilian inhabitants and at worst acts in a sinister drama staged by the PCF.

After the liberation of France was completed on the day after Germany's unconditional surrender of 8 May 1945, it was understandable that French and other Allied leaders spoke highly of the courage of the male and female volunteer fighters who suffered so cruelly at the hands of the anti-partisan forces of Generals Pflaum, von Jesser et al. These tributes to French heroism were politically necessary at the time when de Gaulle was reconstructing a sense of national identity in a population riven by the political divisions of the pre-war Third Republic and deeply traumatised by the horrors of the occupation and the liberation, in which Allied bombing and shelling cost the lives of many thousands of innocent French civilians in the north of France.

There was also an unconscious collective guilt to be assuaged because a small minority of French people had actively collaborated with the Wehrmacht, the Waffen-SS, the SD and the Gestapo.

The resultant 'romance of the Resistance' enabled many people who had done nothing but keep out of trouble to feel a reflected glory, as though they had personally played a part in the struggle to free their country from alien domination. It would have been politically and morally wrong to ignore the sufferings of the families that had lost their menfolk and the women who died, often after atrocious torture, in the conviction that they were sacrificing themselves for France. For each victim tortured and killed, there was also the grief of those they left behind. At a time when modern welfare state legislation was just a dream, the lives of many thousands of children and other dependants were impoverished emotionally and materially by the loss of breadwinners and parents. Families had to leave homes that could no longer be afforded and live in undeserved poverty, unalleviated by the eventual certificate of the Legion of Honour that recognised the sacrifice of the heroic dead.

If one is, with the benefit of hindsight, to add up all the suffering, including that inflicted in the German reprisals against thousands of innocent civilians, it is impossible to complete the other side of the equation by a compensating military gain.

Allied leaders used to say, during the liberation and afterwards, that the Maquis and Resistance partisans who took on regular German forces in the summer of 1944 had diverted from the Normandy front this or that number of German divisions which might otherwise have helped to drive the Allied invasion forces back into the sea. Yet, when one looks at the military quality of the troops deployed against Clair and Anjot in the Glières, Huet in the Vercors, and Colaudon and Guingouin on Mount Mouchet and Mount Gargan – and against all the other open insurrections in France – it is hard to find many units that would have made a great difference in Normandy. These were not first-line troops like the Wehrmacht and Waffen-SS units who fought so tenaciously to counter the Allied invasion – and who might well have succeeded had the Luftwaffe not been a spent force in the west, giving virtually undisputed control of the skies to the RAF and USAAF.

Pflaum's and von Jesser's anti-partisan troops were formed by OKW in large part as training units and were heterogeneous assemblies of men, many conscripted by force among German-occupied nations in Central and Eastern Europe and the USSR plus Soviet POWs from as far east as Central Asia. They fought in many different German uniforms. Yet, a uniform does not imbue the wearer with the fanatical motivation of the Waffen-SS Panzer divisions, nor the solid, stubborn discipline of the average Wehrmacht soldier and his officers fighting for their country's survival at that stage of the war. Many of the conscripts, like the Czechoslovakians at Aubusson, hoped sincerely for Germany's defeat and the eventual liberation of their countries. Cannon fodder Pflaum's men and von Jesser's could have been, but how effective they would have been in the front line, combating the Allied armies, navies and air forces driving through the north of France towards the Reich in the second half of 1944, is an open question.

What cannot be denied is the heroism of the French men and women, mostly but not all young, who volunteered to risk imprisonment, torture, the slow death of the concentration camps and the swifter death by firing squad – all from a spirit of patriotism. That was magnificent and should not be forgotten. Their memorials, dotted all over France and still regularly decorated with fresh flowers, are a testimony to much that is best in any nation. Losing people of this quality was a great loss to post-war France, which had already forfeited so many of its brightest and best in fighting the German invaders in the First World War.

In the 1950s the PCF displayed posters reminding voters that France had been invaded by Germany three times in seventy years[1] and occupied wholly or partially each time. Britain and North America are fortunate never to have known that humiliating experience, but in the past this was due more to geography that gave them the protection of the sea – and in Britain's case the potent shield of the Royal Navy – than to the political astuteness of their leaders or the military prowess of their generals.

In 1940 it was easy for British people to bolster their own damaged self-esteem after the humiliation of Dunkirk by saying that the British Expeditionary Force had to retreat across the Channel in 1940 because 'the French had lacked the will to fight'. The achievement of the *résistants* and *maquisards* who voluntarily risked torture, deportation and death unprotected by any Geneva Convention – and many of whom paid such a terrible price – demonstrates beyond all doubt how wrong that glib alibi had been.

NOTES AND SOURCES

All translations are by the author, unless otherwise attributed.

All illustrations are from the author's collection.

Every effort has been made to trace copyright owners. In the event of any infringement, please communicate with the author, care of the publisher.

1 Raising the Resistance – Tracts and Terrorism

1 US casualties amended by the Statistical Services Center, Office of the Secretary of Defense, 7 November 1957, as quoted in *Encyclopaedia Britannica* 2002 Deluxe CD-Rom edition.
2 Diamond, H., *Women and the Second World War in France*, London, Longman, 1999, p. 60.
3 Lazare, L., *La Résistance Juive en France*, Paris, Stock, 1987, p. 105.
4 Guillemin, H., *Parcours*, Paris, Seuil, 1989, p. 400.
5 Doenitz, K., *Memoirs*, London, Cassell, 2000, p. 409.
6 Pryce-Jones, D., *Paris in the Third Reich*, London, Collins, 1981, p. 120 (abridged).
7 Lagarrigue, M., article in *Arkheia*, No. 17–8, Montauban, p. 11.
8 Amouroux, H., *La Vie des Français sous l'Occupation*, Paris, Fayard, 1961, Vol. 2, p. 58.
9 Also spelled *Natzweiler* in German.
10 Paris, E., *Unhealed Wounds*, New York, Grove Press, 1985, pp. 98–9.

2 Putting the Dirt in 'Dirty War'

1 Dalton, H., *The Fateful Years*, London, Muller, 1957, p. 368.
2 Jenkins, R., *A Pacifist at War*, London, Arrow, 2010, pp. 54–6.
3 Marshall, R., *All the King's Men*, London, Collins, 1988, p. 253.
4 Foot, M.R.D., *SOE in France*, London, HMSO, 1966, p. 302.
5 Kemp, A., *The Secret Hunters*, London, Coronet, 1988, pp. 776–8; also Kramer, R., *Flames in the Field*, London, Michael Joseph, 1995, pp. 115–27; also documentation at Natzwiller.

3 The Making of the Maquis

1 He held this office July to December 1940 and April 1942 to August 1944.
2 Subsequently historians have disagreed over the extent of his responsibility for the slave labour programme.
3 Amouroux, p. 29.
4 Burrin, P., *Living with Defeat*, London, Arnold/Hodder, 1996, p. 249.
5 Amouroux, p. 39.
6 Quoted by L. Chabrun et al. in *L'Express*, 10 October 2005.
7 Ibid.
8 *The Unpublished Diary of Pierre Laval*, London, Falcon Press, 1948, pp. 187–98, facsimile in Appendix V.
9 Firemen in Paris and Marseille are still technically members of the armed forces.
10 Amouroux, p. 43.
11 Ibid., pp. 47–8.
12 Ibid., pp. 49–50.

4 The Loneliness of the Long-Distance Agent

1 More details at www.militarymuseum.org/Ortiz.html.
2 Dalloz, P., *Vérités sur le Drame du Vercors*, Paris, Editions Lanore, 1979.
3 See www.militarymuseum.org/Ortiz.html.
4 Ibid.
5 Jenkins, R., *A Pacifist at War*, London, Arrow, 2010, p. 3.
6 Ibid., p. 52 (abridged).
7 Quoted in his Afterword to Masson, M., *Christine*, London, Virago, 2005, p. 278.
8 Interview by Jeremy Clay reprinted in *Leicester Mercury*, 30 June 2009.
9 A short-range radio communication system for speech between the ground and incoming aircraft.
10 Jenkins, pp. 106–7 (abridged).
11 This can be seen at http:www.maquisdelain.org/media/11-11-1943_01.avi.
12 Krivopissko, G. (ed.), *La Vie à en mourir – Lettres de fusillés*, Paris, Tallandier, 2003, pp. 268–9 (abridged).

5 Live Free or Die!

1 Quoted in Azema, J.-P., *De Munich à la Libération (1938–1944)*, Paris, Seuil, 1980.
2 More details on http://alain.cerri.free.fr – a site developed by Roger Cerri's son to publish his father's wartime diaries.
3 Also spelled Montiévert and Montiévran.
4 More details at http://alain.cerri.free.fr.
5 Other records suggest earlier, at 1630hrs, but all agree that it was as the light was failing.
6 Noguères, H., *Résistants contre SS 1943–44*, Paris, Editions Tallander, 1987, p. 1576.
7 Vistel, A., *La Nuit sans Ombre*, Paris, Fayard, 1970, p. 362.
8 Code-named Operation Anvil during the planning phase.

9   Noguères, p. 1569.
10 See www.militarymuseum.org/Ortiz.html.
11 Ibid.
12 He also received the honour of a Chevalier of the Légion d'Honneur, the Croix de Guerre with five citations, the Médaille des Blessés, the Médaille des Evadés and the Médaille Coloniale. His other American awards included the Legion of Merit with Combat 'V' and two Purple Heart medals.
13 See www.militarymuseum.org/Ortiz.html.
14 More details on site of USMC www.marines.mil.

6 The Trojan Horse

1   Joseph, G., *Un Combattant du Vercors*, Paris, Fayard, 1972, pp. 24–7.
2   Ibid., p. 36.
3   Rosencher, H., *Le sel, le cendre et la flame*, Paris, Félin, 2000, pp. 269–301.
4   Picirella, J., *Mon journal du Vercors*, Lyon, Rivet, 1982, pp. 13–8.
5   Ibid., pp. 18–9.
6   Rosencher, pp. 269–301.
7   Picirella, pp. 22–5.
8   Rosencher, pp. 269–301.
9   Joseph, pp. 208–9.
10 Krivopissko, pp. 325–6 (abridged).
11 Joseph, p. 125.

7 Dream of Victory, Reality of Death

1   Joseph, p. 222.
2   Todorov, T., *Une tragédie française*, Paris, Seuil, 2004, p. 37.
3   Ibid., p. 78.
4   Rosencher, pp. 269–301.
5   See www.memorial-vercors.fr.
6   Dreyfus, P., *Vercors, citadelle de liberté*, Geneva, Famot, 1975, p. 14.
7   Interview with Madeleine Masson during preparation of Masson's book *Christine*.
8   Picirella, J., *Mon journal du Vercors*, Lyon, Rivet, 1982, pp. 63–8.
9   Ibid., p. 69.

8 Ransomed from the Death Cell

1   Interview with Madeleine Masson.
2   Jenkins, R., *A Pacifist at War*, London, Arrow, 2010, pp. 236–7.
3   Interview with Jeremy Clay reprinted in *Leicester Mercury*, 30 June 2009.

9 From the Sky Came Death

1 Joseph, p. 193.
2 Dreyfus, p. 76.
3 Unpublished Picirella diary.
4 Joseph, pp. 200–3.
5 Dreyfus, p. 9.
6 Ibid., p. 27.
7 Ibid., p. 32.
8 Ibid., p. 36.
9 Ibid., pp. 81–7.
10 Ibid., pp. 89–90. An alternative, but disputed, version of this signal is given in Dreyfus, pp. 295–302.
11 Joseph, pp. 239–40.
12 Jenkins, p. 182.
13 Ibid., p. 178.
14 Joseph, p. 287–8.
15 Dreyfus, p. 102.
16 Rosencher, pp. 269–301.

10 They got what they Deserved

1 Rosencher, pp. 269–301.
2 Jenkins, p. 181.
3 Dreyfus, pp. 138–9.
4 Amouroux, pp. 82–4.
5 Dreyfus, pp. 148–50.
6 Ibid., pp. 152–3.
7 Ibid., pp. 156–9.
8 Ibid., pp. 161–3.

11 Failure is an Orphan

1 Testimony of Denise Noaro on website of Les Ecoles de Villard de Lans.
2 Full details in Joseph, G., *Combattant du Vercors*, Paris, Editions Curandera, 1994.

12 Atrocities on Both Sides

1 Article by G. Beaubatie in *Arkheia*, Nos 17–8, Montauban, pp. 50–5.
2 Some sources put the estimate as high as 700 men, but this may be a confusion caused by including the GMR and Milice.
3 Interviews included with report of Maurice Roche at www.malgre-nous.eu/IMG/pdf/doc89.pdf.
4 According to some accounts, these were smoke or tear gas grenades, left there by the GMR.
5 Nossiter, A., *France and the Nazis*, London, Methuen, 2001, p. 250.

6 Now the Hotel Mercure.

7 Beaubatie, pp. 50–5.

8 Report of Adjudant-Chef Conchonnet, quoted in *L'Express*, 6 October 2005.

9 *Arkheia* magazine, Nos 17–8, 2006, p. 58.

10 Ibid., p. 57.

11 Ibid., pp. 58–9 and Nossiter, A., *The Algeria Hotel*, London, Methuen, 2001, pp. 231–51.

12 *Arkheia* magazine, Nos 17–8, 2006, p. 58.

13 Roche report.

14 ibid.

15 *Arkheia* magazine, Nos 17–8, p. 59.

16 Roche report.

17 Letter from the Minister of the Interior dated 27 June 1954.

18 Nossiter, *Algeria Hotel*, pp. 272–3.

13 The Worst Atrocity of All

1 In his book *La Bataille du Mont Mouchet*, Villebois, La Plume du Temps, 1996, p. 2.

14 'Understand? Officer, Bang Bang!'

1 Divisional orders signed by General Lammerding exhibited at the Centre de Mémoire, Oradour.

2 Letter to OKW complaining of these problems, signed by Lammerding, exhibited at the Centre de Mémoire, Oradour.

3 More details on family website http://acroy.perso.neuf.fr/cave.htm.

15 The Town Where Nothing Ever Happened

1 *Guide du Routard – Berry*, Paris, Hachette, 2011, pp. 61–2.

16 A Recipe for Disaster

1 J.-W. Müller (ed.), *Memory and Power in Post-War Europe*, Cambridge, CUP, 2002, p. 64.

2 Kriegel-Valrimont, M., *La Libération*, Paris, Minuit, 1964, p. 31 (abridged).

3 Guingouin, G., *Quatre ans de lutte sur le sol limousin*, Paris, Hachette, 1974, p. 175.

4 Todorov, p. 30.

5 Ibid., pp. 17–23.

6 Azéma, J.-P. and Bédarida, F., *La France des Années Noires*, Vol. 2, Paris, Seuil, 1993, p. 396.

7 His curious family name, which means 'year's end', was due to his grandfather being found newborn and abandoned on 29 December 1850.

8 Todorov, p. 40.

17 A Country in Chaos

1 Delalande, B., *De la milice au maquis* (self-published), St-Amand, 1945, p. 19.
2 Sadrin, R., 'Souvenirs d'un maire', published as an annexe in Todorov, T., *Une tragédie française*, Paris, Seuil, 2004, p. 180.
3 Todorov, pp. 64–5.
4 Ibid., p. 76.

18 No Time to Waste

1 Delalande, B., *De la milice au maquis*, self-published, St-Amand, 1945, p. 105.
2 Todorov, p. 222.
3 Ibid., p. 224.
4 Delalande, p. 200.
5 Ibid., pp. 218–9.
6 Parrotin, M., *Le Temps des Maquis*, Aubusson, 1981, p. 458.

19 Bodies in the Trees, Bodies Down the Wells

1 Todorov, pp. 117–20.
2 Ibid., p. 128.
3 Although French, he held the SS rank of Scharführer (sergeant).
4 *Bulletin municipal de Bourges*, 1944, BYP11.
5 Article in *Le Patriote Résistant*, January 2009.

20 Kill the Hero!

1 Real name Philip (or Philippe) Liewer.

21 Rough Justice

1 Interview in broadcast of France 3 Limousin, date unknown.
2 Obituary notice in *The Guardian*, 3 December 2005.
3 Article by Professor Cécile Vaissié in *Arkheia*, Nos 23–4, pp. 46–71.
4 Extracted from Aron, R., *Histoire de l'épuration*, Fayard, Paris, 1967–75.
5 Statistics compiled by the Comité d'histoire de la Seconde Guerre Mondiale and its successor, L'Institut d'Histoire du Temps Présent.

22 Punishing the Women

1 Vergili, F., *La France Virile*, Paris, Payot, 2000.
2 Ibid., p. 88.
3 All the women's names have been changed at their request.
4 J.-P. Guilloteau article in *L'Express*, 31 May 2004.
5 Ibid.
6 Ibid.

7 The cases of Mlle Z, Anne S. and Anita A. are condensed from Guilloteau's article.

8 Saubaber, D. *Pour l'amour d'un Boche*, quoted by Guilloteau in *L'Express*, 31 May 2004.

9 Vergili, p. 276.

10 Ibid., pp. 23, 29.

11 Argument expounded in Vergili, *La France Virile*.

12 For black marketeering, 14.6 per cent; denunciation, 6.5 per cent; political/military, 8 per cent; foreign nationality, 2.1 per cent; unknown, 26.7 per cent.

13 Morris, A., *Collaboration and Resistance Reviewed*, New York/Oxford, Berg, 1992, pp. 85–6.

14 Vergili, p. 226.

15 Burrin, P., *Living with Defeat*, London, Arnold/Hodder, 1996, p. 207.

16 See ibid., p. 207, although no information is available as to how this figure was computed.

17 Article by J. Tronel in *Arkheia* magazine, Nos 17–8, pp. 26–45.

18 Name changed at her request.

19 Personal communication with the author.

23 Paying the Price of Love

1 Her name and the name of the town have been changed at her request.

2 Saubaber, D., *Pour l'amour d'un Boche*, quoted by Guilloteau in *L'Express*, 31 May 2004.

3 Marie-Rose's story is as recounted by her to the author.

Epilogue

1 Including the Franco-Prussian war of 1870–71.

INDEX